JOB

By DANIEL BERRIGAN

Prose

The Bride: Essays in the Church
The Bow in the Clouds
Consequences, Truth and
Love, Love at the End
They Call Us Dead Men
Night Flight to Hanoi
No Bars to Manhood
The Dark Night of Resistance
America Is Hard to Find
The Geography of Faith (with Robert Coles)
Absurd Convictions, Modest Hopes (with Lee Lockwood)
Jesus Christ
Lights On in the House of the Dead
The Raft Is Not the Shore (with Thich Nhat Hanh)
A Book of Parables
Uncommon Prayer: A Book of Psalms
Beside the Sea of Glass: The Song of the Lamb
The Words Our Savior Taught Us
The Discipline of the Mountain
We Die before We Live
Portraits: Of Those I Love
Ten Commandments for the Long Haul
Nightmare of God
Steadfastness of the Saints
The Mission: A Film Journal
To Dwell in Peace: An Autobiography
A Berrigan Reader
Stations (with Margaret Parker)
Sorrow Built a Bridge
Wheron to Stand (Acts of the Apostles)
Minor Prophets, Major Themes
Isaiah: Spirit of Courage, Gift of Tears
Ezekiel: Vision in the Dust
Jeremiah: The World, the Wound of God
Daniel: Under the Siege of the Divine
Job: And Death No Dominion
The Bride: Images of the Church (with William McNichols, S.J.)

Poetry

Time without Number
Encounters
The World for Wedding Ring
No One Walks Waters
False Gods, Real Men
Trial Poems (with Tom Lewis)
Prison Poems

Selected & New Poems
May All Creatures Live
Block Island
Jubilee
Tulips in the Prison Yard
Homage (to G. M. Hopkins)
And the Risen Bread

Drama

The Trial of the Catonsville Nine

JOB

And Death No Dominion

DANIEL BERRIGAN

with art by Robert McGovern

Franklin, Wisconsin

As an apostolate of the Priests of the Sacred Heart, a Catholic religious congregation, the mission of Sheed & Ward is to publish books of contemporary impact and enduring merit in Catholic Christian thought and action. The books published, however, reflect the opinion of their authors and are not meant to represent the official position of the Priests of the Sacred Heart.

2000

Sheed & Ward
7373 South Lovers Lane Road
Franklin, Wisconsin 53132
1-800-266-5564

Printed in the United States of America

Cover and interior design: Madonna Gauding

Library of Congress Cataloging-in-Publication Data

Berrigan, Daniel.
    Job : and death no dominion / Daniel Berrigan ; with art by Robert McGovern.
        p. cm.
    ISBN 1-58051-074-4 (alk. paper)
        1. Bible. O.T. Job--Criticism, interpretation, etc. 2 Sociology, Christian (Catholic) I. Title

BS1415.2 .B47 2000
223'.107--dc21

                                                                00-028534

1 2 3 4 5 / 03 02 01 0

Contents

To my Sisters and Brothers
of the "Depleted Uranium Plowshares"
imprisoned for peacemaking;

Susan, Elizabeth,
Stephen and Philip—

Blessed are you.

Foreword

Although I did not meet him until 1981, Daniel Berrigan had profoundly affected my life since his early and frequent nonviolent protest actions against social injustice and the war in Vietnam during the raging sixties. I was particularly struck when he was sent to federal prison, with his brother Philip, for burning draft cards with homemade napalm at Catonsville, Maryland, in 1968. He reasoned that it made more sense to burn the draft cards of young American men than permit the American governement to burn Vietnamese children while remaining legally unaccountable and morally unchallenged. Such a rare and conscious and uncompromising morality, "though devoutly to be wished" by both, was equally feared by church and state. And Berrigan was charged full fare to yearn for such freedom and moral integrity. Thus the brilliant American Jesuit was rendered "a meddlesome priest" and in the process came to comprehend something very fundamental about Job early on.

Raising the ante of personal involvement so high struck fear into the hearts of fellow travelers as well. Shortly before he began his sentence, Dan was confronted by a pacifist with a resonable lament: "It's different for you, Father Berrigan; you don't have any children. What's going to happen to our children if we go to prison for opposing the war?" Father Berrigan's response was no less lamentable, "What's going to happen to them if you don't?" And they took him away.

They were taking him away again in the summer of 1981 when I came to New York to play the judge in a docudrama on the trial of the "Plowshares Eight." Long after his release from prison and the end of the war in Vietnam, long after the American Peace Movement had virtually dissolved, Dan—again with

his brother Philip and now with six close friends—entered a security area of the General Electric plant in King of Prussia,
Pennsylvania, and "attacked" the nosecones of two MX-12
nuclear missiles. They poured their own blood over them and
beat them with hammers in a powerful and symbolic fulfillment
of the ancient command of the prophet Isaiah, "Beat swords
into plowshares and study war no more." The action struck at
the very heart of American militarism and the immorality of
the arms race, and this small group of Catholic radicals would
pay dearly. Found guilty, the eight defendants were facing over
ten years in federal prison. However, they were free pending an
appeal, and director Emile de Antonio took advantage of the
situation while he made a documentary film on the group and
their action. Denied permission to film in court during the trial,
Antonio decided to dramatize the proceedings using the trial
transcripts with actors playing all the members of the court and
the defendants "playing themselves." Thus I made my entrance
into Daniel Berrigan's life! Granted that reality must shed image in order for friendship to begin, still I was not prepared for
such an extraordinary reality or friendship.

Berrigan was perhaps the most admired and beloved Catholic priest in the United States and by far its most famous Jesuit.
Yet he wore second-hand clothing with no Roman collar and
lived in a tiny apartment in a New York City working-class
neighborhood. And though this thin and handsome Daniel
had spent considerable time among lions in many dens, he was
gentle and friendly with a quick smile and a hardy laugh. He
was openly engaging as well, with a sharp and brilliant Irish
wit, but there was something in his eyes, or I dare say *behind*
them, that spoke another language altogether. And a part of
me that understood some of that language knew that knowing
him would change my life fundamentally.

I had only recently returned to Catholicism after a long absence, and I was searching for a way to unite the will of the
Spirit to the work of the flesh. What better example to follow

than this "meddlesome priest" with the enviable courage to challenge Christianity to block the slouching beast's path to
Bethlehem and rediscover the reality of the nonviolent Jesus!
Who spent his life speaking out and acting against war, violence, and nuclear weapons. Who had stood with the suffering
masses, the victims of war, the starving and the poor from Vietnam to Central America to South Africa, the homeless on our
own city streets, people with AIDS, and those on death row. Who
despite his age and fragile health has been arrested scores of
times, always with a peaceful plea that the killing might stop,
that injustice might cease, and that the healing might begin.
Who has stood with the suffering and suffered with them from
north Vietnam to Northern Ieland and the Middle East and along
the way recorded his journey with volumes of poetry and more
than fifty books, including his powerful autobiography *To Dwell
in Peace.* Who continues to teach and preach at universities and
give seminars and spiritual retreats all over the world. Who better indeed! And how fitting that he should take up the Book of
Job to find meaning and insight into our world of suffering and
his own lifelong solidarity with it.

The haunting story of Job is an image of the world's poor and
our response and/or lack of response to it. It is ultimately a story
of faith despite our doubts, of hope despite our despair, of love
despite our indifference. Berrigan unlocks the mystery of
Dostoevsky's intriguing quote: "My greatest fear is that I will not
be worthy of my suffering" and he calls Job "a summons to live
humanly in a bad time" as it places into question our own response to God and to one another in the face of human suffering.
Like Berrigan's own life, it summons us to live more humanly;
to be people of peace, compassion, and nonviolence; and to remain faithful to the God of peace and justice even though the
world and our own doubt tell us otherwise.

Together Job and Berrigan summon us to trust in God despite
all, to remain faithful to the way of nonviolence, and to walk in
solidarity with the suffering peoples of the world so that we may

come to know ourselves more humanly as God knows us and
find more of God in each other's suffering.

Finally, Berrigan reminds us that nearly all of humanity's
suffering is inflicted from the First world on the Third, that personal suffering is universally necessary for spiritual growth, and
that the worst suffering of all is to suffer alone.

Martin Sheen
2/2/2000

Preface

"I know that my redeemer liveth . . ."

Not much to hang one's hopes on, we are told; the words are a limping translation of a corrupt Hebrew text.

And yet, and yet, how the words resonate, amid conflict and opposition, luminous, teasing with hope!

The story is ancient—and new. A chieftain, a giant among his people, grows prosperous. He is favored of God, honored among his own.

Then, a sea change. In multiple guises, from above and around, from Deity to demon to companions, from bodily illness to ecological ruin, death moves on him. Job is stricken ill, family and goods are snatched away. His scene of torment; an ash heap, or a town dump.

And in the midst of such travail, those words, "I know that my Redeemer . . ." are left hanging there; a future vindication, integrity restored, a sane universe, restoration of all . . .

On the cusp of old age I took a serious, extended look at the book of Job (rather ruefully, and with an eye over the shoulder, knowing I'd already exceeded the biblical allotment by years).

It was perhaps inevitable, that tardiness; at least I so console myself. I had first to make my way through the *selva oscura* of Dante's *purgatorio*—a tortuous passage through American alarms and wars, bombs and incursions, from '67 to — when? circa 2000 at the least.

Meantime, for years, I studied Job. By common consent of the ages, it offered a singular version. Better, a vision.

Job, an exemplary human being, persuasive, bracing—and hard to take.

A character unlike any other in the Bible. Of no prophet is so excruciating a story told, in such relentless detail.

Job stands under a veritable firestorm. It assails his physical integrity, his virtue, his faith. God, Satan, and a coven of humans bear down on him. Each is intent on a curious, not altogether admirable project—the "testing" of the just.

An awful book, in the biblical sense. A book that made me pause in the reading, ponder, often tempted to lay it aside. Simply too much.

Too much, this *laissez-faire* God. Who was he anyway, by what right did he bargain his friend away? This sinuous world-weary Satan, too clever by half. And that trio, pouring a salt of contempt into a friend's wounds.

And too much—Job himself. A mighty protagonist, a prince among men. And more; one who, as is strongly implied, speaks for us all, speaks in our name, bespeaks the human predicament.

Speaks for my condition, and yours? The notion is appalling. He confronts the illusions we live by, the empty fealties we offer a culture of death, our dismal, rote pieties.

The book is a judgment. We meet our match. We, the masters of the world's game, as the game is rewarded—and punished.

The quintessential American game; for every winner, many losers. Winners inside the borders, losers beyond. The military thrives on such assumptions, in principle. So does the world economy, runaway, set in fast-forward gear.

We know there are losers in the world. In an honest moment we might even admit that Americans create them, multitudes of losers. But the fact is after all, somewhat inert. Hardly impinging or breaking the skin. Or leading to ethical change, as goes without saying.

Then comes this book of Job, the drama of a born loser.

And, perish the thought—what if we ourselves were, in someone's eyes, losers? What if Job were an image, straight from the hand of the Maker of Images—an image of the American plight, the first world plight, of our uneasy place in creation, our larcenous wealth? What if Job bespoke the effect on the flesh of humanity, of our spiritual "underdevelopment," our intractable violence?

Job, image of the human—precisely as loser; Job afflicted—and as such commended to ourselves. Figure him out.

I studied Job; and I learned—some few things. A summons to live humanly in a bad time. A faith that verges on despair, that looks that dark eminence in the face and is not turned to stone. A faith desolate before the injustice of the world. A faith that survives a barrage of nostrums, accusations, insults. A faith that would not be put to silence.

A faith kindred to the one discovered by Jacques Sommet, French Jesuit who died in Dachau; "a new faith, the faith of the charnel house."

Job's faith. A faith that in conventional eyes—those friends again—very much resembles blasphemy.

Job the loser, and Job the teacher. I was put off by contradictory, litigious squabbling, by endless entrances and exits, doors that open only to slam shut, refusal of comfort or assurance, argument and counter-argument, characters insulting and demeaning one another, even as they invoke competing gods . . . What a welter!

I longed to have done with this imbroglio, a drama that dares question my status in the universe, in history, before God—before the victims of American bombs-at-the-ready, a carnivorous world-throttling economics, an internal combustion machine of violence.

And questions. Not new ones by any means. I sensed that somewhere in the dark spaces of the American psyche (in my own psyche), a question was lodged. What if a heavenly being, an eye resting on America, grew frosty? What if a thumb were to turn down on us. And we declared the unchosen?

The book brings such suspicion to the fore, mercilessly. It implies a radical reversal of roles, one after another. And this, even as everyone is apparently mortised securely in place. God in heaven, only slightly concerned with the plight of his friend; more concerned to prevail in his shady bargaining. And Satan prowling the earth, a hand of death laid on Job.

And the plight of Job, for forty-two interminable chapters, is driven home. Followed by a brief, scarcely believable summary of relief and restoration.

Unsettling, shifting, no firm ground underfoot. Every character, no matter how high and mighty, every lofty repute, held up for fierce reappraisal. No one, not even God himself, justified, approved, allowed to come off as morally admirable, untinged by selfishness or ego.

God enters into a vile bargain whose prey is the life and well-being of—a friend. Satan is thoroughly—Satan; which is to say, twisting goodness to bizarre ends. And Job, complex, truculent, near blasphemous, his moods veering between despair and ecstasy.

And of those friends, less said the better—surely among the least attractive companions ever assembled around a figure of woe. Cocksure, petrified in orthodoxy, discrediting the suffering one, peddling their version of God as judge.

And they sum Job up, dissect him like a corpse on a gurney. He is self-deluded and secretly given to wicked ways.

One can only advise; beware, sensitive souls, this cast of characters!

But the author asks in effect; will you understand?

He presents a human passing through the knothole of actual, awful life. Not Job, the prospering chief secure in possessions (only slight attention is lent that circumstance, a prelude to the main act).

The main act is terrible. Utter downfall, wounds, pettiness, and grandeur, bursts of anguish and fear and dread. A story that shocks, a kind of Greek recognition scene, a devastating cultural critique.

And an offering too; of a possible healing, even a kind of rebirth, a new sense of ourselves in the biblical "scheme of things."

Connections. When I turn from the book to the world, I see Job as a social image. He is multiplied, from one era and culture to another and another—and on to our own.

Today Job is an image of those who dwell in a world we Americans have both named and created; the "third" world.

But more than "out there," he dwells in our own assaulted humanity. As well as in the slain, the bombed, the refugees, the unwanted, and undocumented. The expendables.

We will never have done with him, this semblance, this haunt. He stands at the end time, the time of no recourse, of no mercy.

We are never done with him, with the summons to stand at his side. In solace, in binding up wounds. In resistance against a vile bargain ("let him prove himself, let God and Satan judge him, and his friends to boot"). A bargain sealed in heaven—or in hell.

Ironically (and this is only a beginning of ironies) we are told that Job was an enemy of the chosen, an Edomite.

A "thank-you," is due, then, to an unlikely benefactor. And a muted "alleluia" as well.

Acknowledgments

The text of Job is a daunting thicket of what experts call "variant readings." Choices of this version over that, arrived at with many a furrow of the brow, must take in account the following items of the history of the book. From time nearly immemorial, scribes, rabbis, the Greek Septuagint, Saint Jerome and his famous helper, the rabbi of Lydda, all have poured fat on fires of conjecture, have aided and abetted (even while striving to restore) the corruption of meaning, one or another producing commentaries that echo ideology or special pleading.

Thus the text of Job, to a degree unknown elsewhere in the Bible, has been severely mauled by time and human hands.

Can there be an implication here, I asked myself, a hidden logic, even a wisdom? I indulge in a hunch; the tradeoffs and patching of editors can be taken as a kind of parable. The medium itself is a message; the variant readings form a kaleidoscope, flashing off images of the story, the agony of Job. And we improvisers, for all our clumsiness, willy nilly are illustrating a truth. Is the text, in the frosty eye of exegetes, a disaster? It is. But so is the human predicament disastrous, our history, our present millennium an incoherent mess of ego, violence, dispassion, greed—nightmarish, yielding no sense.

This being lamentably true, should not the tale of Job be as hard to decipher, as surreal as a page of Kafka or Ionesco or certain gruesome episodes of *Bleak House?* Talk about cold comfort!

✦ ✦ ✦

As to versions of Job, I've generally stuck close to the Tanakh of the Jewish Publication Society (JPS). A scholar of the eminence of Jaroslav Pelikan, I thought, would prove a sound guide in obscure matters.

The Bible of Jerusalem (JB) in its original French fascicles, has been helpful if at times pedantic, pious, chary of controversy, rarely exciting. So too the Revised Standard Version (RSV), New American Bible (NAB), the Good News Bible (GNB), and so on. Each has strengths, each limps.

✦ ✦ ✦

A word concerning my method, such as it is. In this I differ sharply from most conventional commentaries.

It may be thought helpful to biblical understanding to have one's family and friends in prison for peacemaking, to be rather constantly arrested one's self, to walk the biblical talk, for years. My longing is to make whatever sense is possible of my own times, which I consider in the American instance starkly demented and dangerous beyond imagining. I gain a small consolation, enough to keep going, by taking the measure of a death-ridden culture, my own, against the biblical version of the human. I want to explore that measure, helped greatly by friends and family who, in bleak times, "measure up"—and then some.

The accompanying watercolors and line drawings of Robert McGovern require a word of special gratitude. *Unafraid* is a word that (perhaps strangely) occurs to me; he ventures into the darkness of Job's plight fearlessly, as though plunging into the *selva oscura* of Dante.

So does the word *modest* seem apt. Robert abides by careful limits, boundaries; nothing olympian or baroque or overbearing in these images. On first receiving his sketches, a group of us passed them hand to hand, reduced to silence. Words were redundant. A master was helping us see.

And thank you, Martin Sheen, famously courageous, overgenerous as is your way.

And lauds to Jeremy Langford—a rare editor indeed, biblical literacy being in such times a highly endangered endowment.

Introduction

Seven prophets prophesied for the gentiles; Balaam and his father, and Job and his four friends

—Talmud

✦ ✦ ✦

Job never existed, was never created; the book is a parable.

—Talmud

✦ ✦ ✦

First as to the author. He is manifestly Jewish, sophisticated, skilled in borrowing and integrating into his work the prophets and their revelatory images. He is familiar with the Sages of Israel, with Jeremiah and the Suffering Servant of Isaiah, with erudite Ezekiel and the author of Lamentations.

He ranges widely, an ecumenical genius of the first order, knowledgeable in the writings of foreign Sages, especially of the Egyptians.

✦ ✦ ✦

The beginning is fabulous; we are to know from the start (God will admit as much, so will we)—our Job is a personage larger than life, archaic, mythical, even archetypal. A patriarch of the stature of Abraham or Jacob or Moses. A towering eminence!

Never again, it is implied, will his like walk the earth.

1

Contrasts, vivid primary colors clash. Job is a non-Jew; more, it is adduced that he springs from a race roundly hated by the chosen. From the Edomites, a people who brought about the fall of Jerusalem, as Ezekiel 35 testifies.

✦   ✦   ✦

He strides grandly into the Hebrew Bible, this outsider confidently at home, for all the world like a grand ancestor of the chosen. As though; of course! he belongs there.

Through the first pages of the book he strides, followed by multitudinous progeny and grand possessions, a splendid sight to behold, sons and daughters, flocks and herds all but numberless.

✦   ✦   ✦

We are to know his title to prestige, to high moral quality. Job is holy and upright, declared such by the most High.

He is a companion in spirit to Tobias, one thinks, to the martyred sons and mother of the Maccabees, to prophets known and anonymous, to the "Suffering Servant" of Isaiah.

In sum, he belongs in the higest ranks of spiritual nobility, to the primordial Hebrew communion of saints.

Is he not of the company hailed by Isaiah, crossing boundaries set in place by enmity and racial fear? Does Job not signal the end of tribal religion?

Isaiah declared it first, an end and a beginning;

> The mountain of God's house
> shall be established as the highest mountain . . .
>
> all nations shall stream toward it,
> many peoples shall come and say;
>
> "Come, let us climb God's mountain . . ." (2:2, 3)

chapter one

"Perish the Day I Was Born"
(1:1–3:26)

1:1–5 Virtue and riches; they go together in this protoCalvinistic universe. Job is "wealthier than anyone in the East"; the abundance is laid on thick, irrefutable, carnal, fabulous.

Assemble the superlatives, enlarge credence.

Job, let it be confessed, is beyond summoning in the flesh. At the beginning, he exists in imagination only, like unexampled, peerless Solomon.

Only later, reduced and demeaned, he becomes credible. Only then does he exist in our image.

His life takes the tormented form of a question. How shall this paragon, summoned to the page by a nameless poetic and psychological genius—how shall he survive the double onslaught; of God, and the parched moralists who arrive to condole with him, and linger only to harrass?

We shall see.

✦   ✦   ✦

At the start and throughout, the setting must upbear a series of furious ironies and contradictions.

We imagine the stage; in the background the gates of a city.

In foreground, a house of mirrors—or a house of horrors. Or both.

The flooring of the house is strangely rickety. Careful, Job, it may collapse underfoot, and tumble the holy protagonist into—Sheol?

No, worse; into this world. A world of friends. Of a certain ilk.

✦ ✦ ✦

These will be confounded; how shall they appraise him? So they will talk interminably of how to appraise him.

Which is to say, they arrive at fantasies, figments, pieces of a life.

They lack simpatico, they care and do not care; ambiguity lies in the voices, the roll of eyes.

They know nothing of what he endures—and do not greatly want to know.

After all, they are untouched by the Hand from the Cloud that creates and destroys, the Hand that touches Job and makes of him a very leper, white as snow.

✦ ✦ ✦

And what of their notion of God?

It is exactly that; notional—complacent and abstract and narrow of scope. Their god fits the narrowed eye of those who appraise life, weigh it close—for a *quid pro quo,* a virtue and reward. A gimlet god.

✦ ✦ ✦

Perhaps we have in the trio early examples of pharisaic religion, or of bourgeois religion.

Whatever its name, such devotion is a cloak; or on the faces of the "friends" of Job, a mask.

Does it cover and conceal reality? One suspects so.

✦ ✦ ✦

In any case, this garment, this mask, renders its wearers self-justified, sterile of mind and heart, indifferent to the plight of others. So clothed, so concealed, they walk safe and sure in the world, stiff with rectitude, purveyors of judgment.

They come down heavy on the faults, presumed or actual, of others. The human tribe, it appears, is Fallen irrevocably, prone and helpless; the central truth of their religion.

Whether the same humans, under an impulse of grace, are enabled to rise once more, is moot.

Words like *love, compassion*, seldom if ever visit their tongues.

✦ ✦ ✦

The friends confront Job under an asumption of close access to the mind of the Almighty. Who, truth told (and they are apt to proclaim the truth loud and clear, on any occasion), much resembles themselves. A god of rectitude, heavy on judgment, an overseer of jots and tittles.

To their god as well, words like *love, compassion*, seldom occur.

✦ ✦ ✦

Such religion, one thinks, can be bought and sold in a flea market of the ancient East. Or in the West as well; one thinks of the scene in the agora of Athens, where Paul encountered a near dead end, and was dismissed by logicians and triflers (Acts 17:16–34).

✦ ✦ ✦

But as to Job, blessings accrue and multiply. "That man was wealthier than anyone in the East." First by reason of a large family; "seven sons and three daughters."

Positively Solomonic, the excess, one revels in it!

And we are dizzied; knowing the outcome, we cannot but calculate the weight, the gravity, the depth of the fall.

The fall. Not into Sheol (Hebrew for *hell*)—into mortal life.

Job falls into the world. The world, carnivorous toward his kind, receives him with open jaws.

✦ ✦ ✦

Job's friends, we concede, are correct, to a point; that world is Fallen; it belongs by inference and more—by befouling claim—to the adversary, ha-Satan (Hebrew for *Satan*), shortly to appear.

So. Let Job perish there, in the jaws; pity, it is a case of like and alike. Job too is—fallen.

✦ ✦ ✦

Such popular tales as ours are very demons of timing and exclusion. At whatever cost or loss, push the action along! is the law.

Thus, of the spouse of Job and mother of his progeny, not a word as yet. Where is she, who is she?

Her too we shall encounter, along with other actors deemed useful to the story. Who talk awhile, or do not; who are nameless or named. But in any case, are expendable.

✦ ✦ ✦

Merciless! Sons and daughters are summarily removed from the earth. They die impersonally, dolls flung aside, limbs askew.

We are in the grim world of the brothers Grimm.

✦ ✦ ✦

We are briefly introduced to the close-knit family of Job, as his progeny gather for a celebration.

Father Job, we note, is absent. Perhaps he lives at distance or is busy with other concerns—patriarch of a huge hegemony, and with many affairs pressing, land, herds, overseers.

✦ ✦ ✦

Of one matter Job is always mindful, if not scrupulous; the religious duties of his family. Their celebrations, he insists, must be joined with prayer.

Job urges; let us celebrate of course. But let us also cleanse ourselves, father and offspring, from even inadvertent fault.

✦ ✦ ✦

As for ourselves, the omniscient readers at the edge of the story, we are invited to praise Job. And who would not?

O admirable man, likened to Tobit; who for a brief moment, honors our page;

> I Tobit walked all the days of my life in the paths of truth and righteousness. I performed many charitable works for my kinsfolk and my people who had been deported with me to Nineveh. . . .
>
> I would often make the pilgrimage alone to Jerusalem for the festivals, as prescribed for all Israel . . . bringing with me the first fruits of the field and the firstlings of the flock . . . (Tobit 1:3, 6).

✦ ✦ ✦

Job and Tobit, content, devout, filled to brim with good fortune.

And we cannot but think (dwelling as we do in a world edgy with premonition, laced with catastrophe)—this fortunate Job, how unready he is, an innocent, seeing nothing of lengthening shadows, hearing nothing of a whisper along a darkening wall. Ignorant as well of a maleficence or envy or evil, hot on the spoor of such as himself.

That whisper.

It is barely audible; and it is furious, barely contained.

One day it will rise to a shout and wrack the earth. Bring Job down!

✦ ✦ ✦

1:6–12 We are transported without preliminary to a heavenly court.

For the storyteller, the passage is easy; after all, creation is "charged with the grandeur of God." And earth is conjoined with heaven, we are told elsewhere, in a burning wayside bush.

Moses has shown the way; converse with God is only slightly removed from face-to-face converse with a friend. We humans are a stone's throw distant from beatitude.

Do our shoes impede? Take them off! (Exodus 3:2–4)

✦ ✦ ✦

Or another event. One night we settle to sleep, and lo! in dream the heavens open, and the "Bene Elohim," angels of the court of heaven, ascend and descend (Genesis 27:42–46).

No wonder the celestial ladder is named for the dreamer, Jacob!

✦ ✦ ✦

So here they assemble, citizens of heaven; God, the Elohim, the "heavenly court."

And another—is he not an interloper in that place where only goodness dwells?

He enters, strangely at home, jaunty even. A demon on holiday?

The "adversary," "ha-Satan." The author makes of him a kind of emissary or overseer of creation, with overtones of malice, envy. A renegade in court?

✦ ✦ ✦

A good storyteller stops us short. Ha-Satan takes his place, nonchalant.

And the heavenly proceeding continues, serenely. This dark one, a kind of Iago, is quite taken for granted.

He can be dealt with? A strange, perhaps perilous innocence rides the air.

✦ ✦ ✦

In this sense perhaps, the "adversary" can be dealt with; goodness knows goodness, goodness also knows evil. And certainly, to the thinking of celestial beings, it is preferable that "ha-Satan" stand visible in their midst. Than that he (*sic*) lurk about on the fringes of heaven and earth.

Let him stand forth then. Let him be heard from.

✦ ✦ ✦

God opens the proceedings, with a word of common courtesy. He takes ceremonial note of the presence of ha-Satan—though perhaps with deep intent.

—Where have you been?

—Roaming all over the earth.

Offhand as well (though perhaps with a darker implication). A later Scripture will add; "seeking whom he may devour."

✦   ✦   ✦

In the question there lurks only the slightest hint. But it is there; ha-Satan has exceeded his rightful place.

We note no such questioning of the other servitors, though the Elohim as well, given the evidence of the famous ladder of Jacob, are busy about human affairs and intercessions.

✦   ✦   ✦

Now to dark matters. Let us dare adduce it; the god makes his first mistake.

A primary rule would seem to hold firm, in heaven as on earth; no discussion with ha-Satan.

Not idly is that tongue described as forked. Talk interminable and tendentious, close woven logic, evidence solid—seeming as a pavement underfoot (but shallow), arguments seemingly irrefutable, making the better the enemy of the good—these are the strong suits of ha-Satan.

These; and the pressing of every advantage. Noting weakness, countering with a pounce.

✦   ✦   ✦

Where are we on the scale of time, as calculated in this world? Is the adversary in the book of Job one with the serpentine agent who brought the first parents to woe?

We recall how mother Eve offered a foolish courtesy to a like dark eminence, with a notorious outcome.

Shall God be luckier, or more skilled?

✦ ✦ ✦

The strong suits of the holy are—silence and contravening deeds.

And above all, refusal to be named.

Evil knows neither itself, nor goodness. But one who gives a name away will shortly suffer control and manipulation.

The naming need not be explicit; as though ha-Satan would dare say, I know you, God. No. Subtler, more sinuous; wind the holy One about, like coils about a Tree of Life. With every word, back, around, forth, the coils tighten.

Until; Now I have you!

Which is to say; Now I have your man Job.

✦ ✦ ✦

To have and to hold.

God, innocent as Eve handing over a fruit, hands Job over.

—Have you noticed my servant Job?

How right and just one thinks, that God boast of Job to the Elohim.

But this praise is dangerous. God would have Job known; but notoriety is perilous; even holy notoriety.

God, so naive as to single out a mortal to ha-Satan—more, praise and exult in that one?—and presume that the one so named will not become a prey?

The innocence of the Unfallen—it is as though Jawe were to point out a solitary deer to a tiger.

This tiger hungers, the liverish hunger known as envy.

✦ ✦ ✦

In the present setting ha-Satan appears neutral, politesse echoing his sense of rightful hierarchy.

He would "test" Job. He would test the one—and best the Other.

Through the just one, he would best God. This "god," who to his mind, can be shamed, discredited, dethroned. Deprived of a capital letter.

He will shame God as well. This, through the fall of Job, soon to be discredited, tumbled down from prosperity and honor.

As Job falls, he will curse; or thereafter. Behold the shaming of God, before elohim and humans!

✦   ✦   ✦

Let us concede something. Evil knows somewhat of goodness; not much, only enough to pursue a conversation, to probe weakness. The weakness of the holy, which is innocence.

Or tactically speaking, a weakness that praises. Praises a goodness that mirrors one's own. Job, mirror of God. Praise him.

God praises a goodness that leaves God and Job vulnerable— to the envy of the wicked.

✦   ✦   ✦

Being wicked, ha-Satan cannot, will not emulate goodness. He can seek only to defeat, humiliate, bring goodness to naught.

Praise of Job before the Elohim befits; *dignum et justum*, "right and just."

But it is not the Elohim who are addressed.

The Lord said to the adversary—

> Have you taken notice
> of my servant Job?
>
> on earth
> none compares with him.
>
> Blameless and upright
> he fears God
> and shuns evil (Job 1:8)

✦   ✦   ✦

The adversary, the testing, the shaming—of God, of Job.

God has wittingly or not, opened himself to a momentous invasion; by the same token, Job is grown vulnerable. Trust is invaded, on both sides.

We note the tactic, the verbal ploy of ha-Satan. Paint with broad strokes a picture of earthly prosperity. A caricature. Make it bright as a child's drawing, all sunlit.

Job's world. Set him down there, patriarchal, somewhat passive, somewhat sated with good living. The smoke of sacrifice rising, easy sacrifice, fat dripping from the bone.

✦   ✦   ✦

Mockery follows, a question put ever so subtly in the negative, a dark nuanced accusation.

> Have you not
> fenced Job about,
>
> him and his household
> and all that he has? (Job 1:9)

A cynical twist on providential love.

Job untested. Possessions; sweet cheats? impediments of true devotion?

In sum, ha-Satan offers a demonic version of Job, of his worth, his life and faith. As though it were impossible to prosper and still love and believe, trust and entrust.

✦   ✦   ✦

A contest begins between God and the adversary, with Job's fidelity as high stakes. It is as though the scene of Genesis, the testing and Fall, must be played out once more.

As though, as though. As though until loss and death find their way into the Jobian garden of delights, nothing of the truth of life can emerge. Only a cartoon of life below, Job exulting in his prosperity, untested, perilously innocent.

A cartoon whose artisan is ha-Satan.

Thus the riposte, coil on coil about the tree of life.

Then—I have him!

✦   ✦   ✦

Even as humans are bound to change, so must the God of humans change. We are in the grand era of Isaiah and the prophets, sources of the book of Job. Questions circulate wildly about. God speaks from a whirlwind, we will be told.

So do humans; they dare, they risk. They are in fact being weaned from deuteronomic, more or less forced fealty, more or less rigid and ruled.

A religion of children is yielding, in view of mature, free worship, freely offered.

Does God desire humans free, or in bonds? Is Job, his fretting persistance, to be embraced as an ideal, an icon of faith?

What of the three "friends" and their clanking theologisms? Is their god of strict requital to be accounted true God?

Uncertainty, conflict within. Conflict above and below.

Shall we infer a kind of insecurity on high?

✦   ✦   ✦

God reflects. Why not then, test this good man, that his goodness be further enhanced; My goodness too, before the Elohim and before ha-Satan, further enhanced?

And God yields. Let Job be the prey, unknowing, of a cruel contest. The terms, be it noted, are set by ha-Satan.

See,
all that he has
is in your power (Job 1:12)

And then, as though over the shoulder, the Deity departing, the audience concluded—

Only this;
do not lay a hand on him (Job 1:12)

But this prohibition too will yield.

✦   ✦   ✦

Point by point, God yields. Job's possessions are given over to this bizarre contest.

And finally Job's person will be handed over.

Shall one judge God?

Like this. Drawn into the tainted drama, who is not made complicit?

God, not complicit?

Having so to speak, consented to sup with the devil. Having neglected to carry a long spoon.

✦   ✦   ✦

1:13–22 It is all done with obscene speed, the wrecking.

A single gesture. We imagine the finger of the adversary stretching out, in mockery of Genetic creation.

And the life of Job, his labor, his large scope, herds and flocks and house and family and—

These fall, as though with the nudge of a finger. Everything down.

✦ ✦ ✦

The scene is skillfully handled, with finesse. One disaster, one messenger on the heels of another.

Messenger 1; oxen, she-asses are stolen, herders put to the sword.

2; fire from heaven (whose heaven?). Sheep and shepherds alike perishing on the instant.

3; poachers descend on the camels; herders killed.

And 4, and most awful, the demise of Job's family.

A mighty wind;

> from the wilderness struck the house
> where seven
> were banqueting (Job 1:19)

The house fell like a house of cards. In the rubble were found no survivors.

✦ ✦ ✦

Is the story beyond belief? Does such disaster, total, all but instantaneous, never befall our world?

The hurricane that struck Nicaragua, Honduras, Salvador, Guatemala in November 1998 destroyed everything in its ambit. Literally everything. An apocalypse, forty hours of anti-creation. Families vanished, together with crops and animals. Entire countrysides were reduced to a flat sea of mud; no verdure, no animals, no survivors.

A Jobian scene, socialized, a rehearsal of the last day.

The infrastructure of entire countries lay in a tangle of wreckage.

✦ ✦ ✦

With Job, the testing is underway, with a vengence.

"But do not touch Job's person."

Is God not aware that ha-Satan has already precisely touched Job's person?

The fourth message has numbed his mind, turned his heart to ice.

Seven days to create the world, how much time required to destroy it?

✦　✦　✦

Good news is astonishing, and reaches us in its own good time; a week of creation. Ill news on the contrary, races toward us pell mell, the world jumbled into a sack of misery; oxen, sheep, camels, humans, all vanished;

> This messenger
> was still speaking,
> when another arrived . . .

> This one
> was still speaking,
> when another . . .

> And yet another;

> Your sons and daughters . . .

For God and the ha-Satan, the wager, the celestial-infernal game is underway. A winner will emerge. A loser already has.

✦　✦　✦

And the hazards, the stakes, the odds? They are held by—Job. Truth told (the truth is a low priority)—Job holds the joker. The first act is but half underway, already he is the loser. With worse to come.

✦　✦　✦

The question arises again and again; what to make of these stories?

How seriously are we to take them, as dramatic emblems of our plight in the world, our faith under seige—the plight of our tribe? Are we to be thought a multitude of Jobs, beset with loss, betrayed, lied to, denied a voice, land and resources seized and polluted?

✦ ✦ ✦

And what to make of this heaven and its drama? What to make of the behavior of God?

And then that "adversary," that "ha-Satan," to whom good sense (with a kind of contempt to be sure) denies a capital letter—what of that eminence, pretender and prosecutor and mocker of the good and valiant, who beyond all good sense, must suffer?

✦ ✦ ✦

> Naked I came from my mother's womb, and naked shall
> I return there; the LORD gave, and the LORD has taken
> away; blessed be the name of the LORD (Job 1:20–22).

The poetry is beyond praise, an image and summoning of a faith that overcomes.

How redundant to praise its grandeur, how unbefitting to harness Pegasus in prose!

The ambiguity of "mother's womb" has been admired, justly so. Mother, mother earth; we have come from both "wombs." We shall return to the latter one, from which we and the ancestors were drawn.

Thus the cycle, sublime and "of the earth, earthly."

Naked Job came, naked he goes.

In loss and desolation of spirit, his world turned to dust and ashes, he comes to know himself.

✦ ✦ ✦

It might have been spoken by a Lazarus risen; he utters a confession close to the bone—the human, its limit, our small land grant in the world—the length and breadth of a grave, all said—the strait boundaries of the human, drawn close in time allotted and place assigned.

And the end; the dribble of a handful of clay on a coffin lid.

Goodness accomplished, goodness laid claim to? Come now, all that is in other hands.

✦ ✦ ✦

> The Lord has given,
> the Lord has taken (Job 1:21)

Life is a gift, better, a loan; on this basis we proceed, now firm of step, now faltering, toward—eventuality. Every debt comes due; alas, even (or perhaps especially) this one. Death is the calling in of the debt.

✦ ✦ ✦

There exists a third party, a third presence—to birth, as to death.

Seven children were born to father Job, the gift of this "third," a kind of tender midwife whose skilled hand urged them forth.

Years passed. The children grew, youth and promise abounded.

Then without rhyme or reason they perished.

There was present at the catastrophe an invisible mourner to receive and welcome them—elsewhere. Or so faith tells us.

✦   ✦   ✦

The "seven" are fitting images of all children who perish, wantonly or by design, unwanted or mourned, by disease or at violent hands.

By unspeakable, inhuman decisions; as the "sanctions" leveled against the children of Cuba and Iraq; as in assault after assault on the people of Baghdad.

✦   ✦   ✦

Job has broken through the cycle that would reason and rage, and raging, lose all reason.

This swift chaos, this death multiplied, is the work of demons; or of impersonal fate, the *fata morgana*.

Shall the survivor shrug, and resume his trudge in a world grown merciless and opaque?

A world of walls, a nightmare, walls that move and move closer, their top rolled round in razor wire; no entrance, no exit?

✦   ✦   ✦

"Blessed be the Name of the Lord." Easily recited, in course of nature's fullness, when the heart overflows. As when a child is born.

But wait. Out of season, out of right reason, the child perishes. And now, in pitch of grief, who can summon the blessing?

Job does. Blessed be he.

We ponder, and admire, and are put to silence. The balance, breathtakingly maintained, as though by a skilled gymnist, in this brief quatrain! Shall we call it Job's unwobbling pivot of faith?

Birth to death, lightness, weight, a single gift. Blessed be the Giver!

✦   ✦   ✦

So much to absorb and take to heart. The death of children is multiplied in this year, in every year of what seems at times a century accursed.

God and the devil in consonance, in a kind of horrid mutuality, curious, detached, bending above the world, testing, testing?

And the house of the family of Job, the human family, falling in wreckage?

✦   ✦   ✦

The "great wind from the wilderness" was no catastophe in nature.

Nothing of that.

Rather, a cruise missile "struck the four corners of the house, so that it collapsed upon the young people and they died."

The literal, horrific scene was enacted in the bomb shelter in Baghdad in 1996. The missile struck, a multitude were incinerated.

✦   ✦   ✦

What of ourselves? Shall we despair in face of this willful infliction of death?

Shall we grow grim of mein, plod the earth unreconciled, burdened with a constricting fury, stalemated, allowing monstrous acts to proceed in our name? Shall we not raise an outcry?

Is not an outcry a sign—is it not the only audible sign—of faith?

✦ ✦ ✦

2:1–10 Act Two.

Heavenly court, angels and ha-Satan in attendance. The latter is by no means set back by what he has seen on earth; Job afflicted, Job faithful.

He would have the man caving in, to despair, to cursing. Such an outburst would offer a peculiar satisfaction to the antagonist; Job would then resemble the undoer of Job.

And God? The Deity would be put to shame, a capital victory.

And on earth would exist a lesser human, a kind of surrogate ha-Satan, lesser perhaps in degree of despair and alienation, nonetheless conformed to a greater.

✦ ✦ ✦

The innocence of God is passing strange, and intact.

The Deity still thinks to prevail in this matter of godly Job. More reasoning with the devil!

A first misstep yields to a second, doubly dangerous—a fire set to contain a fire.

No containing this fire.

✦ ✦ ✦

The Deity starts;
Shall you
even you,

not be moved
to praise of Job,

having heard
his praise of Me,

his trust
in face of the worst? (Job 2:3)

The hoof is cloven, the tongue forked. A sneer;

Why,
a skin
buys a skin!

Only touch
his sweet skin,
and we shall see him
turn about (Job 2:5)

Turn about, to me, not to you!

✦ ✦ ✦

In the first round, as we noted, firm boundaries were set by the Deity; no touching the person of Job.

In the second, the boundary is dissolved; now, only "spare his life."

Swift as a shot arrow, the ha-undoer and -afflictor moves against Job. And the victim is touched by a leprous finger. "Head to foot" he is stricken, a leper white as snow.

✦ ✦ ✦

. . . the story which declares our total incurable aban-donment is repugnant and will not be heard for long. There are no such stories which have won the abiding interest or loyalty of the human species—neither in the Bible nor in the perhaps older surviving tales from Mesopotamia nor in any subsequent literature. Why?

A reflex reply whould be; "because such claims are literally intolerable for long." But the reply of the Yahwist,
the Elohist, their oral predecessors, of the Christian evangelists and of most human beings would certainly be;
"because they are false." (Reynolds Price, *A Palpable God*)

✦   ✦   ✦

Job sits apart, solitary, motionless in grief. The image has
haunted the centuries. Reduced to this; naked, dust and ashes, a
potsherd to scrape his sores for phantom relief.

And for the first time, we hear from his wife.

It is as though she exists only as a kind of found object. Found,
exhibited briefly on stage, for the moment useful to the tale.

By no means to be thought equal to her celebrated, honored
spouse. Indeed, up to the moment of her sudden outburst, we
knew literally nothing of her.

Now, curiously, she plays a kind of domestic ha-mocker, an
enticer.

Is it because she has yielded to despair?

How could it be otherwise, how could she not yield?

✦   ✦   ✦

She stands in the mind, a question. We are ignorant of her
name, her emotional life, this partner in affliction.

Shall she wander the earth among the distrait ones, the
Erinyes? Shall she have no part in the Great Debate, the drama
named for Job?

✦   ✦   ✦

Job sits apart, his life in ashes.

Does she sit there at his side? We are not told.

She enters the text as a wraith, a voice, a fury. Then the scroll
closes with a sigh.

✦ ✦ ✦

We recall the wife of Lot departing the burning city, her backward look brimming with loss and sorrow. One verse, and she is disposed of (Genesis 19:26).

Lot's wife, Job's wife.

Lot's wife is by no means disposed of. She is—transfigured, made permanent on the landscape of time.

That glance of hers! It lends savor to an otherwise parched, savorless text. She looks back, she weeps. Thus she offers a human response to a world plunged in (male) inhumanity and ruin.

✦ ✦ ✦

A woman's backward glance, and now a woman's word; each is badly received, awry, each stops the text short. To a first glance the gestures, the words, form an unseemly smear on the page.

But. Like other great biblical moments, these gestures are by no means unseemly.

The outburst of Job's wife marks the text, a stain of tears, the cry of one ignored, unheard from.

Hers is a befitting plangent accompaniment, a choral ode giving voice to Job's numb acquiescent grief.

At the start he is dumb as a corpse. And she? She rages, she questions. She will not be silenced.

Hers is thus to be accounted a proper biblical search, for sense, for meaning. She is like a crone in a wrecked world; she pokes about in the debris of life, fingers things inanimate, discarded, used up. She weighs them, mourns them, finds them wanting.

✦ ✦ ✦

Weighs her spouse? Weighs God?

Is the "test" proceeding without her, the cards held by God and ha-tongue-in-cheek, the odds constant and contrary, raised and raised against herself and Job and their family?

✦ ✦ ✦

Is the test to proceed in exclusively male fashion, which is to say, adamant, ironic, parched of all tears?

And will faith in God emerge as a male vindication, a male overcoming of fate, the satisfaction of a male God who tested male virture and rejoiced in the work of his hands, Job holding steady?

✦ ✦ ✦

She, her "no," denies the domination. She and her furious outburst. She is lightning in a summer sky.

✦   ✦   ✦

Such clashes and contrasts she offers, so rich! What seems in
Job a victory over malificent circumstance, in her is pure struggle.
No outcome, nothing to glory in. She wrestles with an evil that
shakes her being.

For sake of fidelity to God, Job turns aside from ha-tempter;
his gaze is pure, in one direction only.

But she? She looks wildly about, scans the horizon near and
far, for sense, for direction. Her fists beat against empty air.

And from Job she earns only contempt; she is the demon at
his elbow. Begone, ha-spouse!

✦   ✦   ✦

Does he judge her; that it were better she had not spoken,
had not been allowed entrance to the page of what must be
accounted his story? Does she not complicate things, pollute the
text with her wild cry?

A text that up to this moment belonged to him alone, to his
godliness, clarity, valiance?

Does she threaten to subvert an otherwise strong proof, for-
warded (that ladder, alight with ascending elohim) to
headquarters? Proof that Job, speaking or mute, is the noble,
sole surrogate for humankind?

She interrupts a drama that in the eye of God, was proceeding satisfactorily.

And the actors, the decor, the text are shaken.

✦   ✦   ✦

And the author of our story. Did he envision one story to be
told, one actor to tell it, to enact it?

She thwarts him. She will not be put to silence.

Let Job insult as he will, in wounded pride of possession;

You talk
as any shameless woman (Job 2:10)

Still it is on record, her interruptive cry, all but self-combusting on the page.

Hers is another form of courage, akin to Job's. Hers too must be taken in account, praised.

✦ ✦ ✦

Entering, crying aloud; then gone. It is as though she were the wraith of his longing, the cry he forbade himself.

✦ ✦ ✦

2:11–13 Then arrive other actors, abruptly, unannounced, these Pirandellan characters. A trio (and a fourth unmentioned, tardily heard from). Momentous, portentous, "friends" from afar;

From afar
beholding Job,
they knew him not (Job 2:12)

So changed he is, so stricken in frame and spirit. And we wonder; will they know him when they grow near, when they vigil and enter combat with him?

Shortly, they will stand self-revealed; rabbis, fine-honed tongues and parched minds. Severe, commonsensical spirits!

Their strong suit is logic. A logical universe, a logical God; together with themselves, a triangulation of logic. Irrefutable.

Whose chief plaint against their friend is; that he is not—logical.

But we shall see.

✦ ✦ ✦

They arrive, they view their stricken friend. By unspoken consent they fall to silence; seven days, we are told, seven nights of silence (Job 2:13).

It is manifestly chosen with care, that measure of silence. A perfect number, the number of the First Week of All. Shall we conclude, they keep "perfectly" silent, for a "perfect" period? And that when at length they speak, their speech also will be honed to perfection? We shall see. Shall see how silence surpasses speech.

And perhaps we may even long, and Job with us, that their silence had continued throughout the text, their part in the drama reduced to—a blank!

✦ ✦ ✦

Still, considering the stage directions, "seven days, seven nights of silence," we think; not a bad start.

The days and nights are hardly wasted; time for these inveterate thinkers and talkers to commune, each with his soul, to consider the tenor of converse ahead, to weigh logical pros and cons.

Even perhaps (but under strict control of mind) to hearken (and that ever so slightly) to the heart's voice. This unaccountable suffering of a friend, What possible meaning or merit?

A good time, we think; good, even great and lofty intimations, hints, directions must come of it.

We shall be right, and we shall be so wrong!

✦ ✦ ✦

Night and day, in a congress of silence, friends surround their stricken friend.

God too, we note, is silent, and ha-Satan as well. Though we are justified surely in a suspicion; that they remain close at hand and attentive.

The scene is like an outpost at the verge of human existence. A handful keep vigil, and in the outer dark, burning eyes pierce the night.

Above, the sleepless stars and moon follow their appointed course. And in our world's vast circle, multitudes slumber on, beautiful, varied, innocent, laved in their banked or fiery dreams.

✦ ✦ ✦

The silence is of import, as the speech will be.

Indeed, the two, silence and speech are as one; joined in fiber and socket, like hip bone to thigh bone, or the word on the page to the word on the tongue.

✦   ✦   ✦

What, we wonder, is our place in that inner circle, daylong, nightlong vigilant, mourning, obeisant to larger rhythms of sea and sky?

What is our place in the world of Job's affliction—and of Job's friends?

✦   ✦   ✦

3:1–26 Silence, Then Speech.

At length, bursting like a birth withheld, the word of Job pours out, nights and days of passion uncontained.

Does he match the brief rant of his spouse? Does he consent to her urging, that he "curse God, and die"?

He stops short of that. He curses "his day." The vast outpouring is compounded with her bitterness. With such woe as curdles the sweetness of life to gall.

And if his outburst must be accounted a curse, the imprecation is aimed not at God, but at the plague of existence, his own.

The distinction is there. One thinks, it is not great.

✦   ✦   ✦

Only imagine; on the biblical page a kind of anti-Bible.

The word of God flares combustible on the tongue of the just, turns abruptly, fervently, explosively, against the gift of God— against life itself.

✦   ✦   ✦

We shall know God in the curse. This is the promise, the meaning under the denial of meaning.

And we shall know Job as well. The curse is a sign; Job takes God seriously, takes life and death seriously. It is the other side, the obverse, of the blessing; "The Lord has given and the Lord has taken away."

And the curse will have its consequence. Has Job been named "just," and by God?

Let him beware; other, less amiable judges surround him. And the face of God darkens.

Denial of holiness will be adduced, sin imputed. Job will be fiercely reproved, then put to silence, first by the trio of friends, then by God.

And from the resultant scandal—arms raised, eyes wide in repudiation of his wild words—from this, we are free to draw what conclusion makes sense, even small sense.

✦ ✦ ✦

It is helpful to recall that in the culture of Job, the spoken word is explosive, immediate—invariably raised to a shout.

The text is something else; a record of events, or of the spoken word. Event and word flatten out on the page; the record cannot summon the raw, original events surrounding Job.

Beginning with the series of disasters, events fall like an explosion and its echo. The original drama is launched on winds of fury and ecstasy, marked (and marred) by attack, rebuttal, vituperation, accusation, insult, denunciation.

✦ ✦ ✦

It is as though God, Job, and the trio of friends were adversaries in a court case. The trial proceeds out of time and place.

Let us say, behind an improbable mirror of Alice.

The antagonists are unruly, contenious, half-mad. The trial is out of control, as it is out of this world.

✦ ✦ ✦

The accusations launched against Job mount on the page, excessive, bizarre, crazily contrary to the praise bestowed by God.

And why not? We are in a courtroom; life is reduced to argument, verbal skill, rhetoric and riposte. This is a culture of the spoken, not to say the shouted word.

Will the plaints of Job not likewise appear excessive, a near curse?

✦ ✦ ✦

Today also we stand in a vortex of events, amid a gigantic irony. An embrace lifts us from earth, from reality. Then we are plunged back once more, fearful and yet in measure restored, our minds first bound close, then enraptured.

This is the mood of the world; a curse, a dark night of the spirit. Death in the saddle. And comprehension evades us; what forces are at work? When will God show face?

Evidence points to a mad governance, or none at all. Even, in the mind of some, to evil at the heart of things.

✦ ✦ ✦

Diagnoses multiply, experts testify. And little or no healing follows. Evil invades and infects high places, the stench of spiritual decay and death mounts to high heaven.

Job's question abides; were it better to be conceived and born, or worse?

Unequivocally one answers Better. But surely not everyone. Not even the fortunate are sure.

Release the dark night then, let it have sway!

Descend, go down. With Jeremiah and Job, enter the bitter malfeasant drama.

Dare one speak of a birth?

But Jeremiah too cries out, against a birth that should not have been—his own;

Cursed be the day
on which I was born!

Let not the day be called blessed
on which my mother bore me!
Cursed be the man
who brought my father the news

and said; a boy
is born to you,
and gave him such joy . . .
Why did I ever issue from the womb
to see misery and woe,
to spend my days in shame? (Jeremiah 20:14–18)

✦   ✦   ✦

And with a difference, the dark hour descended like a pall on
Jesus, a death before death;

> He withdrew . . . about a stone's throw, then went down
> on his knees and prayed in these words; "Father, if it is
> your will, take this cup from me; yet not my will but
> yours be done."

An angel then appeared from heaven to strengthen him.

In his anguish he prayed with greater intensity, and his
sweat became like drops of blood falling to ground
(Luke 22:41–44).

✦   ✦   ✦

The Friday We Name Good

You come toward me
prestigious in your wounds,
those frail and speechless bones.

Your credentials;
dying somberly for others.
What a burden—
gratitude, fake and true vows,
crucifixes
grislier than the event—
and then the glory gap—
larger than life
begetting less than life,
pieties that strike healthy eyes
blind.
Believe! Believe! Christians
tapping down the street
in harness to their seeing-eye god.
Only in solitude,
in passing tic of insight
gone as soon as granted—
I see you come toward me
free, free at last.
Can one befriend one's God?
The question is inadmissable I know.
Nonetheless a fiery recognition lights us;
broken by life
making our comeback.

DB

✦　✦　✦

Job has not cursed God; he has cursed the night of his own conception, the day of his birth. Thus too Jeremiah.

Are we dredging up a useful, indeed crucial distinction here—or are we playing at casuistry? If one curses his own existence, is he not cursing the God of life?

Still, we go slow.

In our book even the ha-Satan does not curse God—though one suspects that reticence is a matter of polity rather than conviction. He longs in his sour guts to utter damnation. But would a curse not banish him from court, diminish his equity in the Great Debate?

✦　✦　✦

Before God, the case is made against God.

This is the daring; and we, launched on a kind of high wire, tread with care. Gravity is all against us—even as grace (the long pole in hand, the sure foot on the wire) is for us.

It would be to no avail were Job to play actor in a charade, put on a peaceable face, "go on somehow," as is said. As though faith were a matter of submitting like a beast of burden to an intolerable yoke.

✦　✦　✦

The metaphors tumble about wildly. Is Job to go on as though the skies had not broken overhead and flung him prone? As though lightning had not struck; dislocation, a universe out of joint, himself flung about like a debris? All this befell him; possessions, riches, flocks, daughters, sons—snatched away.

✦ ✦ ✦

What is he to do, this just one, whose justice is not canceled, though nearly so? Whose justice is tested under a pounding pestle of distain and contention?

How comport himself, in the post-deluge of his life?

✦ ✦ ✦

The story of Job, his words, lie on the page, "for our instruction."

His questions, as they touch us and our world, are of pressing, immediate point.

A handbook for surviving humanly, and this when the pillars of existence shake about our heads.

✦ ✦ ✦

As a first "instruction," we note how Job descends, step by step, to the depths. From there, he surveys the wreckage of his world and reports on it; bleak, darkness, emptiness.

But the dark is not all. Despite all, light breaks through—wisdom amid loss.

Dawn

Dawn is up, the man walks
behind a smear of shadow.
He sings to himself; "Darkness,
cast by me, begone from me."
His soul
he holds aloft,
a burning glass.
Concentrate of dawn
burns in him—soul, his own.

DB

✦   ✦   ✦

Job tastes it, lives to tell of it; gall and wormwood, postdeluge, poststorm, postincursion, postflocks and herds, postfatherhood. His response is a poem—a shocking poem. In no conventional sense can it be called a prayer.

Is God invoked? Yes, but this is the minim God, the God who almost is not, the God of no logic, of good sense run amok. The God of broken lives.

A broken God?

One can only say; in Job's circumstance, praise of God would sound both foolish and false.

✦   ✦   ✦

Job asks only a rock-bottom favor; let God turn aside from him, ignore him utterly.

Has He not already done so? May God have no concern for it ("that day, the day of my birth"). For this God must be accounted far from providential or loving; He has "hemmed him (Job) in" (NAB), has "hedged him about" (JPS) (Job 3:23).

✦   ✦   ✦

Job longs for an end of it all; for death. Not extinction; death. The man Job, living (or as he might say, "so to speak, living") conjures images of a "postlife," images both somber and wonderful. What might Sheol be like?

The images speak of a great longing, of a heart broken in pieces, a dropped pottery—and he striving to gather and repair the shards.

✦ ✦ ✦

That state, that "place" implies, invites, conjures up all that life first gave, lavishly, then snatched away; "repose . . . sleep . . . rest." Twice denied, because first bestowed.

His Sheol is populated with all sorts and conditions of people; it reflects the variety and scope of the world's tribes; "Kings . . . counselors . . . princes . . ."

More; Sheol dissolves social classes, levels all, grants surcease from toil, from evil or oppressive behavior;

> The wicked
> cease from troubling,
> the weary
> are at rest . . .
>
> prisoners at ease,
> hear not the voice
> of the slave driver . . .
>
> small and great
> alike are there,
>
> and the slave
> free of his master (Job 3:17–19)

✦ ✦ ✦

It sounds like paradise. Beautiful, we think, plangent, seductive. And finally impossible, this longing, this dream of a postworld world, in which the dead enjoy a surrogate life, a life "of sorts."

A place where, faintly to praise (or perhaps not so faintly), the inequities and iniquities of life in the flesh no longer plague.

✦ ✦ ✦

Evidence

A blank, a knowing nothing
as though all day, shilly-shally
drizzle drowned the sun. Light
is lackluster, a blank face.

Rain or tears falling,
who knows?
Both.

And the mute landlocked trees

And no one sees
leaves that may be, may not.

DB

chapter two

"A Friend Owes Kindness to the Despairing" (4:1–9:35)

4:1–2 Comes the "turn about is fair," the hour of the Great Rejoinder.

Eliphaz undertakes to speak first.

His mind, we shortly note, is clad in homespun, he revels in home truths.

The trouble is; Job has been cast out. Where then shall such truths come home?

In the wild sea of event, no spar to cling to.

For his part, friend Eliphaz admits of no doubts, whether concerning God or his stricken friend—or for that matter, concerning a favorable outcome of Job's trouble.

No doubts. His faith is secure, a bird in the hand.

And that would seem the nub of the trouble, that sense of being in command of event, in possession of outcome.

But, but. One's mind is set to stuttering. Something, some dire event, has turned the world on its head. And one is led to ponder. The world of Job the just has gone to ruin.

Then whose world shall remain firm underfoot, unwobbling, ordered, sane?

An event has rendered clarity deceptive, security insecure. The "event" stands before Eliphaz, in the sore estate of a friend.

Job, the just one brought low—this is a clue, a text lying open to hand and eye. Can the friend seize on it, read it, reverence it? And go slow?

✦ ✦ ✦

Alas. Can Eliphaz "read the signs"? He must be thought in this regard near illiterate.

He is a great one for speechifying; words trip beautifully, lightly on the tongue. His world is a garden of innocence, his logic untrammeled by event.

Has a horrid finger touched Job, withered his vine, blasted his fruits? Not to worry; Eliphaz will make sense of it. Good will come of it.

✦ ✦ ✦

Out of the rigid, logical construction Eliphaz has made of God and the world, out of a secure life and a clear mental script, he proceeds to instruct.

To wit; the world's moral fabric is close woven, tightly deuteronomic. To wit; the just are vindicated, the wicked, for their misdeeds, suffer.

The logic is airtight, watertight, landtight. In heaven as on earth, every jot and tittle, whether of deed or desire, act or omission, is touted up, closely.

The God of Eliphaz? An image emerges; God is a supreme lawgiver, overseer, logician. He much resembles—Eliphaz.

✦   ✦   ✦

One is well advised not to slight this teaching of accountability and judgment.

It is soundly elaborated in the Pentateuch, part of the patrimony of the faith. It has been fiercely tested in the world, by the wicked and unaccountable. It has sustained generations of victims and martyrs. Prophets have had recourse to it.

The teaching is a bulwark against encroaching dark.

So we grant Eliphaz much; accountability frustrated, the universe is chilled, absurd, pointless.

✦   ✦   ✦

The teaching also has an appealing Zen-like quality, it allows for zigzag and chancetaking. It grants place to the crooked lines, the fault lines—as well as the song lines—of life.

It has its own mantras, composed one thinks, by the just under duress, clinging against odds, to hope. "All shall be well, all manner of things shall be well." "What goes around, comes around."

✦   ✦   ✦

Still, we find something lacking, even faintly offensive in the rejoinder of the first friend.

Something like this; the instructive tone, the sour whiff of "religious" disapproval. It is as though Eliphaz walked the world, his nose elevated in distain.

His religion is conventional, cool, somewhat parched.

A favorite theme is of strict retribution; a teaching, granted, apt to hearten the just in their sufferings.

Still, a question. What if, as in the present encounter, Eliphaz were to turn the teaching about, casting doubt on the goodness of Job, deducing with icy detachment, guilt as implied in his plight?

✦ ✦ ✦

Let us grant Eliphaz a measure of uprightness and integrity; but it is all untested. He has not known evil times.

He has not lost everything—flocks, family, bodily health. His faith follows, to all appearance, on good fortune.

Logical. No wonder he proclaims a God of right reason, a comprehensible God.

He stands steady in the world. He takes his stand, one thinks literally, and certainly in metaphor, above Job. Posture and argument are one.

But how shall he come to understand the shaken grandeur of his friend?

He is a theologian; he is not to be thought a suffering servant.

The God of the whirlwind passes him by.

✦ ✦ ✦

Eliphaz stands, as though superior to stricken Job, crouching there in a stew of misery.

Does he dare play rabbi to his friend, condemned to a Sheol in this life?

Does he know nothing of Jeremiah plunged in a dry well, of Ezekiel sent to exile, of Daniel condemned to the stoked furnace and lions' den?

And now he stands before Job, condemned to a heap of offal, to the pits of the world, an offscouring of all?

✦ ✦ ✦

So too, the timing of Eliphaz is awry. "All shall be well," he proclaims.

And the saying may one day come true. We, the omniscient audience, know that it does, at the end, come true.

But what if, for the present and whatever bleak future, every-thing comprising life's benefits, family, flocks, home—everything is manifestly unwell, chattels and family torn from life, van-ished, seized?

✦   ✦   ✦

Questions, what of the questioning mind? Is a mind free of questions to be thought a human ideal?

The mind of Eliphaz is free of all encumbrances, nuances, revenants of a lost paradise.

His habitual mode is the declarative or imperative, the sure and steady.

✦   ✦   ✦

What a different planet, the world of Job! Earthquakes under his feet, life is a boiling cauldron of questions.

By what means is that "shall," that sure and shockproof future announced by Eliphaz, to be verified? Are the dead to be restored to Job? And his leprosy healed? And the ruined house.

✦   ✦   ✦

Nothing in Eliphaz of this perplexity, uncertainty, no doubt, no contrary surmise. Period.

His self-confidence, his ready, steady access to the divine Will, is confounding. His soul's grammar requires only a clear asser-tion. Period.

✦   ✦   ✦

We contrast the faith of Job, and are stricken and silent.

He is belabored, pummeled by fists of disaster.

No clarity, finality. His life has taken the grotesque form of an interrogation mark.

✦   ✦   ✦

4:3–11 Eliphaz begins with a concession, lovingly one thinks. Of the three friends, he is the elder; by implication, he knows his friend best.

He concedes the noble qualities of Job; beyond doubt he has helped others stand firm in adversity, has offered truths that abide and heal.

✦   ✦   ✦

How comes it then, wonders Eliphaz, that when disaster stikes close, Job cannot gather his stated belief, hold it like a full sheaf, lift it for all to see?

Is the truth of loving providence a truth only for the good times, is it beneficial to others only—good but hypothetical, good but in the breach falling short?

✦   ✦   ✦

4:12–21 This Eliphaz is indeed someone to be reckoned with!

His confession begins; better, it breaks like a firestorm. It is momentous, personal, shattering, a bold ecstatic claim.

The claim, the instruction run through the scroll like a rope of fire.

It is as though his oracle issued from a burning bush. His word is not his own, and his own. He has been touched by the Holy; or so he claims. Terrified though he be, he must speak the word abroad; that is the sum of his claim.

✦ ✦ ✦

Let Job take it or leave, and ourselves as well.

Eliphaz has seen (better, has heard) That Which (One Whom) Elijah heard on Mount Horeb (1 Kings 19:12 ff.). Eliphaz has seen the One Whom Daniel saw "by the bank of the great river Tigris" (Daniel 10:7–9).

Why tell the vision?

It seems designed to put the likes of Job firmly in place. A place whence by implication, he has strayed.

Let Job confess; he is human, no more, he is vastly less than the angels. And if the great angels can be faulted for, in some sense or other, falling short; what then to say of

> the dwellers
>
> in houses of clay
> whose origin is dust
>
> who are crushed
> like the moth,
> shattered
> between daybreak and evening,
>
> perishing unnoticed (Job 4:19–20)

✦ ✦ ✦

Such images of mortalilty, our fragility—images sublime and downputting at once!

Such an incursion of pessimism! It is as though death spoke an obit over every human effort, every work of genius or high nobility, the blood of martyrs, the courage of confessors—rendering all void, null, redundant.

✦ ✦ ✦

Does Eliphaz secretly despise Job, this subdued inarticulate victim—with, be it noted, no visionary claim to stake all on?

Let Eliphaz speculate further, let an implication stand. (After all, it is for Job's benefit!)

Has he brought this misery upon himself? in ways secret, well concealed?

✦ ✦ ✦

We grant it; the revelation of Eliphaz conveys a truth. Human life is fragile, death easily disposes of the living.

His vision goes further; it conceals, only half reveals a deeper fault in our condition;

> Can mortals be just
> before God,
>
> can humans,
> face to face
> with their Maker,
>
> be pure? (Job 4:17)

Judgment runs like a vein through his discourse.

A vein brimming in blood.

Bad blood or good? Job it would seem, is the "human" in question—unmentioned by name, implicit throughout.

Let him take the instruction to heart. He is but a human, of lesser dignity than angels. Can Job then claim that he stands under no judgment?

He cannot. Claims of justice and purity are vain.

Let him search his soul, turn out his pockets, hold his sin to the light.

Let it be said plain. His losses, his leprosy, these are no arbitrary or absurd befallings. An awful effect postulates a dark cause. Let Job look to it; in contrition lies redemption.

✦　✦　✦

And we wince for Job, and sigh. Does he require this dire instruction? Does it mitigate his misery, a balm in Gilead?

No, a sorry word for a suffering servant!

✦　✦　✦

Seduced by the account of an epiphany, we might conclude that God has spoken through Eliphaz. Had spoken a final, sinaitic word concerning God's management of human affairs.

A visionary word was uttered, and eventually set down here. The message ended, and a firm period was placed. Period.

And the scroll closed, once for all.

But wait.

✦　✦　✦

Open the scrolls! This dim, platitudinous view of the human! We are perhaps justified in doubting its divine origin.

Eliphaz claims a nocturnal revelation; it is literally "hair-raising," more in the nature of a nightmare.

True or not, it contributes little or nothing to our knowledge of God or ourselves. Its message seems the voice of his conscious mind, a nocturnal echo chamber of convictions awake.

✦　✦　✦

We have a more exalted, even reverential anthropology offered elsewhere in Scripture, bearing a better credential;

God created humans
in His image,
in the divine image
He created them,
male and female He created them (Genesis 1:27)

You have made them
a little less
than the angels,
crowned them with glory and honor;

You have given them rule
over the works
of Your hands . . . (Psalm 8:6, 7)

✦   ✦   ✦

5:1–7 Indirection, innuendo is the preferred ploy of this inspired pessimist. A little, malevolent parable lays bare the skill;

I myself saw
a fool
who had struck roots;

impulsively
I cursed his home;

may his children
be far from safety,
be crushed
at the tribunal,
without rescue.

May the hungry
devour his harvest . . .

> may the thirsty
> swallow his wealth (Job 5:3–6)

✦   ✦   ✦

Logic is a vise; it bites close, and holds.

In its grip Job languishes; behold his sorry fate. For every ill effect, an ill cause;

> Evil does not grow
> out of the soil,
> nor does mischief
> spring from the ground.
>
> Humans themselves
> beget mischief
> as sparks fly upward (Job 5:6–7)

Hard-nosed, adroit, is the insinuation.

✦   ✦   ✦

5:8–16 Eliphaz stands with a God whose creation is a system humming with rational energy.

The system, how define it? A complex mechanism of reward and punishment, in consequence of good deeds or ill.

✦   ✦   ✦

Job, too bad for him, is hardly to be thought secure, or in place.

Nor is he likely consoled by the God of Eliphaz, or by his systematic universe, ticking away, exact and exacting, a kind of supernal Swiss timepiece.

✦ ✦ ✦

5:17–27 The logician continues, taking a different tack.

Only let Job turn his mind to the benefits accruing to this plight, to loss of family and possessions and soundness of limb. Let him summon to mind a truth that, it would seem, he has neglected to take in account.

Has he lost everything of his sweet life, leaving him a snail's passage, an eked-out, quasi existence?

The loss may well be a gain; his moral improvement may be underway, his necessary correction;

> See, how happy
> is the one
> whom God reproves! (Job 5:17)

✦ ✦ ✦

And if Job, for the nonce, strikes us as failing to leap with joy and bound away from his dung heap—why, too bad for him.

The indefatigable three, these normative believers, can but conclude that the divine exaction has not borne fruit in the delinquent.

Eliphaz has so concluded. The corrective has not taken hold.

✦ ✦ ✦

Still, the moralist has done his part.

What pharisee could improve on the lofty ethic of the Eliphazian speech, on its orthodoxy, its antiquity—and more, the quality of its poetry?

Let the masterpiece shimmer on the page, hand-illuminated. It is indeed noble.

Will it be taken ill if we add—it leaves the heart cold, is fruitless?

✦   ✦   ✦

Human

No great miracles, no
not even small ones.
They're terra incognita, *lunar.*
Omega doesn't walk there, even anonymous.
Comes then, a dark clue—

eyes that see,
heart heard from,
tongue, a prisoner of conscience
parsing truthful words,
necessary silence. Thus the human. The difficult, step
     by step, hard-won
eventual glory.

DB

✦   ✦   ✦

6:1–7 For Job's part, little remains to to be said, and literally nothing to be done.

Let rot, let death-in-life speak for him.

One cannot but note the strange, uninviting, adversarial role friendship has taken.

No answer, no point in something so futile and wearing as a "refutation" of Eliphaz.

✦   ✦   ✦

Willy nilly, Job must content himself with the discontent, bone-deep, of his predicament.

Let him say something though, about the medicinal virtue of this "temporary" correction.

Easily said, "temporary." But his sufferings bear no promise of relief, no hint of being lifted. To all evidence his affliction is to be lifelong; death will come as his sole relief.

Come then, death!

✦ ✦ ✦

6:8–9 Come then, death.

So Far, So Good

Listen
if now and again
you hear the dead
muttering like ashes
creaking like empty
rockers on porches
filling you in-filling you in
like winds in bare
branches like stars
in wintry trees—
so far
so good
you've mastered finally
one foreign tongue

DB

✦ ✦ ✦

6:10–13 And for sole consolation, we are offered three radically different readings; "that I did not rebel against the decrees of Providence" (BJ). Or, "that I did not suppress my words against the Holy One" (JPS). Or, "that I did not conceal the words of the holy One" (KJ).

Elements of each? In the first version, Job admits to an innocent directness and vigor of soul. His obedience is intact.

In accord with the second and third, his honesty stands
beyond impeachment. Let him confess that "God's most deep
decree" lies utterly beyond human ken. The Holy One has become a stumbling block, a scandal.

Let his friends codify, even prettify the brutal scramble called
life. Job will have none of it. How could he?

How grave, how impossible to fathom, the judgment that
has reduced his life to a rubble!

✦   ✦   ✦

6:14 A key turns in its socket; a clue lies beyond, a hint of a
moral landscape, of the religion of the prophets (and the religion of Jesus!).

Unlikely

Here
in a cell like honeycomb
swells
the formic future—
the sublime human creature

DB

✦   ✦   ✦

Among the difficulties at the heart of the debate, this; a radically different understanding of friendship and its entailments.

Eliphaz has set the tone; of necessity, a friend is also an adversary. Friendship has its mission; to rebuke and correct the moral
impairment, the conscience gone awry, the truculence and ar-
rogance and baffled obstinacy—of a friend. Of this friend, Job.

Shall a friend allow ills to supporate, to worsen, a leprosy of very soul?

Never; such would betray a holy office.

Standing face to face, friends also stand before God. The friend is burdened with a mission; he must set his friend aright.

No sentimentality permitted, infecting and weakening!

✦ ✦ ✦

For Job, the matter of friendship is simpler; a matter of the heart.

Again we have various readings—which perhaps come to the same;

> To refuse pity
> to one's neighbor
> is to reject fear
> of the Almighty (BJ)

> A friend
> owes loyalty to one who fails
> even though that one
> forsake
> fear of the Almighty (JPS)

> A friend
> owes kindness
> to one in despair
> though that one
> forsake
> fear of the almighty (NAB)

> To the afflicted
> pity should be shown
> from his friend;
> though he forsaketh
> fear of the almighty (KJ)

✦ ✦ ✦

Do we have here a hint of the sensibility of God incarnate?

In any case, Job's illness is hardly of the spirit; his moral vision is intact here, it pierces to the quick.

To wit; a friend has other responsibilities than chiding the unfortunate and victimized.

A fellow human is not a dray horse, to be flogged uphill. How degrading to both driver and beast!

No, if the decrees of God be opaque, draconian, then let be.

Let a friend be content to stand by, or sit by, or vigil by. In a silence that signals a heartfelt simpatico, an assurance; I am with you.

Let the friend cast aside even a hint of the icy imperative mode.

Is not the decalogue itself a heavy burden? Must a friend elaborate and embroider litigious niceties, his countenance severe, his soul parched?

✦ ✦ ✦

Growing

The fiery
are fiery to the end.
The sun huffs like an adder—
burn, baby, burn!
Everything burns,
sanity, eyeballs.
Old age is cursing God,
antistrophe
to that sublime dawn bird
that mourned its preincarnate
maidenhead and murder.
Now I remember.
And

if I dance
algebraic as an angel
it is
because You are
motive intractable,
staggering burden—
old Father I heft to shoulder
fleeing the burning city.

DB

✦ ✦ ✦

6:15–30 Job grows audacious, his eloquence is fueled by a piercing sense of betrayal.

To what shall he compare these friends, who embroil him and themselves in judgment, who weigh him to a pennyworth, only to find him wanting?

He will turn matters around, will launch an offensive.

His fury pours out, a very torrent of imagery; these friends are dry riverbeds, stony wadis; streams that have run their course, and are no more.

—Does a caravan depend for direction, even for survival, on a watercourse that runs true north, or south?

Alas, the parched bed twists this way and that, like a snake's shed skin. No true north.

The travelers are set off course, lost.

✦ ✦ ✦

What an indictment! Direct of speech, no missing the point, not by a jot;

Such
are you to me,
at this hour.

Or, more trenchantly still—
So you are
as nothing.

At sight of me
you grow terrified (Job 6:21)

✦   ✦   ✦

Misfortune has made Job strong, even as his plight has turned the friends to water.

Overwhelmed as they are by dread and fear, how can they minister to a friend? Impossible.

The connection is subtle, painful, bracing; fear wreaks the death of friendship.

Could they admit to fear?

Never, not so!

✦   ✦   ✦

Fear of what? of their own death, staring at them in the wild mirror of Job's ruin?

They must mask their dread with bravado, with a righteous assault. And by an equally imperious necessity, Job must un-mask their fear.

✦   ✦   ✦

He has heard Eliphaz out, as his friend hurled God about like a blunderbuss. And then the codicils, the terms and bribes, urging repentance upon a sorry delinquent.

Thus Eliphaz and his like behold Job; we shall see more of it. He is duped by self-will, his plaints fester away, importunate and profitless.

✦　✦　✦

Need it be said, we behold Job otherwise?

Backed against a wall of existence, stricken, immobilized, he arrives at the truth of his predicament.

Face to the wall, he is also brought face to face with the veiled Mystery.

The wall, the Mystery. Are the two One?

The irony breaks his heart. In the stews of misery, he confesses to knowing little or nothing of God.

✦　✦　✦

One thing he has done. (It stops us short too, with admiration; and it gives heart.)

In effect he has turned the tables.

It is the friends, not he, who stand under indictment, who are—unjust;

> The fatherless
> you overwhelm, for your friend
> you dig a pit (Job 6:27)

Which is to say, they are strangers to the heart's native vocation of mercy and compassion.

Strangers also to God?

Let us say; strangers to the God of Job, the Mystery.

In his eyes they lay claim to a fictive god, a god cabined and confined to the blind box of their morality.

In our eyes as well?

Yes. It is they who are cabined and confined, they who are unjust. We stand with Job. Let them repent;

> Relent!
> Let there not
> be injustice;

> Relent!
> I am still
> in the right (Job 6:29)

Job, knowing the good, knows evil.
Not an "evil" God, be it noted.

✦ ✦ ✦

As for Eliphaz, has he claimed a word from on high? Let him be told plain; his revelation tastes of—damnation.

The evil lies elsewhere than in a God who allows evil its day.

It lies close at hand, as Job strongly hints; close as ashes in the mouth;

> Can my palate
> not taste wickedness? (Job 6:30)

✦ ✦ ✦

7:1–10 Human dignity, son of God, etc., etc.?

The friends would push the notion hard. "Notional," like their understanding of God.

In a torrent of scornful images, Job will counter their lofty (and deadly conventional) "religious" estimate of human behavior.

✦ ✦ ✦

Are we humans free? Far from it. Rightly understood (and following BJ), we are in "militia," in military servitude.

And our plight is no temporary, passing metaphor; it is in fact lifelong. We trudge along, in lockstep with other unfortunates, clothed in the same dun, ragged clothing.

Worse; the law of the jungle rules. We are armed against other humans.

Army recruits; doomed, damned to permanent warfare. War defines us, even as it places us under orders, at risk, for reasons worse than meaningless, witless reasons that damn, extinguish our human sense.

And in any case, the "orders" are sealed, never laid out by the supreme Commander.

What an image for the twenty-first century! Everyone inducted in the new world order, that dominion of darkness in which a few thrive, and the many go under. In which the devil takes the hindmost, as armed violence supersedes human exchange. In which voices of sanity are to be reckoned—voices in a wilderness.

Another metaphor, defeating an easy optimism.

We are hirelings, day laborers. Deprived of dignity, security, community, we stand in a marketplace, amid the debris of hope.

O to be hired before sunset closes the market! Hired even for a meager price, a bitten coin, the currency of edgy survival.

We are items for sale, along with dumb cabbages and hanged chickens. For sale, ourselves; stoop labor, day labor.

Dignity? We are redundant, disposable.

As are many, under the dominion of NAFTA and its international cartels, its economic slaveries.

Or another trope; we are slaves, no more.

Commanded and forbidden, shunted about, no sense or meaning governs life. "A master's will is one with God's will,"— one and the same, God the slave master, the owner of humans, playing god.

No validity of our own.

Dignity? We are branded, bent like an iron in the fire of mere use.

✦   ✦   ✦

Or a final image. Call us—and this at best—"workmen."

We whose worth is functional, base matter passed hand to hand; money.

Worth so much, and no more. Never "the roll, the rise, the carol, the creation"—a worker of worth, proud amid his work.

✦   ✦   ✦

7:11–21 How pay tribute to this stark, altered tone?

In the bitterness of his fate, Job turns to prayer.

He will address God—though hardly in terms acceptable to his gimlet-eyed friends.

This is the God of bitter fruit, of no outcome, of a life of fidelity counting for nothing, going nowhere. And worse than nowhere; to a dead end whose signpost reads; "Futility," or (take your choice, you humans) "Absurdity."

No choices?

Nevertheless. Job prays.

He

Hands, calloused with the long failure
Of prayer; Take my life, he says
To the bleak sea, but the sea rejects him
Like wrack. He dungs the earth with
His children and the earth yields him
Its stone. Nothing he does, nothing he
Says is accepted, and the thin dribble
Of his poetry dries on the rocks
Of a harsh landscape under an ailing sun.

(R. S. Thomas)

✦　✦　✦

Let not the irony be lost; it is both delicious and tragic.

To the friends, God is a "third party." They are pleased to "explain" God.

They succeed only in explaining Him away. They never once have recourse to prayer.

But Job turns to God. No subject—object, useful to discussion, no "third person," no enigma to be "solved" by human ingenuity.

None of the above.

You; a Torment.

A sleepless vigilant Eye.

An Examiner, a Scrutinizer.

A Hound of heaven, close to heel, tripping me up.

A "Thou," unutterably mysterious, spurning the devices of logic.

Unto Yourself. Brooking no interference. Taking no bribes.

Allowing the wicked to win, place, show.

As You choose, sustaining or abandoning virtuous losers.

Eccolo, Me, Job.

The game, the dance; touch Me, touch Me not.

✦　✦　✦

What are humans
that You
are mindful of them,
that You should care for them?

You have made them
little less
than the angels,
have crowned them
with glory and honor
given them rule

over the works of Your hands,
putting all things
under their feet (Psalm 8)

The solemn anthem, exalting our humanity on high—how
Job turns it to his own bitter, ironic ends!
His tone is close to Psalm 144:3;

God, what are humans
that you take note of them,
that You take thought of them?

They are like a breath,
their days
like a passing shadow

✦   ✦   ✦

A prayer for dire times.
A prayer for the Era of Job, for Job worldwide, the Job of this
unspeakable millennium. Unspeakable, whether in past or
future; whether the second draws to an unsteady close, or the
third looms overhead. Cruise missiles flare over Baghdad in monstrous mockery of the Savior and his command of love,
millennially ignored and put to naught.
A prayer for our tribe of suffering servants—and for those
who wantonly inflict the suffering. For our common humanity,
violated in the hubris of the bombers, for those stricken to ground.

✦   ✦   ✦

Are we humans stuck in horrid, inhuman roles, executioner
or victim—deprived of all alternatives?
The Living Theater still performs "Not in My Name" in the
middle of Times Square, whenever someone on death row is
executed.

The actors celebrate the life of the victim at the hour of his death, then go out to spectators, touch them, stare them in the eye and say; "I will swear to you that I will never kill you. Can you promise me the same?" (Sara Boxer, *New York Times*, 29 August 1998)

✦ ✦ ✦

Is there a third way, a way out? Can it be the way of Job, of the suffering servant?

A way that must cope with purgation and loss.

In the American instance, to this point. My brother Philip, my fellow Jesuit Stephen Kelly, and others were imprisoned repeatedly for actions against nuclear weapons and war.

We witnessed their dignity amid public indignity, their grace in the disgrace; they were tried as criminals, convicted, and jailed for works of peace. For refusal of the blood-ridden game of tit for tat, bomb for bomb.

Thus casting off the politics of contempt, the deadly beat of the war drum. All honors to the suffering servants of the God of Job, those awaiting trial, those in prison!

Their crime; they dramatize the imperative of Isaiah; swords must be beaten into plowshares.

✦ ✦ ✦

Sour, stuck in Job's throat. The taste of You (Job 7:19);

Will You not
look away from me
for awhile,

let me be,
until I swallow
my spit?

And again (Job 7:20);

> If I have sinned,
> what have I done to You,
>
> You close Watcher of humans?
> Why make of me
> Your target?
> If, if . . . as adduced by those who surround me,
> assuring me that sinner I am.
> For if not a sinner, what logic governs this catastrophe
> thrice compounded?

✦ ✦ ✦

I shall argue with You.

For a start, let us take the contrary for a fact—my sinful estate.

And You, are You not the God of forgiveness?

Look, soon (in a sublime non sequitur) I shall clutter the world no longer. Seek me, I shall be gone, out of Your hands, dust to dust.

✦ ✦ ✦

Job is at the wall, at resource's end.

And he stands rebuked; for dire complaint, for a prayer of pure effrontery. In sum, for mistaking who this God is.

Rebuked that is—by his friends.

There are conventions to be observed, politesse, seemliness; sandals off then, before the Holy!

There are attitudes befitting, and attitudes outrageous, offensive.

You, Job—you neglect the conventions, refuse to pay tribute to creaturliness!

✦　✦　✦

8:1–8 The second round of argument, this one induced by friend Bildad.

Heavy, heavy from his tongue falls the burden of implication, the close dovetailing of vice/virtue and consequence.

And worst of all, a prejudgment falls like the blade of a guillotine, remorseless. The argument would decapitate the already dead, demolish good repute, destroy one who is powerless to defend himself.

Presuming, judging, condemning; and this weighty activity, we note, is undertaken with audible aplomb—though whether the judgment of God concur, remains unknown.

Does not a single verse express the spleen? We witness a culture of recrimination and inflated charges. Bildad utters the abusive words;

> If your sons
> sinned against Him,
> He dispatched them
> for their transgressions (Job 8:4)

Job will let it pass. The words are beneath contempt.

✦　✦　✦

8:8–13 Another implication. To illumine the plight of those neglectful of God, Bildad appeals to Egyptian lore.

These wilful ones are like papyrus, river grasses; under a merciless sun they dry up, turn to a powder.

✦　✦　✦

What light the metaphor might be thought to shed upon Job, his anguished prayer, his plight, is unclear. Or perhaps it is all too clear.

Perhaps that notorious prayer of his proved scandalous to the ear of God (beyond doubt to the ear of Bildad). Perhaps such words should never have passed human lips?

✦   ✦   ✦

8:14–20 Let us venture further.

These friends, as has been clear, are masters of innuendo.

A canny rhetoric works wonders; accusation gains double weight for being insinuated rather than expressly laid down.

An implication lies there, a stain on the page. Is Job himself that "impious one, whose confidence" (in a marvelous image, we must grant this demon his due) "is but a gossamer thread, his trust in the web of a spider."

Job? One who "forgets God"?

Have these vigilers lost their moorings? Do they—or do we, venerating Job as a suffering, believing servant of God—dwell in coocooland?

✦   ✦   ✦

8:21–22 Nothing daunted, this lyric leaper Bildad takes flight into am empyrian future.

In this wise. Only let Job give small attention or none at all to his present plight—and all shall be well!

✦   ✦   ✦

9:1–13 A void beyond measure separates Job from God; it were best that he, a mere human, know the truth, the void, and acknowledge it.

Now we grant it; there is no gainsaying, on Job's part or our own, that immeasurable, unbridgeable void.

And beyond doubt as well, the truth places all winning cards in one Hand.

Against the Maker and Sustainer of all, what is one to do—a mere human, and less; one who is reduced to dwelling among slugs on a dungheap?

✦　✦　✦

Who am I, Job, to question the One who admits of no obligation to respond? One moreover, before whom all analogies fall to face?

Am I then to confront God as I would an interloper, impeding the ruffian from breaking and entering my dwelling, crying out; Who are you, why are you here? Explain yourself!

God explains nothing.

How, when justice has fled the world—how summon illusions of equality before the law?

✦　✦　✦

9:14–19 Justice! Job is impassioned for justice. It wreaks havoc upon havoc, that passion. It runs through his being like a killing current, a torment.

Shall he, shall he not "be justified before God"? Shall he "contend with God"? Dare he "choose arguments against God," "appeal to God," "issue a summons to God," "call God to account"?

9:20–23 He knows it, his bones tell him. The outcome of any such fantastic legal proceedings is set beforehand, set in stone;

> Even though
> I were right,
> I could not answer Him . . .
>
> If I appealed,
> and He answered my call,
> I could not believe
> He would hearken
> to my words (Job 9:20–21)

✦ ✦ ✦

Shall a mere human, wounded in his inmost parts, dare summon God to judgment?

Shall Job stand as prosecutor of the divine Design?

To wit; I have a case against Him; "He destroys the blameless
and the guilty alike!"

So He does.

Still, the idea of a "summons" issued against God is to be
accounted absurd. If not blasphemous.

The trio would have it named, clear and dire—blasphemous.

✦ ✦ ✦

Blasphemous.

(Absurd or no, blasphemous or no, the author has set it down;
the metaphysical unlikelihood of the "summons," the "case,"
must be stated, if only to be named for what it is—absurd.

Named for what it is—the word of God.

Name it then! Thus we unmask the rules of the game—rules
that the Author of the game never willingly reveals.

Rules that the impeding friends would keep as firmly masked
as Furies playing at Eumenides!)

✦ ✦ ✦

This intolerable Job, how he turns conventional religion on
its head!

We had thought, and often since childhood were sternly reminded, judgment awaits every mortal.

Job's impeding, harranguing chorus—how hard they push
the thought, like a bolus down the throat.

To their own advantage? Special interests at work?

Wrapped close in rectitude, they repeatedly call Job's attention to immanent, indeed ongoing judgment that hovers over (over him!), like a bird of prey.

What need of argument on the matter—is he not sunk in a stew, scabrous, pathetic? Does he not stink to high heaven?

Does not crime have consequence; is not consequence proof of crime?

✦   ✦   ✦

Sublime, valiant Job! Let us give the lie to these hectoring true believers, let us turn the moral universe on its head—if only to show its intolerable present form, the stacked deck, the inequity of it all, the Goliath of the universe lording it over his race of homunculi!

Come then God, in presumption intolerable, I Job summon You to judgment. In outrage, perhaps in excess of outrage and wild contravention—I shall show forth the terror of the human, our predicament, a horror!

Perhaps I shall show You a faith the world has not seen. A faith You have not seen?

✦   ✦   ✦

The orthodox trio surround me like an eighth plague, hem me in, suffocate. They own the scrolls and the logic and the Sages, from Egypt to here. They would have me cribbed, cabined, confined in the airless box of their own orthodoxy.

They own You as well, or attempt to. They would have You—even You—cabined and confined.

I Job love You. I would free You. To be Yourself, terrifying, inexplicable, untamed in the world.

✦   ✦   ✦

The need is not for the total consolation of narcotic fantasy—
our own will performed in airless triumph—but for the credible
news that our lives proceed in order, toward a pattern which, if
tragic here and now, is ultimately pleasing in the mind of a God
who sees a totality and at last enacts His will.

> We crave nothing less than a perfect story, and while
> we chatter or listen all our lives in a din of craving—
> jokes, anecdotes, novels, dreams, films, plays, songs, half
> the words of our days—we are satisfied by the one short
> tale we feel to be true; History is the will of a just God
> who knows us. (Reynolds Price, *A Palpable God*)

✦   ✦   ✦

The entire speech (chapters 9 through 10) is the plaint of a
distraught Lear; magnificent, brooding, laced with wonderful
half-mad images, flickering in the mind's dark like a cloud of
fireflies.

No respite, Job's memories assault him, tigrish, fevered.

It touches on his existence, on the truth of life, this obsession
of his. It will own his dying breath, this confession. He has been
faithful, he is no renegade or reneger.

Read not the condition of soul from the decay of his body.
Fidelity has made firm his bones and given health to his flesh.

✦   ✦   ✦

Health also to his understanding. He knows himself, where
he stands in the scheme of creation. Before God, before his own
soul he affirms it; he is just.

And then—all he loves, all the holy accumulation of the years
is seized and swept away.

And he is to believe in the justice of the vast larceny? To believe (it comes to the same thing) that his loss is the just desserts of infidelity?

It is the world, and God, and the theological tormentors hemming him in—these are gone mad.

✦ ✦ ✦

We wonder; is an inkling, a hint, a suspicion lodged in his tormented bones? Has a bargain been struck, a bargain that has given him over to loss and anguish, he a bait, a hostage of misfortune?

And this, in order to prove a secret point, of import to deity and devil?

✦ ✦ ✦

9:24–35 Such ruminations stir in him! Job is dangerously close to knowing what we, the omniscient observers, know—the truth, the celestial debate, the swapping of challenges and claims;

> The earth is handed over
> to the wicked one;
> He covers the eyes of its judges.
> If it is not He,
> then who? (Job 9:24)

✦ ✦ ✦

Such images, such provocation. He all but dares the lightning to strike!

And why not? What after all remains to him, has he not lost everything?

This is an entreaty so near despair, as perhaps—at long last—to touch, like the fingers of the blind, the face of hope;

> It will be I
> who am in the wrong;
> Why then should I waste effort?
>
> If I washed with soap,
> cleansed my hands with lye,
> You would dip me in muck
> till my clothing
> abhorred me (Job 9:29–31)

✦   ✦   ✦

From "you" to "he" and back, Job's mind veers. God is absent and can only be talked about; no, God is present, and must be faced.

Of that "he," the distant one, only this can be said: what "he" is not;

> For he is not a man like myself,
> that I should answer him
> that we should come together in judgment . . .

And a longing for someone, neither "friend" nor ha-Satan, to intercede;

> Would that there were
> an arbiter
> between us . . . (Job 9:32–35)

chapter three

"Let This Cup Pass" (It Will Not Pass) (10:1–14:12)

A man is more than two sticks crossed. He is more like
the sea, bringing up God knows what at any hour.

—Joseph Conrad

He

Nail him to sticks,
he stands free, makes sense
of agony, of sticks and stones.
No grafting him on;
                his fruits
are free—more years'
intensities.
          He ranges, rejoices
the horizon sorrow lifts him to.

Look how hands refuse
all but that pinioning.
                Blood flows
red against bitter
hemlock, maple sweet.

          Blood writes
what heart provides;
                God knows what

that sea brings up.

God bring that sea safe
—safe is no word for him—
> *a*

surf home, shuddering its coast,
crying hoarse in its falling—

Victory!

DB

✦   ✦   ✦

10:1–8 That prayer, that prayer of Job!

He has imagined himself aright, he has imagined God aright.

He, Job is the accused; of what, he is uncertain. But accused, and all but convicted beforehand!

And of this we too are witnesses.

Recall the history, along with its protagonist, first in prosperity, then standing raw in his flayed bones.

At the beginning Job stood before a God of large benefits, lavishly conferred.

Then came the celestial bargaining. And all was abruptly withdrawn.

This is the source of subsequent ills, this cruel arbitrary game of winners-losers. The start of an adamantine judgment, and of conviction as well.

✦   ✦   ✦

Has the face of God hardened? Has God become wintry, implacable?

One thinks; the harrangues of those fervent partisans, their harrassing, has seized on Job's soul. It is as though the claw of an eagle grasped his entrails.

For the moment they own him.
And their version of God—the implacable One!

✦   ✦   ✦

Nevertheless, Job perseveres in prayer.

So doing, he reminds us of another judge, an unjust one, and another client, much resembling himself;

> Jesus told them a parable on the necessity of praying always, and not losing heart;
>
> Once there was a judge in a certain city who respected neither God nor humans. A widow in that city kept coming to him saying, "Give me my rights against my opponent."
>
> For a time he refused, but finally he thought; "I care little for God or human, but this widow is wearing me out. I am going to settle in her favor or she will end by doing me violence."
>
> Jesus said; "Listen to what the corrupt judge has to say. Will not God then do justice to his chosen who call out to Him day and night? Will He delay long over them, do you suppose? I tell you, He will give them swift justice" (Luke 18:1–8).

✦   ✦   ✦

Is the God of Job just or unjust?

To the hectoring trio, the question is inadmissable. Job is impertinent in raising the question.

And worse; at a point of anguish, he dares answer negatively; God is unjust;

Therefore I say
He destroys the blameless
and the guilty . . .

He mocks as the innocent fail (Job 9:22–23)

✦   ✦   ✦

We of a later millennium take our cue from Job. Is the God of Jesus just or unjust?

Again, the seeming impertinence.

Seeming; we must tread softly here. Jesus Himself has wrestled with it; "Abba, if it be Your will, let this cup pass from me" (Luke 22:42).

It was not that Will, the passing of the cup. That Will was the quaffing of the cup. It must be drained, to the dregs.

And another evidence, hardly ambiguous, was wrung from his throat as He hung dying.

"*Eloi, Eloi, laba sabachthani.*" "My God, my God, why have You forsaken Me?" (Matthew 27:46)

✦   ✦   ✦

Are we in waters too deep for sounding?

Is our question, the justice of God, not so much out of order, as—beside the point?

It was not God who capitally condemned Jesus the Innocent. It was the world, the Fallen systems, the principalities adroitly named by their sponsors "law and order," the officials of Rome and temple, a polity enamored of death.

And this interruptive One—He put Himself in the way, He spoke out, became an obstacle. A scandal even.

✦ ✦ ✦

Disposing of Him wrought a very epiphany, a justification of the justice system, of "things as they are."

Had the imperial system not prevailed? Pilate, Herod, the high priest could question their souls, sure of the answer. The system works, and works well!

✦ ✦ ✦

Jesus was tried, convicted, duly executed. And a law stood revealed, a law of the Fall.

Which is to say, human authority is bound to the wheel of Ixion, bound over to death as its (our) dominant ideology.

In the "case" of Jesus Christ, the law was promulgated by its architects and guardians, Pilate, Herod, Caiphas.

Did they know it, did they sense that their hands, their hearts and minds, were bound over, hostages to an awesome principality known as "the law of the land"?

✦ ✦ ✦

And if God be so minded as to enter the world, God is bound over to the same law.

The world's "normal" functioning must go on; normal murder, normal imperial usurpation, normal larcenous economics, normal seizure of land and people. Normal religion.

And this God? He put Himself in the way.

Crucify Him.

And the dossier of Jesus Christ was closed. Or so it was proclaimed.

✦ ✦ ✦

This at least can be ventured. In anguish, Job and Jesus turn to the same God.

Prophet

He paused, and spoke; "Coopers, craftsmen, shepherds—
blessed is the prophet
whose blood speaks in his stead. Search death out!"
And sought death in their cities, and was taken
young years and all, composed in ground
like wintering bees

and after respite stood again
in tremendous mime—doors sprung,
world grown permeable—

all we would come to.

DB

✦   ✦   ✦

Whom the two, Job and Jesus, are granted to see with the eyes of faith, Whose countenance turns to them, what outcome of torment may be thought to lie ahead—of these we have differing reports.

An outcry is raised, as though from a tragedy beyond compass, of tragedy come home.

We have heard that cry, torn from other throats—from an Antigone, a Hecuba, an Oedipus.

✦   ✦   ✦

Let us venture this. In the heyday of his prospering, Job's prayer would be charged with a sense of mutuality.

On his part, gratitude to a God of gratuity and large heart.

And on God's part, a congratulatory mood; Job is a stalwart, beloved son, irreproachable.

And blessings follow, in abundance.

✦ ✦ ✦

At this point of prayer and prospering, would horrendous questions intrude, like a dark flock of harpies? Questions like, "Is my God just?"

Hardly, one thinks.

Then the scene changes, a sea change. Awful events rush one on another. Messengers hurry to announce the next catastrophe, to shout loudest, to be first in the contest darkened by awful news.

"Possessions destroyed and stolen, flocks, herds!"—then the apple of his eye, his lineage and hope, "sons and daughters, dead by mischance!"

And the spouse, her losses as well, her lineage and hope plucked from her. Distraught, the woman mimics and mocks in agony.

His agony and hers; "Curse God and die!"

✦ ✦ ✦

We are like spelunkers, digging down and down in all but total darkness.

Who is this God of Job, who the God of Jesus?

Is there correspondence-in-God?

Do the tormented heroes turn like heliotropes in the same direction, face to face with a just God?

✦ ✦ ✦

Let us try a parable.

Jesus conjures up an earthy judge; by implication, He issues a moral judgment on this eminence; "He [the judge] respected neither God nor humans." And again, abruptly; "He was corrupt."

Yet the judge, no paragon, yields before a widow, a woman

hapless and powerless. Evenually she wears him down. Before her vigiling and outcry, he confesses defeat.

He yields not a whit to any demand for justice. Merely, prudently, eye to the main chance, he "reverses himself."

And what of the woman's tactic? It was a last-ditch measure, a sort of anti-bribe, a pressure exerted by one whose sole resource was her ingenuity and steadfastness.

Measured on the scales of Lady Justice, how small a weight this widow could claim. Justice after all is blind; and how shall she weigh a passionate soul?

Yet on the awful scales, the widow's pressure exerted a different force and gravity than that of law and obligation, a pressure extraneous to blind weighing.

✦　✦　✦

Which is to say, the law is placed on the scales for sake of public scrutiny, for a secular passionless outcome of *dignum et justum*. Of *prosit*. Of *stet judicia*; "approved, let the verdict stand."

All this is a matter of the "law of the land," the habitual course of the world's system. Which, need one add, is hardly to be thought concerned with the fate of a mere widow, or attentive to her rant.

✦　✦　✦

She ignored the system.

Her hope, whatever form it took, must be sought elsewhere. Must be created whole cloth, by herself.

Has not justice been denied her, again and again?

Far from giving up, she transformed herself to a very witch of invention.

We picture her, vigiling at the judge's dwelling, crying out, night and day raising her ululation, her noisy embarrassing fuss.

By hook, by crook, she would prevail.

She, the ancestor of a Gandhi?

✦　✦　✦

So rich the plaint, so nearly incoherent the images, reflecting as in a distorting mirror, deep trouble of mind.

Or like a rudderless vessel. Veering this way and that in a sea gone daft, the S.S. Job laboriously plows the terrible waves.

Themes emerge, we hear a cry, then it is stifled, a voice lost on the winds.

✦　✦　✦

He addresses God, at length.

As to the existence of this redoubtable Someone, Job has no doubt. No doubt, though the evidence, the bestirring of storms, is arbitrary, unpredictable, the ship all but scuttled, borne under.

God exists.

I Job exist, barely. I and Thou.

You created me, for reasons (as matters turned) best known to Yourself.

✦　✦　✦

Here, Job

Events are orthodoxy, he would say,
submitting like any son.
The way a fruit tastes of itself
he tasted sacrifice,

no thirst but for that cup
engendering thirst.
Credo is event, would say
to a brother's face
by birth or death brought near—
a descending god he saw, a god

sprung from his tears.
Piety of experience
bound him in web.
He wore the world for wedding band.
Here, Job,
a few notes toward a life.

Words words we buried.

Look. Time wears new features; time takes heart.

DB

✦ ✦ ✦

10:9–22 As though Job admonished his soul; let us go back and back—to beginnings.

To You, in act of fashioning me, of clay.

And would You name me a faulty vessel, breaking in Your hands? Would You toss me aside, grind me underfoot?

✦ ✦ ✦

You, fashioning me in my mother's womb, skin and flesh, bone and nerve. I and Thou, from the beginning.

And a maternal eye looked to my well being; Your eye;

Grace and favor
You granted me,

Your providence
watched over my spirit (Job 10:12)

✦   ✦   ✦

Then; disaster, loss upon loss.

And how shall I, faith gone to rags and tatters, utter more than a half-strangled cry, carried off in contrary winds?

✦   ✦   ✦

The charges of the distempered trio are leveled, again and again. And they strike home. Job begins to doubt himself. Is he perhaps guilty; is not this suffering, as they claim, proof of malfeasance?

Can he adduce that searching his heart, he comes on nothing of sin? Is not his passionate disclaimer in fact a woeful form of self-deception?

What Job refuses to see, does God see, and turn away, casting over this life a distaining shadow?

Unfinished

The world is somewhere visibly round,
perfectly lighted, firm, free in space—
but why we die like kings or
sick animals, why tears stand
in living faces, why one forgets
the color of the eyes of the dead—

DB

✦   ✦   ✦

Who is this God, in merely human fashion judging and punishing?

Job dwells on the theme; shall God ape the worst, the most corrosive human behavior?

Job longs that God be—godly.

With this implication, flung back at his tormenters. Let God resemble less these logicians, whose judgments pummel him giddy.

Who in sum, seek to unseat his sound perception of God;

> Do You have
> eyes of flesh?
>
> Is Your vision
> that of mere humans?
>
> Are Your days
> the days of a mere mortal,
> Are Your years
> the years of a man,
>
> that You seek my iniquity
> And search out my sin? (Job 10:4–6)

✦   ✦   ✦

They do unseat him; his perception of others, his righteous sense of himself.

His moral estimate is torn between protestation of innocence and their staccato mutterings of guilt.

He veers wildly in those weird weathers, a vane torn from its anchor.

> First, wildly northward;
> You know
> that I am not guilty . . . (Job 10:7)

And again, what make of this, due south?

> I know
> You had this in mind;

to watch me
when I sinned

and not clear me
of my iniquity . . . (Job 10:13–14)

✦ ✦ ✦

Guilty, innocent; these are not terms of an inner debate, to be settled to the satisfaction of one party or the other.

Guilty, innocent? The alternatives are pure torment; an upper and lower millstone, and Job crushed between;

Should I be guilty,
the worse for me!

And even when innocent,
I cannot lift my head,

So sated in shame
so drenched in misery (Job 10:15)

✦ ✦ ✦

The upshot; only death promises relief.

We have heard the plaint before. It recurs, is driven home like a nail in a coffin lid.

Best relief were briefest life.

Womb, then tomb. If only birth and death were so intermingled that on the spur of a moment, the first issued in the second!

One must add a third; womb, tomb—gloom. Job envisions no Edenic setting as his eternal estate of choice. Rather;

. . . the land of deepest gloom
a land whose light is darkness,

all gloom and disarray,
whose light
is like darkness (Job 10:21–22)

✦　✦　✦

A Babylonian text, we note, summons a like conception;

> a house of darkness, a house from which none issue
> again, a path from which a voyager knows no return,
> where the sole food is dust. . . . They see no light, they
> dwell in twilight. (*The Descent of Ishtar*)

✦　✦　✦

11:1–20 Finally, Zophar, third of the assembly of Job's advisors, Job's "friends," launches forth.

Mercifully his tirade is brief; mercifully, since he has little to offer beyond contempt, clear and pointed.

From innuendo to insult. The final speaker of the present cycle is determined to sum things up, once for all.

Like a skilled prosecutor, in the spirit of ha-Satan he would clinch such matters as his companions had left somewhat untidy—had sullied even with a faint stain of compassion.

Out, damned spot!

✦　✦　✦

The language is loaded with scorn.

Job's plaints, for a start, are evidence of mere garrulity.

His arguments? windy, without substance, babblings, derisive of others (of his betters?).

We have here, only half unveiled, a lapsarian anthropology.

Given his conception of God, the fallen estate of humans (which is to say, Job's dramatic Fall), must follow.

The logic is a darkness, night following night in a Sheol of the mind.

✦   ✦   ✦

And what of God?

Zophar is a passionate Platonist, his Deity is a living, breathing oxymoron, parched and severe. God is defined as a surpassing perfection.

And what of us humans, one wonders, under so firm a ferule, its Wielder ever on the ready?

God is a perfection eternally on the *qui vive*, taking close note of the imperfection, iniquity, injustice endemic to our sorry selves.

Endemic to Zophar himself, his inner disarray dramatized in this distempered outburst?

Such is of course, never stated.

✦   ✦   ✦

Of us humans, more to come.

At source, the offense of Job (let us by all means concentrate on him) is his unyielding talk of "innocence." Intolerable.

A spurious innocence, to be sure. Like all such claims— spurious.

Let Job know it, the only wisdom is a syllogism tight as a noose. To wit; humans are "worthless . . . iniquitous . . . empty." But Job is human. Therefore.

✦   ✦   ✦

Even granted the conclusion, "Job is worthless, iniquitous, empty"—let him not despair. Recourse abides. Only let Job own up, and confess his sin;

> Correct your thought,
> stretch out your hands
> toward Him! (Job 11:13)

We pause there, amazed. Has Zophar seen and heard nothing? Has Job not turned again and again in supplication to God?

Perhaps so. But hardly in a manner apt to win relief for his plight. Too hedged about is this "confession" of his, hesitating between yes and no;

> Say it clear. I have sinned!
> Repudiate the evil
> which soils your hands,
>
> banish injustice
> from your dwelling! (Job 11:14)

✦   ✦   ✦

An impasse.

Promise of justification is held out by this protopharisee. And Job cannot submit. Cannot accept it, the bribe and its spurious beatitude.

Long before this debacle unfolded, we were privy to the divine praise heaped on Job in the heavenly court. Then his skies fell in.

And we say in our hearts; if God be for him, who shall rightly accuse?

A feeling in the bones; one can only suspect that the spirit of ha-Satan is abroad in these earthly clones.

✦   ✦   ✦

Promises, promises, Zophar is awash in them.

It is as though a mortal the key to treasures untold. Submit, and all will be yours;

Then you will lift your face
in innocence,
will stand firm and unafraid.

Then you will forget misery,
recall it like waters
that have ebbed away.

Your life
brighter than noonday,
gloom transformed to morning.

You will be secure, for there is hope,

entrenched,
you will rest secure . . . (Job 11:15–18)

✦   ✦   ✦

Imagine

If the world's temperate zone,
then too
its cruel weathers,
torrid, arctic.

If freedom, then two wills
conflicting; wild Cain,
smooth-phrased Abel, too good
for foul actual life.
If shelter for sad shepherds,
then the wild verge of the heart—
extravagance, violence, the lamb
murdered, rot and stench.
If the way,
then no way at all; way lost,
last chance, a potter's waste.

If fiery vine, then sour lees at heart.

If silence, forebearance
under all malice—
O when
when will You have done
imagining?

DB

✦   ✦   ✦

12:1–12 Job, uncowed, yields not an inch of the field. Accusation strikes fire. His tongue flares with mordant irony and ridicule.

In effect, he has had his fill of cliches and commonplaces and moral tags;

> No doubt
> you are the intelligent,
>
> with you,
> wisdom shall die.
>
> But I have intelligence as well as you—
>
> who does not know
> such things as these? (Job 12:1–3)

What have they, "the undisturbed," to teach one bent low under the lash?

He knows too the rumors surrounding his plight, the common feeling that circulates like a miasma;

I have become
the sport of my neighbors;

The one whom God answers
when he calls upon Him,
the just, the perfect man
is a laughing stock.

In the thought
of the complacent
is contempt for calamity
such as awaits those whose foot slips.

While robbers live
untroubled in their tents,

while those who provoke God
are secure . . . (Job 12:4–6)

✦   ✦   ✦

Job's is a culture of shame. Prosperity justifies the fortunate as godly. But let disaster strike, and a dark imputation races abroad.

The "friends," as would appear, have like-minded friends—a multitude of such. Then how is Job to rebut the reproaches?

Worst of all are the dark urgings—that he own up, and be saved!

He will not. He will counter, strongly.

He too has advice to give.

It is this; the method, the counsel of the three, is drawn from lore of the animal realm; it is subhuman. Animals flourish; instinct serves them well.

These harrassing counselors also live by instinct, by mechanical arousal and measurable spasm.

Their minds are unshadowed, half lit, unnuanced.

Thus too their god; an image in their own likeness, unshadowed, unnuanced.

✦   ✦   ✦

And the regimen of their god bears a like character; like god, like creation.

Their understanding of creation is airless, subterranean.

The virtuous and the wicked, nicely distinguished by the illuminati, flourish or languish.

Truth is easily available to the deserving. On them no misfortune falls, about them no demons lurk.

✦   ✦   ✦

A suspicion arises. The underpinnings of our story are destroyed by the god of the timeless, tireless trio. Their deity cannot be imagined bargaining with a ha-Satan.

And to clinch present matters, such as Job could never become a bargaining chip in a divine-demonic contest.

✦   ✦   ✦

In sum, their god, in stark contrast to the Deity of Job, is pleased to show his hand in the world.

Clarity, clear evidence! Devotees are granted to see reality, neatly bundled; wheat here, tares there; merit here, damnation and loss there; disciples, deviants.

✦   ✦   ✦

Whereas with Job, God appears only as blind catastrophe, absence, darkness.

This peculiar paradox, the insistence on God's existence in the face of His apparent disappearance, derives from the kabbalah, the tradition of Jewish mysticism, in which the world in its imperfection is created by God's recession. He draws a curtain of darkness down before Himself in order to allow light to appear, darkness serving as the necessary foil for illumination.

The thought rests at the center of Jabes's poetry, which turns on paradox and contradition. He writes in "The Book of Questions": "G-d is image in the absence of images, language in the absence of language, point in the absence of points."

The counterintuitive thrust of this thought leads to the imperative . . . that we have to "take the contradictions into our keeping / at the edge of emptiness."

This is a religious thought without irony because it stems from a religion based on the indispensability of irony, of dialectic and dialogue. (Carolyn Forche, *Against Forgetting*)

✦   ✦   ✦

A first round of debate is winding down.

All unaware, the trio of friends stand in the presence of a mystery. Why this atrocious suffering of a friend?

One thinks, so dark a question, embodied, visible, should overmaster tongue and logic, set hearts on pilgrimage into a wild place of silence, longing and dread.

Alas. Job's high repute, his favor before the Deity, his awful diminishing, these work nothing of the kind.

✦   ✦   ✦

Sense of mystery? Under frosty eyes Job is reduced to a mere "case," a "problem." He, his losses, the dungheap and leprosy, the death of loved ones—these are pieces of a logician's game. Only contrive the right move, and the puzzle will be "solved"!

These *eminences grises* have in fact "solved" his "problem"— beforehand.

✦   ✦   ✦

To what shall we compare Job, abandoned to the hardly merciful hands of his friends?

A splendid butterfly dead in their hands, a specimen impaled on the pin of vainglorious assurance?

His utter losses have become a—problem!

Intolerable, inhuman.

He will have none of it. He will not respond.

✦   ✦   ✦

But of course he will. He is not dead as yet, nor have his wits fled him.

Under their contempt, their juggernaut judgment, wisdom breaks through.

Truth told, his wisdom is hardly to be thought inferior to theirs.

✦   ✦   ✦

12:13–25 At least in one respect, Job stands in the line of the great prophets.

He knows the God of the living, the God of humans. Knows that the power of God lies beyond human—or logical—limit.

Creation is at His explosive command;

When God
holds back the waters,
they dry up;
When He lets them loose,
they tear up the land (Job 12:15)

✦　✦　✦

Then on to ourselves, speedily.

A like power scrutinizes, limits, unmasks, rebukes the institutions that fuel the engine of this world.

In unaccustomed detail Job enumerates them; these great ones are brought low, confounded, their follies and pretentions laid open to all. Mockery is the tone;

To God belong
strength and resourcefulness;

erring
and causing to err
are from Him.

He makes counselors
go about naked,
causes judges
to go mad.

God undoes the bonds
fastened by kings,
about them
fastens mere loincloths.

He makes priests
go about naked

pulls down
every establishment.

He deprives
trusted officials
of their speech,

plucks away
the minds of elders (Job 12:16–20)

And so on. Political and religious systems, legitimated by time
or tradition or power or money or gender—these lie under the
regimen of a merciless scrutinizing Eye. Veritably, Job becomes
an oracle of the politics of God;

God exalts nations,
then destroys them,
spreads people abroad,
then abandons them.

He deranges
leaders of the people,
makes them wander
in a trackless waste.

They grope in darkness
without light.

He makes them stagger
like drunken men (Job 12:21–25)

This Job; one thinks him a disciple of Isaiah. The prophet
had spoken in a like vein;

Where then are your wise men . . . ?
The princes of Zoan are fools;
The princes of Memphis deceived.

Egypt has been led astray
by the chiefs of her tribes.

God has mixed within her
a spirit of distortion.

They have made Egypt stagger
in all her undertakings
as a drunkard staggers in his vomit (Isaiah 19:12–15)

The theme is woven close, in a history of hope against hope.
Worldly systems thrust their victims down and down, to the
base of the social pyramid. And suddenly, these nameless ones
find voice through Isaiah and Job (and Jesus). Whom the same
systems have thrust down and down, sightless piers of the imperial aggrandizement.

✦   ✦   ✦

We stand in a far later era, and hear a village maid proclaim
the like, the overthrow of death-ridden principalities;

God has shown might with his arm,
has confused the proud in their inmost thoughts,

has deposed the mighty from their thrones
and raised the lowly to high places.

God has given the hungry every good thing,
the rich God has sent away empty . . .

The tradition is long and honorable, and here celebrated;

Even as promised to our ancestors
to Abraham and his descendants forever
(Luke 1:48–55)

✦   ✦   ✦

The "good news," literally unkillable, rises from the page of
our testament. From the mouth of a pregnant maiden, daugh-
ter of a brutally occupied people.

A woman deprived of worldly recourse; and yet—what
Recourse she summons to her side—to our side!

✦   ✦   ✦

Darkness engulfs our world, as we cross the threshold of the
famous millennium.

Intense, relentless greed and violence are the hallmarks of
official behavior. The ecology is insulted and endangered.

The skies seem closed against all dawns.

And the past once more is present. In the era of prophets, the noblest of humans languished in foul places; Jeremiah in the pit, Isaiah banished and put to silence, Ezekiel in long exile, Job on his dungheap.

Nonetheless, today also the "good news" seeps through the gates and bars and locks and chains, those monstrous odds. From jails and gulags and kangaroo courtrooms, from death rows, the good news, all unexpected, rings out.

Jail Senses

Sound—
>   tv noise
>   jingling keys
>   slamming metal doors—

listen to the silence!
Sight—
>   graffiti walls
>   mildew showers
>   roaches, mice—

Canadian geese fly south!

Smell—
>   stale air
>   bleach
>   lice soap—

cookies baking!

Taste—
>   Luke-warm diluted coffee
>   Kool-Aid
>   canned vegetables—

fresh fruit!

Touch—
  stainless steel toilets
  plastic mattresses
  cold cement walls—

circle of hands in prayer!

(Sister Carol Gilbert, OP;
Gods of Metal Plowshares, Kent County Jail)

✦ ✦ ✦

The Long Reach of Love

If I am not built up
bone upon bone
of the long reach and stride of love—
if not of that
as stars are of night,
as speech of birth and death; thought
a subtle paternity, of mind's eye—
if not, nothing.
A ghost costs nothing.
Casts nothing either; no net
no fish or failure, no tears like bells

summoning across seas
the long reach and stride of love
dawning, drowning bitter waters.

DB

✦ ✦ ✦

13:1–13 The words fairly shout from the page. Let no one conclude that our Job is lacking in fierce verbal skills, strong invective!

Suffering is an emory wheel; on it his language is honed to a wounding edge.

Job sees within, he speaks of what he sees. And what he sees lurks beneath the self-serving declamations of his "friends."

The trio are to be accounted mere "charlatans," "quacks." According to Job, they are not simply confessing a faith at variance with his own. They are deluded. They fancy they speak for God. But their arguments are mere windy palaver, self-deceived;

> Your briefs
> are ashy maxims,
>
> your responses,
> mounds of clay (Job 13:12)

Truth told, they denounce for sake of a—thesis.

Which is to say, in support of an idol; their "god."

So deep in the debate, and we can scarcely credit their behavior. A fellow human, purportedly a friend, cowers under a lash of misfortune. And they rebuke and hector; sinfulness has tainted him, flesh, blood, bone, possessions, family. And their god applauds such inhumanity?

✦ ✦ ✦

An atrocious claim! Job is ablaze with anger.

Unconscionably, they stand where ha-Satan, the prosecutor, stands; they speak on behalf of an ominous principality, the adversary of God.

Their witness joins that of the tempter of God and God's own.

Will they join in this dark enterprise?

✦   ✦   ✦

They will, with a vengeance.

And Job, his heart's might doubled with outrage, counters their attack.

In a relentless cross-examination he questions them, their motive and method;

> Is it for God
> you speak falsehoods,
>
> for His sake
> you utter deceit,
> for Him you lean
> this way and that,
> playing advocate for God?
>
> Will it go well
> when He searches you out?
>
> Will you fool Him
> as one fools men? (Job 13:7–9)

✦   ✦   ✦

13:14–17 We have seen it before; rumor goes around, comes around. Now, with a difference—it is wildly inflated.

It takes this form; the "just one" is nothing of the kind. Job is a sinner. His lowered estate comes in consequence of sin, a punishment, inexorable, befitting.

The friends must be accounted chief architects of this awful logic of crime and consequence. They are also by implication, its inflators.

✦ ✦ ✦

Nothing for it. In response Job must risk everything.

Everything? but everything has been snatched from him!

Has he nothing then to place on the scales of chance-mischance? He has something; his existence, miserable as it is;

> I will have my say,
> whatever comes of it.
>
> I will take my flesh in my teeth,
> my life in my hands.
>
> Though God slay me
> yet will I trust,
> arguing my case before Him (Job 13:13–15)

✦ ✦ ✦

It comes to this; all or nothing.

Nothing to lose that has not already been lost. He will risk what is left to him; life itself.

And we recall, with a start of recognition, the original bargaining chip offered by God to ha-Satan.

First, a concession; "He is in your power."

Then a boundary set, a taboo; "Only spare his life."

✦ ✦ ✦

Now the boundary is down, the taboo robbed of force. "I will take my life in my hands." Not certainly by way of contemplated suicide; by way of a wager.

It is helpful to recall; we know more than Job of Job's story. We know of the celestial bargain, and its final outcome.

So an implication denied to Job, dawns on us. If God can

bargain with ha-Satan—and if, over and above the bargain, the adversary wins to his side a coven of tormentors—then Job too shall bargain with God.

✦   ✦   ✦

And the terms of the wager? They are more exigent than the restoration of goods and chattels—or even the raising to life of the dry bones of his family.

At stake is his name, besmirched as it is; the vindication of his integrity, called wickedly in question by the acolytes of the adversary.

Short of this outcome, no gain, no material resoration will suffice.

✦   ✦   ✦

13:18–19 A different image, and a recurring one; Job seeks a formal juridical process. On its outcome (as above), he is resolved to stake everything;

> See now,
> I have prepared a case;
>
> I know
> I will win it.
>
> Who then
> makes a case against me?
>
> Then I shall be put to silence,
> and perish! (Job 13:18–19)

The challenge to an adversary, the terms set by the servant in Isaiah, are strikingly similar to those of Job; Who dares contend with me?

Let us appear together!
Who would be my opponent?
Let him confront me!

See, God is my help—
who can win a verdict against me? (Isaiah 50:8–9)

✦ ✦ ✦

13:20 To all intents the encircling "friends" have ceased to matter. The issue with Job is—faith. Faith to be maintained, though it lies prone beneath a megatonnage of disaster.

Faith, a "therefore."

Though it must also be a faith "in despite."

Despite the massive adversity befalling him, despite even the awful trio—Job will believe.

He addresses God, directly. (Which, we note, the friends never do.)

God is present. The God of Job.

✦ ✦ ✦

Inscrutable though the deity be, the trio and their arguments are declared—redundant.

It is as though, like their logic, they were reduced to "ash" and "clay."

Let me, Job, address God vis-à-vis; the Thou, the Sole Reality, the Despite All, the Last Ditch Leap.

✦ ✦ ✦

13:21–22. Thus the prayer.

Two favors grant me. First, withdraw that hand of Yours; it presses me to earth. I would come to You in another mood than terror.

And second, issue Your summons, and I will answer You. Or if it please, I will speak first.

✦   ✦   ✦

Let me speak.
Why do You hide your face from me, treat me as Your
    enemy?

Will You harrass
a wind-driven leaf,

Pursue dried straw? (Job 13:24–25)

Which is to say, in an incomparably moving and apt image—have you not already done Your worst? Was not the season of verdant leaves and tender grasses, the season of my flourishing youth, long since canceled by You?

As though a human were to know but one such summer. Then alas, heart and enterprise fade, lie in a permanent winter—icy winds, sere leaves, withered straw.

✦   ✦   ✦

Would You have me answer for "faults of my youth," for sins of inadvertance or fragility, devoid of all malice?

Thus Job would put the best face on his guilt, if guilt there be.

And why not? Has he not been commended repeatedly by God?

And is the praise to evaporate at the whim of those who tarry about, only to bait him?

✦   ✦   ✦

"You put my feet in the stocks" . . . how apt to his condition of helplessness, of immobility!

(We recall the like, literal punishment of Jeremiah [20:2], and centuries later, of Paul and Silas [Acts 16:24].)

Feverish, Job blows hot, blows cold.

For the moment his sense of God turns bizarre. It resembles that of his friends; the god of suffocating surveillance, watchful, hemming, weighing deeds to a feather weight. A god worlds apart from a loving Companion and Friend, the God of Job.

✦　✦　✦

Can this be the God he has served with wit and wisdom from his youth, the God of steadfast love and ample gifts?

Or are they right after all, those artful theoreticians, their minds dark, peripatetic as carrion birds smelling death on the air?

Is their god to be accounted true god?

✦　✦　✦

It is as though in a low mood, Job were slipping his firm moorings. What to conclude, but that he is taking seriously the adversaries' version of the deity?

And more, their version of the human as well, dire and downputting as it is.

He ruminates, tormented, doubting his own mind. As though he drew a pitiful garment close; close as a shroud, head to feet a dark bundle of misery.

✦　✦　✦

14:1–6 A long threnody follows, *sotto voce.* Mouth against knees Job crouches there, covered in sackcloth, disembodied, as though his words issued from a Sheol of the mind.

His "friends" flourish, nothing of loss touches them.

Are they exempted from all misfortune? Or is God pleased merely to delay their ruin?

Pay them no heed, their inviolable assurance, their hammers
of judgment pounding out a last hour—his own.
No. Crouch there, endure there, die there!

✦   ✦   ✦

His condition, not theirs, is simply to be accounted the human condition. Dare it, look it in face, this Medusa;

> Humans
> a stick of worm-eaten wood,
> a moth-eaten garment
>
> Likewise;
>
> They shall all wear out like a garment
> You change them like clothing and they pass away
> (Psalm 102:27)
>
> —like flowers of the field; bud, blossom—and fall.
> A voice says, Cry out!
> I answer, What shall I cry?
>
> All humankind is grass
>
> and all their glory like the flower of the field;
>
> The grass withers, the flower wilts
> when the breath of God blows upon it . . . (Isaiah 40:6, 7)
>
>
> Like unabiding shadows, here and gone.
> Humans are a breath,
> Their days, a passing shadow (Psalm 144:4)

And a question, always a question. The religion of Job is a welter of questions.

Can a human be found who is clean of defilement?

To bring wisdom to bear on the dolorous matter, Job requires no God. He answers for himself; and so answers for all. No one is innocent of fault.

He has had experience in the matter, close at hand. First, it would seem, through his suffering at the hand of God.

✦   ✦   ✦

And we wonder, and are saddened. Is Job slipping into the sterile formulas of the adversaries? Is he falling victim to their logic; misfortune as proof of guilt?

✦   ✦   ✦

14:7–12 Indeed (so goes the sad rumination) on the scale of renewal and regeneration, we humans are less potent than— flora.

Trees fall to stumps; rain comes, and lo! new shoots appear.

Human fate is otherwise; we are streams once for all gone to drought.

Poor Job waxes eschatological. What is, is ineluctable, and shall be, in *saecula saeculorum*. A threnody of inexorable fate;

> So we lie down,
> and rise not again
>
> Till the heavens are no more,
> we shall not awake
> nor be roused from sleep (Job 14:12)

✦   ✦   ✦

Is Job doing his tormenters one better? As though to say; Very well, no recourse. The text, the outcome, is written beforehand, no hand avails to alter it. Providence? Nothing of the sort exists. Illusion.

The wing of Fate is overhead, shadowing all endeavor. Night claims the day.

chapter four

"Wearisome Comforters, All of You" (14:13–16:17)

14:13–14:22 Let me, says Job to his lamenting soul, let me dream the impossible. Let me construct a hut, a shelter from Your wrath.

So. A parable concerning a shelter.

I shall name Sheol anew, call it a shelter from Your storms.

Someone to Die For

I had a nightmare—
the rickety shack brought down
I was sheltering in;
from sleep to death
gone, all coped in dream.
What then? I had never lived?
it well might be.

Without friends—what?
dead, unborn, my light
quenched, never struck.
The piteous alternatives
life simulates!
streets haunt, faces hang—
still, I mark
like an unquenched man
merciful interventions—
a clean end or beginning,

someone to die for
some love to sing

DB

✦   ✦   ✦

Let me, Job, grow grandiose, let me suppose even greater impossibilities of mercy.

Day upon day, night upon night I would abide in that hut of Sheol, would wait there, a shade among shades. Would await the passing of Your wrath, would work out my servitude in patience.

Until You, filled with longing for the work of Your hands, call my name. Summon me. And lo, I would return from death, and walk the earth once more.

All that mercy, that love restored!

✦   ✦   ✦

And yet, in the bitter here and now, what a difference!

Here, now, You count every footstep of mine as faulty.

And yet, were my parable of hope to come true, You would keep no record of sin, would seal my misdeeds close. As though they were not.

✦   ✦   ✦

Job's rumination. All in vain, or nearly so, his hope, his dream of return.

It cannot be; the naked "facts of life," pushed by merciless interlocutors, reveal his predicament—different, of another order altogether.

Of what use these dreams of "return," of a love that summons the beloved, even from Sheol? They dissolve, the suffering one is left with—near nothing.

Diseased hands and feet, death without and within, injustice clinging like a leprosy of the soul.
   Only consider;

>   Mountains collapse and crumble
>   rocks dislodge and fall,
>
>   water wears away stone,
>   torrents wash away earth—
>
>   So You
>   exterminate hope,
>   You overpower us forever,
>   we perish.
>   You disfigure
>   and dispatch us.
>
>   Do sons attain honor? the father knows nothing.
>   Are they brought low?
>   Nothing.
>
>   He feels only
>   pain of the flesh,
>   his spirit lamenting within (Job 14:18–22)

✦   ✦   ✦

The Word

> *A pen appeared, and the god said;*
> *"Write what it is to be*
> *man." And my hand hovered*
> *long over the bare page,*
> *until there, like footprints*
> *of the lost traveller, letters*
> *took shape on the page's*

*blankness, and I spelled out
the word "lonely." And my hand moved
to erase it; but the voices
of all those waiting at life's
window cried out loud; "It is true."*

(R. S. Thomas)

✦ ✦ ✦

A mournful mingling of worlds!

We wonder, awed. Does Job dwell in this world, or by anticipation in Sheol?

Does he linger as yet in this world, his flesh absorbing the dark hues of the underworld, the sun of his life extinguished? (Those daughters and sons of his, untimely taken!)

Or does his brooding spirit flit hither and yon, now in this world, now in that, bewildered, ruminant, pathetic?

✦ ✦ ✦

One thing is certain; he dares the Almighty to strike, knowing that no further insult awaits, short of death (ignorant as he is of the instruction to the ha-Satan; "Spare his life"). Still the question lingers; does he sense in his bones, victimized yet prophetic, something of a mysterious bargaining and taboo?

After all, has he not accused God, has his tongue not parlayed at the edge of a curse?

And despite all, does he not linger in this life?

✦ ✦ ✦

In our testament, Paul too gives a poignant account of suffering and setback. The litany bears comparison with Job's;

Brothers and sisters, we do not wish to leave you in the
dark about the trouble we had in Asia; we were crushed
beyond our strength, even to the point of despairing
of life.

We were left to feel like men condemned to death, so
that we might trust, not in ourselves, but in God who
raises the dead. God rescued us from the danger of death
and will continue to do so. We have put our hope in
Him who will never cease to deliver us.

But you must help us with your prayers . . .
(2 Corinthians 1:8–11).

✦   ✦   ✦

Yet, what a contrasting tone! Paul is all hope and vigor; God
has not failed, has only tested him. His labors are heavy—still,
they buoy him up. Let adversity show face, his vigorous spirit
exults, he will overcome!

Was he never brought up short, we wonder, never overwhelmed by rejection, distain, dismissal?

Of course, one thinks—in such a world, bearing such a message, how could it not be so?

The bitter moment came, and passed. No reproaching God
for the misadventure in Asia. He shows an uninjured face of
hope. All is well, despite all!

✦   ✦   ✦

And the tone, one notes, is firmly pastoral; Paul is surrounded
and upheld by trustworthy friends; companions of a far different stripe than Job's hangers-on.

For respite and consolation, Paul turns instinctively to his
community. He takes for granted mutuality of word and work.

He and they undergo these tests together, his people are at prayer on his behalf.

✦   ✦   ✦

No such community stands with Job; indifference, overt hostility, heartlessness wrapped about in a cloak of orthodoxy—these are a mix of gall in his cup. Unconscionably, he must stand alone.

How, in so dark an impasse, can he suffer profitably?

✦   ✦   ✦

And the question of work. Paul is a colossus of voyages and labors, fairly bestriding his world. His tongue is fiery with the word of Christ.

The task is always unfinished; he is consumed with it. Passion outruns his feet, his chariot, his ship.

And all the while, a lofty mind and a large heart preserve him from obsession, keep him balanced, candid, single of purpose.

✦   ✦   ✦

A regal figure, at the helm of event, never out of kilter—and quite prepared to do battle!

In touch with God, and with his people.

We sense the consonance of hearts; in face of misfortune, it heals. To right hand and left stand Luke, Titus, and the others.

There are setbacks, arduous marches, wild sea voyages. Betrayals too, and the sowing of dissent. But consolations abound; does God not walk, sail, ride with the enterprise, ratify it, bless it?

The truth, the truth to be proclaiamed; this is his passion. The Word of God must be spoken, and spoken again, the community of faith formed, strengthened, ratified, reproved. Here and there and everywhere in the world he speeds, sails filled with a wild wind of the Spirit!

That world is a harsh testing ground; but it is also infinitely serendipitous, its peoples grand in variety and gift. They await him, and he them.

✦   ✦   ✦

A second spring! Under God he, Paul, is bringing it to pass! The gentile church is in bud, an ineffible odor is wafted abroad. "We are the aroma of Christ." A fine flowering is to come, and shortly.

Nothing can impede; nothing. Therefore it follows (and the logic has the tautness of grace under pressure)—nothing is to be feared, nothing regretted.

Even as his vision flings him abroad over land and sea, Paul turns the world on its head, counts every loss a gain, every setback and trouble.

✦   ✦   ✦

Is the Pauline comparison odious, made in Job's despite?

This is by no means the intent. In Job, we have a man isolated, lonely, beset, derided by heartless minds.

Worse; God has made him a kind of chess piece in a questionable contest, a battle of egos.

Job must play a game whose rules are concealed from the player.

No wonder this God of his seems a dark enigma. No wonder Job is beside himself with the absurdity and cruelty of life, the injustice.

And then this bizarre coterie, pressing him back and back as though with a phalanx of spears—their logic, their retributive minds, their straightlaced god!

✦   ✦   ✦

Job must be accounted a hero. And more; a teacher—of limits, and of the surpassing of limits—a surpassing that faith itself makes altogether necessary.

Through Job we learn of the widening, better, the forcing apart, of the boundaries of faith.

It is as though he, captive to misadventure, laid a shoulder against the walls of his prison. And lo! the wall was pushed back and back.

And the pressure he summons is, we note, exerted against mighty counter pressures; companions who read the text of his life wrong. And more; who press upon him the wrong reading, the wrong god. Hearken to us, learn from us, submit!

Their god. True God?

Here in progress, is the dark drama of faith, the withstanding of the tragic hero.

✦   ✦   ✦

Those eldritch friends, four against one; outside the prison, they push in and in. Job, to the wall. There, narrow logic inhibits breathing, fresh air, light, access to the Mystery.

What a sour fervor they show! Like raw converts, they renounce the courtesy of open minds. They would push the walls inward, until this presumptuous breather were suffocated and subdued.

✦   ✦   ✦

Yet we must grant the quaternity their due.

Almost despite themselves, they stand within a great tradition, the breakthrough of Ezekiel; they insist on personal responsibility.

Each human must heft the burden of his own behavior;

consequences may not be avoided or sloughed off on another, whether here and now or in the future. Descendants for their part must not be burdened with the sins of ancestors.

Thus the argument, as it is applied time and again to Job.

Let him assume responsibility for his life, for darkness, faults, omissions, perhaps even sin.

✦ ✦ ✦

The "friends" are merciless surrogates of a merciless deity. They apply the principle whole cloth, abstract, deprived of affect. Those absent hearts!

In place is a parched severity of mind. So they come to know little or nothing of Job.

Religion has petrified compassion.

✦ ✦ ✦

Suspicion rankles in their minds; is not Job intolerably free and easy, does he not play hobs with tradition, with the law?

They would "improve" Job.

✦ ✦ ✦

Another mystifying aspect, as the interminable diatribes drone on. We hear not a word of mutuality. Do they never converse with one another? Who are they among themselves, these formidable intellectuals, so assured of their status before God?

✦ ✦ ✦

In the presence of Job they see and do not see.

Does a suffering servant stand before them? Can they not see his anguish, smell his supporating sores, comfort him, bind up his ills?

Their hands are lax, their minds overtaxed.

They summon the mind-set of ha-Satan. Dare one venture; they think like him?

✦ ✦ ✦

And what of God, the God of Job?

He would save His servant, but barely. A salvation reduced to the dry bones of Ezekiel's vision.

The Deity would lay claim to Job's fidelity as His own triumpth, to His credit. Only look, see this peerless one, the apogee of My human tribe, this unswerving hero!

And who is Job to say otherwise?

✦ ✦ ✦

Still, in effect he says it. He goes counter.

He, a mere human, dares call the Deity to accounts.

And this wild fling, this unheard-of venture is all to our advantage, instructive.

Even though to many, including the intrusive trio, Job's words are a dark scandal.

Call God to account—for what?

For destroying him.

✦ ✦ ✦

We are privy to the first act; how God parlayed with ha-Satan, how terms were laid down.

Without Job's knowledge or consent the contest is played out—in his own putrefying flesh.

The terms hold fast, the adversary has his say, his day.

God bargains a life (and what a life!) all but away.

✦　✦　✦

We have noted the stark contrasts that mark the life of two great spirits, Paul and Job.

There are also likenesses to consider. Paul writes in considerable detail of his sufferings—and in harrowing detail we learn of Job's losses.

But we have no comparable account, we note, of the sufferings of Jesus. It is as though the evangelists take common resolve; to limit themselves to the barest of narratives.

Only once or twice in the gospel of Luke, emotion breaks out, a near anacoluthon. It is as though the quill trembled in the scribe's hand and he broke into tears in the telling. The agony in Gethesemane, the prayer of Jesus for surcease, the sweat of blood (21:41–44).

✦　✦　✦

Paul would also have believers know the price of discipleship.

Always within the text, a common currency is passed. From the price he paid, Christians can tot up the price accruing to ourselves;

> We are afflicted in every way possible, but we are not crushed; full of doubts, we never despair. We are persecuted but never abandoned; we are struck down, but never destroyed.

> Continually we carry about in our bodies the dying of Jesus, so that in our bodies the life of Jesus may also be revealed.

> While we live we are constantly being delivered to death for Jesus' sake, so that the life of Jesus may be revealed in our mortal flesh . . .

We do not lose heart, because our inner being is renewed
each day even though our body is being destroyed . . .

The present burden of our trial is light enough, and
earns for us an eternal weight of glory . . .
(2 Corinthians 4:8–12, 16–17).

✦   ✦   ✦

Suffering? It goes without saying; it is a condition of the work
to be done. He suffers willingly, and passes the implication to
ourselves. Only take up the task; the suffering will come. And it
will all be bearable.

Whereas, for his portion, Job has only—suffering. It is his
sole work, his testament and witness.

Do others have errands in the world, consuming, distracting,
heartening?

Urgent, single of mind, the apostles of the momentous Task
come and go in the world, in time.

✦   ✦   ✦

Say, What?

And what are we?
Not the rich,
a fist of worms for a heart,
nor the poor
consumed with making do.
Say, a slum child
in a filthy yard—
a spool, a few crossed sticks—

the doll wound on a bobbin
almost talks back,
almost stalks away.

Was this the way He meant us?
meddlesome,
proud, not docile—
to stand to Him, thwart, amaze Him still!

DB

✦ ✦ ✦

In his heyday Job had been "busy about many concerns," family, herds and flocks.

Now he has—nothing, no task but suffering.

No response to his anguished "why," no answer. His questions hang on the air like hooked meat in a shop window.

He has nothing but his suffering.

And in the eyes of his friends, he suffers badly. He refuses to take into account the implication, obvious to the inner eye, of his travail. Sin has brought him to this sorry pass. Repent, recover!

✦ ✦ ✦

A Laocoon in bonds, he twists and turns about, contending against the tight logic that forges in one, cause and effect, sin and punishment. Logic as they insist, that keeps the stars in their courses, and the moral world making sense—to sensible folk.

✦ ✦ ✦

15:1–6 Eliphaz resumes the attack.

Job admits no moral limits. Good sense, sound argument—these avail nothing. His shield is of adamant, his will perverse.

He draws from his quiver a series of discommoding questions, discharging them like arrows—if one can credit the hearing! Insulting, apodictic, truculent, surly—worse than questions, indictments!

The nostrils of the righteous fairly quiver with indignation. Only conceive of it—Job's words are rife with impiety, the recourse of the wicked. He would indict the Almighty!

✦　✦　✦

Does he require an adversary to reveal his true estate?

He does not; he stands self-condemned. The more astute his arguments, the more convoluted his emotional charge—the more closely he is trapped.

✦　✦　✦

The battle is joined, worlds collide.

The charge; impiety.

Two versions of reality, radically different?

More. The attack of Eliphaz all but ignites the page, the words leap from place, nonsensical, frenzied. Job—accused of impiety!

> You subvert piety
> and restrain
> prayerfulness before God . . .
> Your own mouth
> condemns you—
> not I;
>
> your lips
> testify against you (Job 15:4–6)

✦　✦　✦

Are we in cloud-cookooland?

Let us merely say; reality is stranger, more bizarre than we had reckoned. The reality before us must include a chorus who stand at safe distance, dictating to an unfortunate the terms of divine dealings.

Passionate, berating they are.

Let Job protest as he chooses.

He is wrong; the game called life is fair. The cards are not stacked.

And what if the Main Player holds the cards close to breast, shall the deity be judged a lesser god for that, shall he be demeaned, hailed into a court of this world—and by so questionable a server of the summons?

Intolerable, altogether. Implied or overt, the Jobian proposal is blasphemous.

✦　✦　✦

And all the while, and all unwitting, these arrogant righteous ones are forging a link. It is tragic, inspired, a consolation cold as ice.

We have noted it before. Job is one with the Suffering Servant of Isaiah (Isaiah 53), as the latter is convicted out of hand, guilty.

The Servant's crime? it is never named. It is literally beyond comprehension.

Crime, consequence. Job joins as well in the punishment accorded the Servant—the scorn and contempt of the godly.

✦　✦　✦

The scene in Isaiah, to all appearance a courtroom, is also a maze, a wordy, incoherent labyrinth, a "justice system" one thinks, contrived by a Kafka.

Surreal, a nightmare. Who speaks, on whose behalf, in whose despite? Who stands with the Servant, who against?

More; of what crime is the Servant accused?

Is the chorus, commenting on the action, complicit in the condemnation? Or are those voices to be judged repentant, remorseful?

✦ ✦ ✦

We are left with this; first, a description of the Defendant, stricken, a veritable Job;

> He had no form or beauty,
> that we should gaze at him,
>
> no charm,
> that we should find him pleasing.
>
> He was spurned and avoided,
> a man of suffering,
> familiar with disease,
>
> a leper
> from whom we veil our face (Isaiah 53:2–3)

We note it, astonished; the Defendant never once speaks for Himself. He stands there, silent as a stele of adamant; He is "commented upon."

Has He chosen, in scorn of His acusers, to say nothing, a Jesus before Herod? Has He been struck mute?

What a show of dignity, if the former; and if the latter, how demeaning!

✦ ✦ ✦

There follows a detailed dwelling on the (adduced) import of the sufferings of the Innocent One.

It leaves one uneasy, this theory of vicarious punishment.

We hear not a word from the accused. Are we then to trust the chorus? Why does not the Victim speak for Himself?

Job does.

✦ ✦ ✦

In the scene in Isaiah, we have a kind of "interpretative theology," much resembling the theologizing of the friends—these lengthy discources concerning God. Invariably as we note, at second remove, or third.

So too, the chorus surrounding the Servant takes the tack of Job's tormenters.

The chorus and the friends of Job are a species of theological inquisitors, impatient with mystery, putting things tight and aright; our sufferings He endured;

> we thought of Him as stricken,
> as one smitten by God, afflicted.

> He was pierced for our offenses,
> crushed for our sins.

> He bore a chastisement that made us whole,
> by His stripes we were healed . . . .

> God laid on Him the guilt of us all (Isaiah 54:4–6)

✦ ✦ ✦

Or so it is adduced. But how astonishing; from the God so characterized, we hear not a word.

Any more than we hear from God, a vindication of the Logical Theological Deity of Job's friends.

✦ ✦ ✦

All of which suggests that both texts, that of Isaiah and of Job, raise questions and invite a closer look than is usually accorded them.

Does the story in Isaiah of the Servant suggest a theory of

retribution, selective and single in choice, and corporate, indeed universal in effect?

Perhaps not. Perhaps it suggests something far different; the mysterious communal condemnation of an innocent, followed by a "whitewashing," a washing of hands.

Tears and grief are expended, copiously.

And all perhaps in view of a cover-up.

✦ ✦ ✦

The chorus suggests a caricature of the classic Greek. Here the voices do not comment on or reveal meaning; they conceal it, deflect it.

They stand apart from the sufferings of the Servant; yet they presume to understand and interpret.

In fact, do they violate the meaning? Are they complicit in the miscarriage of justice, the kangaroo court, the condign punishment?

✦ ✦ ✦

They much resemble Job's tormenters, assigning arbitrary meaning, flattening out the mystery.

The Servant moves through the text like a ghost, silent, unsubstantial.

Not so Job! In marvelously wild and wooly scorn, he shouts a spate of scorn, his fiery poetry of the oppressed, rejecting the "meaning" nailed like a signboard against his body.

✦ ✦ ✦

The speechless Servant stands there, at the mercy of the theologizers.

Under His silence the chorus grow bolder. They know God, how God conducts the world.

In casu, how God conducts the present affair; the trial and punishment of the Servant, the disposition of the "case," the closing of the dossier.

They are confident, sure exegetes. And in the text they seemingly prevail.

In fact, they do not.

They invite judgment on themselves. They are manipulators, userers of the Word. They debase It.

Their God, it appears, is a crude bargainer. He (*sic*) conducts the world like a theater of cruelty, engages in a vile tradeoff;

> God chose to crush him by disease,
> that if he made himself an offering for guilt,
>
> he might see offspring and have a long life
> that through him God's purpose might prosper . . .
> (Isaiah 53:10)

✦   ✦   ✦

And more of the like.

The Servant's role is assigned. He is protagonist in a drama written by others. The indefatigable chorus are pleased to name it "Divine Plan."

"Assigned" is a key word; the Servant is indentured to a higher will, is allowed no choice. He is a victim, He accepts the indignity.

And the arrangement, one thinks, does small honor to anyone involved; to the god or servant.

And to the chorus? No honor at all.

✦   ✦   ✦

Still, one is led to ask; to whose "instruction" is the episode of the Suffering Servant offered?

To the religiously righteous it might be of benefit. To name
the god, which is to say, to proclaim a god useful to their ideology.

All said, theirs is the ideology of Caiphas, the high priest;

> It is better for one person to die for the people . . .
> (John 11:50)

Chances are that the god so named, so "explained," will thus
receive a credential of sorts. Will be publicly sanctioned as the
official deity, the god embraced in good faith by the devout, the
god of the church. And of the nation.

✦ ✦ ✦

So; on to scapegoating. Someone must be singled out, laden
with the sins of all, must die on behalf of all.

In accepting such a life and death, the Servant is promised a
surpassing glory. The text is, to say the least, ambiguous. Does
the fate of the Servant imply a true image of God?

Or does it urge reflection concerning a religion devoid of compassion and justice?

The answer, it would seem, is left to ourselves.

✦ ✦ ✦

The servant image of Isaiah undoubtedly influenced the author of Job.

Two suffering Servants, with a notable difference.

The contrast lies in the responses.

The Servant in Isaiah passively submits—or appears to.

Is He in fact (and usefully) put to silence?

✦ ✦ ✦

Job for his part will not be gagged.

His harping friends, like the chorus surrounding the Servant, are intent on scapegoating him. They press hard; confess your sin, and be saved!

Job grows ever more indignant and voluble. He spurns them.

How dare you assign guilt, place a stigma on me? How dare you instruct me in the ways of God, even as I suffer under His hand?

✦ ✦ ✦

If only, if only you Job, will turn and turn about!

And promises, promises accrue, dazzling restorations! Your lofty place in the world restored, a cornucopia of bounty will again tip in your direction.

Likewise with the Servant. Only let Him be led like a lamb to the slaughter, let Him consent to His fate, and

> he shall see his descendants in a long life . . .
> he shall see the light in fulness of days . . .
>
> I will give him his portion among the great
> and he shall divide the spoils with the mighty . . .
> (Isaiah 53:10–11)

Or so it is said.

But the promissory note is signed by an all-too-human hand. As for God, the Deity conceals His hand.

✦ ✦ ✦

15:7–16 Press him, press Job hard.

Does he bethink himself a very Adam, an ancient, an ancestor of all. And more—wiser than all descendants?

> The Lord God formed out of the ground various wild
> animals and various birds of the air, and brought them
> to the man to see what he would call them.
>
> Whatever the man called each of them, that would be
> its name.
>
> The man gave names to all the cattle, all the birds of
> the air, and all the wild animals . . . (Genesis 2:19–20).

Or perhaps—the tormenters grow bolder—Job was present to
God from eternity, along with Wisdom Herself?

> The Lord begot me, the firstborn of his ways,
> the forerunner of his prodigies of long ago;
>
> from of old I was poured forth,
> at the first, before the earth.
>
> When there were no depths I was brought forth,
> when there were no fountains or springs of water.
>
> Before the mountains were settled into place,
> before the hills I was brought forth,
>
> when as yet the earth and the fields were not made,
> nor the first clods of the world (Proverbs 9:22–26)

Or perhaps like a Prometheus, Job has furtively stolen Wisdom, and to his own benefit borne Her off?

We are awed—and uneasy in spirit.

The questions are posed with unselfconscious irony, even self-
parody. Questions like a closed circle, a serpent swallowing its
tail. Questions that offer by implication their own answer.

Thus the questioner hurries on. No listener, he.

Why await a response from one unendowed with good sense?

> What do you know
> that we do not know,
>
> what intelligence have you
> which we do not? (Job 15:9)

If only Job and his like would hear them out, and submit!

But then of course, the drama would resolve, the crisis pass.

Just as, if the friends came to a better mind, if they grew wise in Jobian fashion, our world would be much improved. Or so the trio avers.

And if the friends arrived at a measure of spiritual understanding, the book of Job would end alas, at that point.

And we would know less of a matter both bitter and urgent; the chanciness of life and fortune, and the fiercely competing versions of God that rend believers.

✦   ✦   ✦

It is as though an ancient serpent, summoned by dour Eliphaz, warmed in midday sun and came to life. The beast has long hibernated in the world outside Eden, sated with the fruit of the tree of knowledge.

Now it grows fiercely aware once more, as though ruminating; this Eliphaz is an ally, he and I know the Fall, the consequence!

> What is man
> that he be accounted
> blameless,
>
> one born of woman
> that he should be righteous?
> If in His holy ones
> God places no confidence,

if the very heavens
are not pure in His sight,

how much less
the abominable, the corrupt—

humans,
who drink iniquity like water! (Job 15: 14–16)

So artful, so lapsarian!

Eliphaz plays upon an old theme—but with a twist worthy of the canny friend of a friend—the serpent.

In face of the onslaught of illness and death, Eliphaz referred in an earlier image to the fragility of mortals,

. . . who dwell
in houses of clay,

whose foundation
is in the dust,

who are crushed
more easily than the moth!

Morning or evening,
they may be shattered . . . (Job 4:19–20)

Now he turns from mortality to morals, contriving his version of God—judge, certifier, naysayer.

He mixes and consumes a pablum for his bitter soul.

And one cannot but wonder; does Eliphaz include himself in the orbit of his tirade?

Or are his strictures aimed only at those others, the irresponsible recalcitrants, the Jobs?

Perhaps he includes himself. Perhaps the knowledge offers a kind of hangman's consolation—to know that the noose tightens about his own neck?

✦ ✦ ✦

15:17–35 One is hard put for a connection here.

Perhaps there is none, and meant to be none. Perhaps we have a critic quite beside himself, carried aloft on the pinions of declamatory rhetoric.

In any case, let Job make no mistake. An indefatigable moralist is clear as to his mission;

> I wish to instruct you.
> Listen to me (Job 15:17)

✦ ✦ ✦

The burden has been touched on before, by colleague Bildad. But now, with a difference.

Bildad's tradition, we learned, was overlaid with Egyptian lore. Eliphaz goes counter. For all his leanings toward human corruptability, he defends the purity of his own people.

Narrow of mind, nationalistic to the core, a divider of sheep from goats, a strangely arbitrary arbiter of the guilty and the pure, this Eliphaz! What I have seen;

> I will tell—
>
> What the wise
> have related
>
> and since the days of their fathers
> have not contradicted,
>
> to whom alone
> the land was given
> when no foreigner
> moved among them (Job 15:17–19)

There follows an interminable expose of judgment against the wicked.

Relevance to Job, to his predicament, to his protestations of innocence, remains obscure.

Obscure, one thinks, but hardly opaque. The dark coloration, the minatory tone, the deep-browed tendentiousness!

Gradually, the innuendo becomes plain, the finger points.

Job. He is bound hand and foot by a deadly filament. Implicated in a web—beyond hope, beyond retrieval?

Thus Eliphez; Beware, Job. Justice, an all-seeing eye, lurks and will pounce.

✦ ✦ ✦

Rhetoric and abuse are in full cry.

In a lengthy monologue, an unnamed wicked tyrant is inveighed against. A Damoclean sword hovers above the throne and its occupant. From the rise and fall of the wicked and powerful, let the common run of mortals, Job included, take warning.

Let them (him) not lightly assume that disempowered as they are, incapable of vast sinning, they are thereby declared immune from all delicts.

Let Job learn; from the greater to the lesser. From palace to dungheap moves the finger of God, probing, dispassionate, tracing in the dust of time a continuity of guilt and consequence.

(One cannot say for certain. But perhaps the above, the image of judgment homing in, is the point of Eliphaz' funerary fustian.)

✦ ✦ ✦

16:1–3 Job hastens to the fray.

> Day and night
> I cry out to You—
> no other,
> no help for me.

Come then, Samaritan—

Out of sight,
out of mind
I wander a no-man's land.

The living
wash hands of me,
the dead
close eyes against me.
Worse;
You
turn away.
In hell
who praises You,
who magnifies Your deeds?

Apollyon's chorus
spontaneous, breathless
striking up
Alleluia, Alleluia?
Misfortunate, maladroit
still I would be
Your faithful servant (Psalm 88)

✦   ✦   ✦

Job has come to a new stage of understanding.

All said (will they never cease speechifying?) these "friends" are capable only of—banalities, moral tags empty of vitality or imagination.

They stand outside the orbit of dire experience, poking and prodding his wounds.

To them Job is a mere specimen under a bell jar.

Or another image; he lies there, helpless before their moral scrutiny, bound to a procrustean bed. And always falling short.

✦   ✦   ✦

16:4–6 Briefly, he imagines them in his plight; a subtle point. They and he dwell in fact, planets apart; how shall they imagine themselves inhabiting his skin—leprous skin at that?

> I also could talk
> as you do,
> did your soul dwell
> where I must.
> I could barrage you with words,
> shake my head with dismay (Job 16:4)

Where is relief to be found? He is between a rock and a hard place, his arguments pass them by, his silence is taken for consent;

> If I speak,
> this pain
> will not be checked,
>
> If I grow silent,
> it will not depart from me (Job 16:6)

✦   ✦   ✦

The implication lies on every page. To the eyes of the suffering one, it is bold print.

The text, its sense, will bear repeating. For all their pretention to superior wisdom, to the "tradition of the ancestors," the quaternity are playing the game of ha-Satan, accuser and prosecutor of the just.

Their religion? It is gone to rot.

They have dared judge the just one.

So doing, they reveal the spirit that urges them on, a berserker.

✦ ✦ ✦

16:7–11 This text is much disputed.

Is God the enemy, are Job's friends the enemy? It could in reality be either.

BJ prefers to have Job here identify his friends.

If such be so, the verses signal the "new stage" of Job's understanding.

Never has he spoken with such flaming bitterness, of these litigious, self-assured harbingers of woe;

> Now I am exhausted, stunned;
> A coterie has closed in on me,
>
> A witness rises up,
> a traducer
> speaking openly against me . . .
>
> My enemies
> lord it over me,
> they gnash their teeth at me.
> They smite me on the cheek insultingly,
> they are enlisted against me.
>
> God has delivered me
> to the impious, into the clutches of the wicked . . .
> (Job 16:7–11)

✦ ✦ ✦

He has never spoken so. He had willingly given ear, shown them respect, due or not. Now the mask is off, the game revealed; they merit neither attention nor deference. Their aim is his destruction.

And hideous to say, God allows them voice;

> God has given me over
> to the impious,
>
> into the clutches of the wicked
> has dashed me (Job 16:11)

✦   ✦   ✦

16:12–17 In a maze of misfortune, Job stands befogged.

How is he to walk the maze, taking accurate note of meaning and direction? Is such and such an event a sign of the malice of humans—or of God?

These so-called friends—what to make of them? What to make of God?

What difference, that single or triple bolts of lightning fall on him? Each kills.

Each is so designed; to kill;

> My enemies
> lord it over me,
> Their mouths gape wide
> to tear me.
>
> They smite me on the cheek
> insultingly,
> they are all enlisted
> against me. . . .
> I was at peace,
> but He dislodged me;
> He seized me by the scruff
> and dashed me to pieces;
> He has set me
> for a target,

His arrows strike
from all directions.

He pierces my sides
without mercy,
He pours out my gall
upon the ground (Job 16:9–13)

✦ ✦ ✦

And then at long last, Job comes to a better mind.
Like Lear on the heath, he returns to sanity.
He gathers strength, rises, voicing once more the great origi-
nal resolve.
As though, after a welter of assaults, from on high, from the
coterie, he shouts; I am sane!

My hands
are free from violence,

my prayer is sincere (Job 16:17)

✦ ✦ ✦

Patience

Patience, hard virtue.

It seems to me when the man
makes meat of us or less,
the less is still the more;
the meat is greater heart.
Cut to the bone, patience
outlasts the butcher's tool. . . .

The universe waits on us,
great patience on a lesser.
A prisoner's days run,
the weeks a slow drawn pain,
the years standing like stone,
great nature doing time. . . .
"Consider the lilies . . ."
good news, good humor, grace. I had so rather live, a few
brothers assailed, than mick-mock
whoring Caesar's strut.
Who pays, who renounces, who
makes that news anew?
Unheard of news, heard now,
seen now, touched now.
I had rather—
but how descry it?
My eyes
flare like a lamp in rain—
Hang around. Patience. Hear it;
the children live, the children
rise from the My Lai ditch.

DB

chapter five

"My Witness Is in Heaven"
(16:18–19:22)

There appears the faithfulness of God, Who forgives by condemning, gives life by killing, and utters "Yes" when nothing but "No" is audible. In Jesus, God is known to be the unknown God.

—Karl Barth, *The Epistle to the Romans*

Knowing God is not knowing and seeing God is not seeing.

—Thomas Merton, *Seeds of Contemplation*

✦ ✦ ✦

16:18–17:16 The sublime outcry intensifies. The blood of Job takes voice; like the blood of Abel, his too cries out from the earth.

Must cry, Retribution!

Innocent blood must not be covered over with dirt; this is the law, oft repeated (Genesis 4:10; Isaiah 26:21; Ezekiel 24:8).

✦ ✦ ✦

No cover-up; the crime of Job's accusers must not be concealed under canards, half-truths and slurs.

Blood, Job's life's blood, has been equivalently poured out in anguish. To this point, a point of no return; with a rush of relief he would welcome death.

No playacting for him, no pretending, as though outrageous losses had not been suffered—or were of no moment.

No covering over the truth; the long bloodletting of his life.

Which is precisely the tactic of Job's dis-comforters and their parched severities; covering over the truth.

In a literal sense (and these harrassers are great literalists) no blood has been shed. There Job sits, alive to be sure, if greviously short of flourishing.

And yet his blood has been shed, equivalently.

The substance of a just life—are they not in effect tossing it away, a worthless libation? They would do so.

They have made it clear, these detractors. In their estimate his life is of no more worth than a chamber pot of urine or a basin of ditch water. Let it go.

To have one's existence demeaned, to be held before public gaze like a dead trophy, an object of divine wrath, justly stricken in view of sins unmentionable—this is to perish in a "second death," to be cast out of the human circle.

Job's great spirit rises in a spasm of NO.

And the NO is preliminary to a greater YES. He has grown in knowledge of his tormenters, their devious tactics, their shoddy moralism;

My friends it is
who wrong me . . .
I am indeed mocked,
their provocation mounts,
my eyes grow dim . . .

You darken their minds
against understanding,

therefore
they do not understand . . .

I shall not find
among you
one wise man . . . (Job 17:6–10)

It comes to this. Job must undergo the onslaught of the "sages of unfaith," of partial faith, of unfaith masked as faith—before he came to a more perfect faith. This is the awful drama. Of faith.

In the biblical phrase, these sages are "dwellers upon the earth." To all evidence they dwell easily there, no conflict is implied, whether with God or the principalities of this world.

Their faith enters the mind's door, we all but hear the sound of closure. The air within is sere, stifling.

No stench of the Fall offends, no hint of faith as consequence or conflict.

Nothing of this.

The Fallen world, its immemorial systems of injustice and folly, of violence and greed—these are no scandal to them. Job is the scandal.

✦ ✦ ✦

It is as though today (and the "as though" is inaccurate; it is in fact so stated)—nuclear arms, cruise missiles, atomic-capable warships, vast fleets of bombers—these offer no scandal to most.

No. It is the nonviolent upstarts who offer the scandal, entering forbidden places as they do, pouring (their own) blood, wreaking (ever so slight, symbolic) damage against the extermination weaponry.

How awful, let them be punished, condignly, to the limit of the law of the land!

✦   ✦   ✦

Job for his part, has come to a resurrection, where only death dwelt. Concurrently, the truth of God, formerly a dark withholding, dawns in his soul.

God is no bargainer with the devil, no gimlet-eyed judge of the living.

Nor does the Deity offer credential and credit to presumptive godlings, to this trio. Job knows it;

> From now forward,
> behold,
> my Witness
> is in heaven,
>
> He who testifies for me
> is on high . . .
>
> That He
> may do justice
> for a mortal
> in His presence,
>
> and decide
> between a man
> and his neighbor (Job 17:1–5)

✦ ✦ ✦

Over against just God, stand the self-justified.

They are pictured here as appalled at Job's misfortune, seized with a kind of vertigo.

Their scandal is proper to the pusillanimous. Their minds decked out in borrowed tags, half-assimilated ideas, they turn aside, swaying where they standway, heads swimming.

Their ideology of a retributive God—a sorry substitute for faith. Gestures of distain give them away;

> At sight of me,
> the "upright" are stupefied,
>
> the innocent
> are roused
> against the wicked.
>
> Yet the righteous
> shall hold to his way,
> the man with clean hands
> shall double his strength (Job 17:8–9)

We have suggested how Job refuses the role thrust at him; a victim, helpless and hapless. Calmly, and not so calmly he reverses the "right order" defined by those who stand over and above, issuing icy decrees.

Let them come down, come near.

Let them also take warning; they are exceeding the human measure.

God will not long tolerate sophists who "make of the worse argument the better";

> Such men
> would change night into day,

where there is darkness
they talk of approaching dawn (Job 17:12)

What better image of minds darkened with a specious clarity, beclouded with an inhuman ethic!

✦   ✦   ✦

The light-darkness theme, heavy with fruitful ironies, is dear also to the Healer of John's gospel.

On one occasion, Jesus heals a man blind from birth. The religious authorities recoil from the event in hatred and denial.

To discredit the event, a first step; they set to demeaning the one healed.

Indeed this is an audacious, disrespectful fellow. Let him be dealt with summarily, expelled from the synagogue!

How better discredit the Healer? Jesus faces them, stops them short;

I came into this world
to divide it, to make the sightless see
and the seeing blind.

Some among the pharisees
picked this up, saying;
You are not calling us blind, are you?

To which Jesus replied;
If you were blind,
there would be no sin in that.

But you say;
We see.
And your sin remains (John 9:39–41)

Wonderfully, abruptly, the curtain falls on the drama, the episode ends.

✦ ✦ ✦

18:1–21 Bildad takes up the cudgels. If words were staves, he would beat Job to his knees.

A first blow. Are we to be compared by you to brute beasts? You, whose anger tears you in pieces?

The gentleman seems obsessed with—wickedness. His tirade heaps images ever higher.

And one thinks; Bildad can hardly be accounted a master of apt speech, let alone a balanced observer of the human scene. He pokes about lugubriously, analyzing the mote in Job's eye, ignorant of the plank in his own.

✦ ✦ ✦

The deity of Bildad has apparently laid on his acolyte a charge; he is appointed judge of the living. Let him take up arms against (strictly hypothetical) wickedness in the world.

The diatribe is hardly to be thought speculative or weightless; it comes down like a hundredweight—on Job.

✦ ✦ ✦

Bildad has cast himself as a kind of prophet Nathan; of necessity, Job must accept the contrary role, that of sinful David.

In the original story (2 Samuel 11), David has caused the death of an officer of his army, Uriah. This, so the king's adultery with Bathsheeba, wife of Uriah, may proceed.

Nathan comes on the scene, righteously, knowing all. He tells the king a seemingly harmless story; an injustice done a poor man by a wealthy.

King David is aroused to a fury, Justice Must Be Done!

Nathan springs his trap; *Tu es ille vir*. You are that man; you, adulterer and murderer.

✦   ✦   ✦

Bildad is capable of none such literary or ethical finesse. He comes down hard.

By strong implication, Job's "innocence" invites close scrutiny. Innuendo again; no names named. Bildad is certain of the dire fate of "sinners."

By no means do the wicked prosper; quite the opposite. The sinner is hopelessly entangled in his own "net . . . pitfall . . . trap . . . snare . . . noose . . . toils."

> The lamp
> of right understanding
> is extinguished (Job 18:6)

Terror dogs the malfeasant.

Worse and worse, his plight! Such a one is prey of the gods of the underworld, the Eumenides. The vizier of the queen of hell is summoned in his despite; so are Nergal and Pluto and the female demon Lileth!

A mighty apparatus of vengeance, all seeing, issues from very hell.

Poor Job. What recourse is left, but that he cower under this avalanche of accusative fury? *Tu es ille vir!*

✦   ✦   ✦

One image surely befits, but hardly in the way Bildad envisions. Indeed Job's "lamp has gone out," his existence darkened by misfortune.

As though this were not enough, Bildad and his cohorts would tumble the shaky pillars of his existence.

✦ ✦ ✦

19:1–12 Job resumes. And we come to the peak of sublime commerce and conflict, between God and human innocence, between the rigorists and the faithful one.

Who is to testify to the truth of God, Job or the chorus of gloom and doom that hems him in?

✦ ✦ ✦

Gradual

I have come to the borders
of the understanding. Instruct
me, God, whether to press
onward or to draw back.
To say I am a child
is pretence at humility
unworthy of me.
Rather I am at one with those
minds, all of whose instruments
are beside the point of
their sharpness.

I need a technique
other than that of physics for registering the ubiquity
of your presence.

A myriad of prayers
are addressed to you in a thousand
languages and you decode
them all. . . .
Call your horizons
in. Suffer the domestication
for a moment of the ferocities

*you inhabit, a garden for us to refine
our ignornce in under the boughs of love.*

(R. S. Thomas)

✦ ✦ ✦

Bildad and Job push hard; but with a difference.

At first glance the arguments appear equally plausible. But the contrast is premonitory.

✦ ✦ ✦

Two versions of God are in contention.

We have noted the tone of the friends; it is stiff, parched, juridical, even merciless. They are logicians; they revel in premise and conclusion, the ineluctable juncture of the two.

The logic heats up, joining iron to iron, red hot. Polemic is their strong suit. Abuse, vilify, humiliate, take the offense!

✦ ✦ ✦

They have merited good fortune; so goes the theory they live by. Not to be wondered then; they see themselves as exemplars, icons of the virtuous life.

Converging on Job, they view dispassionately a far different exemplar; one whose punishment befits a crime, perhaps a series of crimes; perhaps even a criminal lifetime. His deviance was skillfully hidden; for years the fictive virtue held intact. Job prospered and was accounted, even by God, as virtuous.

Then, the heavens cracked and fell about his head.

While, be it noted, their own status stood firm, their goods and perquisites intact.

✦ ✦ ✦

Will Job refuse to take note of this—their grace, his fall from grace? The implication lurking—their prospering, his downfall? Will he not confess his sin, and thus purge himself?

✦ ✦ ✦

What an onslaught!
The social ramifications are vast, in time and culture.
They press close, illustrating our own times.
To celebrate American prosperity in the world (some of us prosper, only some)—fortunate citizens can count on squads of historians, clergy, churchgoing politicians, a frenzy of self-congratulation pouring from the omniscient media.
God on our side! The myth of national righteousness survives every counter-event or argument; crimes of war, economic piracy, internecine and international violence.
To these no sin is adduced; quite the contrary.

✦ ✦ ✦

Other sins are adduced, if only now and then, and as a distraction from true crime.
True crime? Sanctioned murder, acts of war, indiscriminate slaughter of the innocent; cruise missiles launched at Sudan, Afghanistan, Iraq, the death of children in great numbers.
And in our lifetime; Vietnam, Granada, the CIA aiding the Guatemalan slaughter against the Mayan people, the contra war in Nicaragua, the slaughter in the Gulf. And so on, a litany of terror; the price of our prospering.

✦　✦　✦

These are built into the "system," fused there, as though in a national monument.

No crime adduced. The crimes are like a bronze rifle resting in the hands of a bronze warrior in a Washington park.

Of what point, in common estimate, is a bronze soldier without a gun of bronze? He would make no sense, he, his uniform, the flag, poised there on the brink of kill or be killed.

✦　✦　✦

The Myth of Innocence has a thousand venues, in arts, anthems, speeches, political drumbeats, *Te Deums*, elections and electioneerings, the collusion of media and money, weaponry and consumerism.

The myth is a powerful caricature of religion, a sedulous ape of faith. It has its pantheon, its assurance of divine approval and predestination, its norms of ethical behavior.

Perhaps most striking of all, it contrives its own definition of sin. Sin is confined to sexual peccadillos. Or the cover-up of same, lies uttered, then reiterated.

✦　✦　✦

Amid the national upheaval, are cruise missiles launched against noncombatants?

They are. A futile distraction, alas.

And no sin is adduced.

Seizure of foreign markets, the imposition of slave labor, waste and pollution of resources, production of ever more lethal weaponry, withholding of essential services from the poor?

No sin adduced.

✦ ✦ ✦

There existed Jobs before Job, there are Jobs after. In our world he has become a dominant, phobogenous social image. Multitudes of Jobs across the world suffer deprivation of human and civil rights, are ill-housed and ill-fed, wounded, untended in body and spirit, carped at, stigmatized by academic and policical harpies.

In Latin America, Asia, and Africa, contemporary Jobs labor on the landholdings of absentee multicorporations; or they slave in factories whose profits flow like a green lava, due north.

It is all one, all slavery.

Our Jobs bear about their necks and shoulders a designating, demeaning sign. It names them, shames them once for all, overtly or by implication; "Third World," or "Overpopulation" or "Sweatshops Welcome." Or; "Minimum Wage Does Not Apply," or "Unions Forbidden."

The sign legitimates enslavement, even as it dignifies slave owners. It declares the slaves redundant, even as it finds them useful.

✦ ✦ ✦

We must be careful not to romanticize our Jobs and their families. In such wise as this; families that "pray together, stay together"; a northern illusion useful in the south.

Job and his spouse and children indeed say their prayers, invoke their God, enduring meantime the self-serving logic of their friends of the "first world."

Friends who have defined those below or beyond borders—as clients, economically useful in the new world slave market.

Perhaps it is unfortunate, from a scientific point of view, that such as these were born. Perhaps they are no more than a human detritus, lumped together under a term both useful and abstract; "overpopulation."

There are in any case, too many of them, hapless and illiterate; no point in wasting time and money on niceties of just wages,
workers' organizations, education, housing, medical care—such
voice in their fate as is granted their counterparts in the mother
country.

These foreign specimens? They are items in the marvelous
market where slaves are bought and sold.

✦   ✦   ✦

Let them also stay in place; let them rot or flourish where
they were planted.

Do they arrive clandestinely in the mother country, seeking
asylum from political or religious tyranny, or perhaps merely
seeking a job, a chance at a decent life?

Let such be seized at the point of attempted entry, and locked
up.

For up to two years, locked up, before a hearing that will
settle their fate, once for all.

That paper chase across the globe! Those magical papers,
parasitical "illegals" transformed into—the resurrected!

Or, the magic failing, the stigma holding firm. Unwanted,
evicted to whatever fate.

✦   ✦   ✦

We take note also; our economic slaves have at hand no cultural myths of worthiness and guilt.

What then shall bring their true condition home?

The myths must be imported in the form of *maquillidoras,*
slave factories, together with their overseers and guards.

These arrive, often accompanied by religious reinforcements;
rigid cults and their clerical hucksters. The latter offer a mitiga-
tion of misery, pouring on wounds and wounded the oil and
wine of the divine Will, a promise of beatitude like a desert

mirage, indefinitely receding in time and denied in place.

The enlightening message is underwritten and verified, daily or weekly or by month, with a few pesos, the wage of slaves—or of sin.

✦   ✦   ✦

Our historical Job, as we have noted time and again, is stubborn, dead set against the cult of guilt.

He clings like a lamprey to a confession of innocence, rejecting vehemently the dire, parched data of the chorus;

> He cries aloud;
> Why
> do the wicked
> survive,
> grow old,
> become mighty in power? (Job 21:7)

The question is classic in the Bible, it is raised by the psalmist as well as Job.

It is also totally at odds with the burden of Bildad and Zophar.

✦   ✦   ✦

> Why do You stand on the sidelines
> silent as the mouth of the dead, the maw of the grave—
> O living One, why?
>
> Evil walks roughshod, the envious set snares,
> high and mighty the violent ride,
> applause for maleficence, reward for crime,
> Yourself set to naught.
> Eyes like a poniard impale the innocent,
> death cheap, life cheaper,
> the mad beast is loosened, his crooked heart mutters

Fear only me!
They call You blind man. Call their bluff,
extinguish their envy.
See, the poor are cornered,
marked for destruction, grist
for a mill of dust.
At the bar of injustice
they tremble, wind-driven birds
under the beaks and stares
of the shrouded Big Ones—
No recourse but You; no recourse
but Your faithful love! (Psalm 10)

✦ ✦ ✦

Zophar is mistaken, woefully so. Job is not to be numbered among the wicked ones.

So the mystery abides; a thorn in his flesh; why must he, the innocent one, suffer?

✦ ✦ ✦

How the dramatic coil tightens! Job and his friends, their feet planted on the earth at the same time, see and report on radically different turns of providence.

Both cannot be true. Either the wicked court ruin—or they prosper beyond measure.

Do Job and his trio see the same "wicked ones"? Is their definition of sin itself at odds?

Finally—and perhaps the pivot of it all, what of their faith?

Do they believe in the same God?

What does their God look like; an implacable judge, or a lover of humankind? What are the divine norms of approval and condemnation?

Is God a Mystery beyond plumbing, a dark Providence lying heavy on the innocent, a stern visaged arbiter, taking note of every jot and tittle of behavior?

✦ ✦ ✦

My friends
wrong me,

before God
my eyes drop tears,

that He may do justice
for a mortal
in His presence,
as a man
pleads
for his neighbor (Job 16:20–21)

We find it persuasive and moving, Job is a man of desires. Though an intractable night lie between, he stands fervently "before God."

And he seeks a response; he would have God act—humanly. Let God make no intractable demands against the just. And let Him grant no exemptions in view of claims of superior virtue.

✦ ✦ ✦

Nothing of this. The quest is modest; let God observe and honor the amenities proper to human justice.

Let God (Job dares say it, or at least imply it), God be to him what his detractors refuse to be, or are incapable of being—a Friend.

✦   ✦   ✦

Grievous differences indeed separate Job from his tormenters. It is as though each were a wounded part of the other. Job
stands before them as well.

They sorely try his soul, badger and prod and even vilify—
still he hears them out.

He must deal with a double adversary; God and this peculiar
coterie.

The game offers no pleasure. How could it? The cards are
woefully, artfully stacked.

✦ ✦ ✦

And could Job be thought to prevail, this solitary crushed man, over the prospering and assured?

They dismember his soul, dispassionatly they weigh his bones, dry bones, finding his picked clean by time and woe. By themselves?

The game must go on, the drama played out to the end. For our sake. We too stand at the dark heart of the Realm of Necessity.

What price freedom in such a world? Job, we think, and tremble at the thought, Job must pay dear.

And what of us?

✦ ✦ ✦

We take close note of him, this icon of faith under fire.

He will not lie prostrate, resigned to a God who has left him all but dead, all but concluding; I were better dead.

No, he recoils, rears up in fury.

He would dare this; indict God for maleficent governance of the world. Of Job's world.

Has not God sought to crush him, the just one?

What then is left to humans, of a fabric of sense and sanity?

✦ ✦ ✦

Thus Job stands at the opposite pole of "resigned," "patient"—tags which milksop religionists have attached to him—this fireball in nature, this lightning unleashed.

No! Is his cry, torn from the throat, launched in the gale of time and the fallen world.

His moral life is suffused with passion, a vortex, furious and tender by turns, conceding nothing into other hands, whether divine or human.

Who are these "friends," to judge him?

Who indeed is God, to reverse the course of a friend, to spin him about and about, to disaster pure and sure?

No, Job will not "go gently into that good night."

✦ ✦ ✦

And all the while, this is his stance, as he insists time and again; he is "before God," face to face with the Impenetrable.

He will not despair, though he comes edgily close to despair.

Not for him the way of the notorious contenders, spinning their theories to fustian.

✦ ✦ ✦

The eye of Job roves wide. He sees at center eye himself and his friends. Himself and they; he the butt of a scorn that widens out and out, instinctive and demeaning.

All the while, they honor the prosperous, withholding a close look into motive or resource. Is not prosperity its own credential and guarantee of divine favor?

For those fallen from grace, on the contrary, a close, moralistic scrutiny befits;

> Am I not mocked
> by those who rail at me?
> their harshness mounts,
> my eyes grow dim . . .
>
> You darken their hearts
> against right reason,
>
> not a hand
> raised in my defense . . .

I am made a byword
of the people,

someone
they spit in face . . .
At the sight,
the upright are stupefied . . . (Job 17:1–8)

We have seen it before; so has the author of Job. The Suffering Servant of Isaiah provoked a like reaction (52:14).

It is as if the scope of a disaster were too much; onlookers avert their gaze, flee the scene, awed, cowed by an awful visitation;

Even as many were stupefied at him,
so marred was his look, beyond the human,
his appearance beyond that of mortals—

✦ ✦ ✦

It is hardly to their honor that the friends of Job do not flee.

Flight would be a confession, minimal to be sure, of a common humanity; a compassion that found the downfall of a friend literally beyond bearing.

✦ ✦ ✦

They linger to their shame, but to our benefit. Without their poking about and issuing menifestos concerning God and the universe, we would be the poorer. We would know less of Job's coruscating greatness.

And we add with a kind of grudging gratitude; apart from the questions they provoke, we would know less of God.

We would not have heard that pretentious pronunciamento; we know God.

And for Job, that distain; you know nothing of God.

And then the classic reversal of fortune, wrought by time as new eyes rest on the text, and ponder deep in search of faith.

How Job is vindicated, and they put to shame.

✦   ✦   ✦

We are in a terrain of new understanding. It is a principle of Greek tragedy that arose in the astonishing period that bore Job, together with Aeschylus, Sophocles, Euripides.

The principle; conflict of wills, against the grain of normalcy, routine, emotional calm—provokes new knowledge.

In the Hebrew instance we have such clashes perennially; prophet vs. kings, prophet vs. ersatz prophet, prophet vs. keepers of the sanctuary or the law.

And the outcome? For us, it is access to new, deepened insight.

We see a simple and brutal outcome; the prophets are silenced, put to shame, cast out from the community, and worse.

Isaiah is banished from court and eventually (as tradition attests) killed by his own. Jeremiah is flung hither and yon, placed in the town stocks, cast in a dry well. Ezekiel's oracles are long denied place in the canon of his people.

Daniel also figures badly; he is no prophet at all, according to the rabbis, is placed in an inoffensive category; "Writings."

✦   ✦   ✦

And yet, and yet. Scorn, exile, punishment, shame; these are not the final word. In time, a staggering irony arises; the losers, the victimzed, these prevail. Subsequent history confers, even half-consciously, high tribute upon these "losers."

We name the great books for them rather than for their tormenters, judges, executioners.

Indeed, the names of the adversaries live on to their shame, as the texts bear witness; named in scorn and loathing for seeking to destroy the great ones.

✦ ✦ ✦

And what of God, as conventional expectation is overthrown, as ironically, horrifically, thrones are toppled?

God arranged it thus.

It is the fifth century before the common era, the time of Job and the prophets. God is revealed anew. It is like a second birth or a second springtime, when the first has gone badly, and frost and ice have conspired to kill the promise.

✦ ✦ ✦

The first birth was of the great ones of earth and heaven; the kings and their god. A god useful to the schemes and perfidies of a Saul, a David, a Solomon.

A god of wars and incursions, of extermination and invasion, of standing armies and world markets and an overbearing, excessive architecture of temple and palace.

A merciless god, in the image of his acolytes, priests, warriors, guardians—the vast bureaucracy accruing to empire and its imperial god.

✦ ✦ ✦

Overweening, it all collapsed, fell apart.

Then, a second birth. God is announced anew on the human scene.

God grants humans a kind of resurrection, a renewed, purified understanding. The prophets announce a God who "exalts the lowly and humbles the great ones." Who stands with expendables and outcasts, with slaves and forced laborers and captives.

Stands also with Isaiah and Ezekiel and Jeremiah, with their words of renewal and hope, their diagnoses of blindness, their denunciations of the high and mighty, their vindication of heroism.

Stands with their prophecies—of ruin and exile and the loss of all. Words as well of the great return and rebuilding. The promise of a second spring.

✦   ✦   ✦

As for Job, nothing of Second Isaiah, that gospel of comfort. He knows only darkness.

If this must be, he will dwell in the dark.

But his perfervid questioning, summoning, indicting—these he will not cease from uttering.

And for his pains, he is granted little of surcease, let alone of approval, whether from his interlocutors or from God.

His world is a death before death;

> My hope?
> it is a dwelling
> in the underworld,
>
> to spread my couch
> in darkness.
>
> to cry to the sepulchre;
> You are my father!
>
> to the maggot;
> You, my mother, my sister!
>
> Where then is my hope? . . . (Job 17:13–15)

✦ ✦ ✦

Job's must be accounted the extreme case, the exemplar. His—the plight of the just before God. I mean plight, pure and simple. No outcome.

Of that, Isaiah, Jeremiah, Ezekiel were granted inklings and more—a Reversal both vast and immanent.

Indeed they were anointed as indispensable in bringing the Reversal to pass. In God's name they were "to root up and to tear down, to destroy and to demolish," then "to build and to plant" (Jeremiah 1:10).

Job was granted nothing of this dignity.

Not for him the biblical assurance bestowed on others; "I am with you." No assurance as to accompaniment, nothing of favorable outcome. Not even the comfort of a here-and-now approval or blessing.

Nothing, need one add, of "impact," "success," "result," "proof of virtue," "self-justification"—those weasel words extruded from the throat of Sheol.

✦ ✦ ✦

We hearken, and tremble. From Job a cry rises; his guts are in torment, the pit is bottomless.

And his cry, to all effect (one thinks, to all intent)—goes unheard;

Voices, a haggle of voices . . .

The big thunderers
play to the hilt
the game You never play—
Lies, a theophany of liars
invades, infests the world!
Then

germinal, untrammeled,
frail as the newborn
Your word is born in us.
O be
for our sake
midwife to that moment! (Psalm 12)

✦   ✦   ✦

We summon those heroes of our century who have given their lives, if only to raise a like cry, the cry of Job.

We join our voices to theirs.

When will they be heard, Ben Salmon, Franz Jaggerstaetter, Archbishop Romero, the Jesuits of Salvador, the nameless prisoners and victims and "disappeared" and tortured, those who perished in the camps and gulags and Devil's Islands of our tormented and tormenting world?

We cry out, on their behalf and our own.

But with this bitter understanding; the cry, its integrity, passion and persistence, cannot depend on a response, a hearing.

Job received none.

And Jesus none;

"My Father,
let this cup
pass from me" (Luke 22:42)

The cup did not pass.

✦   ✦   ✦

The friends are obsessed, as we have noted, with an ironbound logic of crime-punishment. The law binds the world, close as bronze bands encircling a barrel.

So goes the theory, cruel, ineluctable; no one is exempt, no one breaks free.

Including Job, whose ruin offers close evidence of—sin.

Were he sinless, were his protest of innocence true, what logic governed human conscience, what sense is to be made of creation or Creator?

✦ ✦ ✦

The trio are implacable guardians of a god-of-small-recourse. They cannot conceive that an upright man be taxed with an affliction that confronts, even denies their terms, definitions, moral niceties, rigors.

The mathematics of merit and demerit!

They set about, in the way of severe ethical tacticians, solving "the problem of Job."

✦ ✦ ✦

On the one hand, theorists; on the other, a mystic.

Job abides with the mystery. Steeped in faith and adoration, he confers on Mystery a capital letter. He abides with God.

He is indifferent to theories and ethical principles. His flesh recoils at these.

No; he brings his anguish and losses, his reeking flesh, before God. He raises the offering, all that is left to him, soul, body, reek and rot.

He will dare ask, Why? And he will persist, face to face, in questioning his plight.

He will dare. And he will bear with the response. He will bear with worse; no response.

✦ ✦ ✦

And let his tormenters know that he rejects utterly their suffocating logic;

Know
it is God
who oppresses me
who envelops me round
in His net (Job 19:6)

It is all tragically personal, all one to One. No theories here!

If I cry "injustice"
I am not heard,

if I cry out,
no redress (Job 19:7)

✦　✦　✦

Job presses his case. And a sublime series of images tumbles
one after another, from the deep heart's core.

This God of his must be held responsible, must be summoned
to the bar, passionately.

As for the logicians, let them hear and be instructed. Let them
even be scandalized.

God has done this, is the agent of Job's ruin;

Half-articulate his words, as though stuck in his throat;

He has barred
my way . . .

has veiled
my path . . .

has stripped me
of glory . . .

has seized
the diadem . . .

He breaks me down . . .
uproots my hope . . .

His wrath
He kindles . . .

counts me
His enemy . . .

His troops advance . . . (Job 19:8–12)

✦   ✦   ✦

19:13–19 Then, what a change of tone!

For the first time in the welter of argument and dissention, Job offers a glimpse of family life, his own. And how endearing!

In effect, ghosts, memories, a void of grief have replaced those tender presences. The spirit of his family is broken, dissipated, turned to gall. His loved ones are ravaged by the deluge that swept him away.

✦   ✦   ✦

A shock; we learn, almost in passing; someone, or some few of his family have survived.

Death, Job hints, would be more easily borne than this; disaffection, shunning, scandal even.

In bitter fact, his world has become a wider image of the friends' circle, suffocating and accusative. The attitude of the trio seeps abroad, poisoning, closing minds and hearts against the sorry spectacle of Job brought low.

The catalogue of those who despise and demean is ruinous, exhaustive. In a kind of fevered anguish, as though summoning each loss, feeling it anew, Job dwells on his losses;

My kin
are alienated,

acquaintances
disown me.

My relatives
have disappeared,

the guests of my house
have forgotten me.

Maidservants
regard me as stranger, outsider
to their eyes.

I summon a servant,
he does not respond,

I must entreat and entreat.

Even youngsters
distain me;

I appear, they mock me.

My bosom friends
detest me,

those I love
have turned against me.

And then the awful climax, the nadir of loss;

To my wife,
my odor
is repulsive

> I am loathsome
> to my brethren (Job 19:13–19)

And a cry is torn from his throat, the cry of a lorn hope, verging on despair.

He is a beggar before the plenty of others.

✦ ✦ ✦

19:20–22 Does his plea reach his friends? Or does it ricochet off hearts of adamant?

Down the centuries an echo sounds; it rattles dry bones, resurrects a dead hope;

> Pity me,
> pity me,
> O you my friends,
>
> for the hand of God
> has struck me!
>
> Why do you
> pursue me like God, maligning me insatiably?
> (Job 19:21–22)

✦ ✦ ✦

It is hard to cry when you are young—and a man. It slows you down. It broaches the wrong questions. It offers the wrong answers. It lets others in. It keeps you too close to what matters, to your true self, and probably to God.

It makes sense for young men not to cry, but to manage, fix and think instead. But soon the patterns are in place, and the young men have become old men—and

human culture has been formed—without wisdom.
I am convinced . . . much that passes as strong opinion
and anger is really disguised grief. Much that passes as
self-protection and fear is really grief denied. Much that
passes as detachment and letting go, is a grief so deep
that there is no room for connection.

Much that is done in the name of justice and peace,
also proceeds from a well of tears and sadness. Much
that is service and compassion comes from the day we
learned how to cry without shame.

An imperial church and a patriarchal culture will always resist tears. Tears cannot be organized or made
orthodox. . . .

The way of tears is the way of the prophets who taught
Israel to groan and lament its servitude. If there is no
groaning there is no liberation . . .

I doubt whether war can be so easily taught once men
learn to cry. . . . I doubt whether the whole system would
work . . . if men could only lament. . . .

This spirituality, this gift of tears, is the stuff of a whole
new world. (Richard Rohr, Introduction to *Griefquest* by
Bob Miller)

✦ ✦ ✦

I sweat like a beast
for the fate of my people.

Is God
ignorant, blank-eyed,
deaf, far distant,
bought off, grown old?

Why endure?
Why thirst for justice?
Your kingdom-come
a mirage, never comes.
I sweat like a beast,
my nightmare life long.
And where in the world
are You? (Psalm 73)

chapter six

"My Vindicator Lives!"
(19:23–22:30)

Behold Your son of excellent intentions!
I said to my soul;
set guard to your tongue—
nothing, no one
take you by surprise.
How little I reckoned!
gall erupted,
fury possessed me, vortex and demon.
The impious took aim,
I fell like a ninepin.
Shamed I walk now.
Healer, Lover,
who will make whole
that pure intent,
that eye of single desire?
Make my heart over

—Psalm 39

✦   ✦   ✦

No man hath affliction enough that is not matured,
and ripened by it.

—John Donne,
"Devotions upon Emergent Occasions," 1624

✦   ✦   ✦

19:23–29 What follows is of capital import to great-souled Job.

He has come to the climax of his argument. With words of a vast (and famously disputed) claim, he seeks to vindicate his faith, lying as it does under fierce assault.

His words are of permanent import; it is as though they were incised in the millennia.

He speaks for the future, for the unborn. He longs to have his words "written down," his claim "placed on record"—and more;

> . . . that
> with an iron chisel
> and with lead
> my words
> were cut
> in rock
> forever! (Job 19:24)

✦   ✦   ✦

Three versions of the passage survive. The ancient text was poorly preserved, we are told; conjecture rules the translations.

One wonders. Is something deeper at work than a literary impasse?

Let us dare a conjecture of our own.

The episode tells of Job's breakthrough, to a new terrain of faith. And no single idiom or tongue can contain the explosion.

The few words (19:25–26) are like a trigger; they explode their charge, break in pieces the fragile vessel of language and culture.

Therefore the variation, the versions, each bearing an irreplaceable nuance, a strength.

—First, the Greek text;

I know that the One who delivers me is eternal, to restore on earth my suffering flesh.

It is God's work to accomplish what I shall know, what
my eye and no other, has seen

—The Syrian text;

I know that my Redeemer lives, and that at the end He
will appear on earth.

And these events include my skin and my flesh. If my
eyes see God, they will see the Light.

—The Vulgate text;

I know that my Redeemer lives, and that on the last
day I shall arise from the earth. Again I shall be clothed
in my skin; and in the flesh, I shall see my God.

It is He whom I shall see, I and no other.

✦ ✦ ✦

Stupifying, this convergence of wisdom, this strange inter-
mingling of the temporal and eternal. And these, be it noted, as
a stage of vindication.

According to the Vulgate, the Promise swings wide, its portal
opens on the savannahs of heaven itself.

A glimpse and more. According to forthright St. Jerome, Job
anticipates our faith;

Job here prophesies the resurrection of the body; no one
has written on the subject so concisely and with such
certainty.

Best to concede the difficulties; they are daunting.

For a start, the Greek word rendered so confidently by Jerome as "resurrect" can also mean simply "restore."

And more, a seeming impasse. Were Job to find his sufferings bearable in accord with a promise, a corporal "resurrection" in the hereafter—then torment over the plight of the just would not continue to haunt the prophets.

But the torment never ended, nor the rage, in Jeremiah and Isaiah and Ezekiel and the others.

And we have no biblical evidence of a mitigating revelation to Job.

✦　✦　✦

Nevertheless. We open the book of Job, in the benighted culture of our third millennium. And God knows we are in search of what consolation we can glean.

Let us grant ourselves a lagniappe, a generous reading of this disputed, crucial passage.

We pause and ponder, we are awed and grateful. It is as though Job and his sad estate were suddenly endowed with the third eye of Isaiah or of parlous Ezekiel.

We linger over the Vulgate; Job leaps across the centuries. It is as though his passionate avowal were set down by a Paul;

> Perhaps someone will say;
> How are the dead to be raised up? . . .
>
> What is sown is ignoble,
> what rises is glorious.
>
> Weakness is sown, strength rises up.
>
> A natural body is put down
> and a spiritual body rises . . .
> (1 Corinthians 15:35, 42–44)

Or it is as though the words of Job formed a "lost" pericope of John's gospel—a message, with respect to human destiny, both mystical and earthy;

> Indeed,
> this is the will of my Father,
>
> that everyone
> who looks upon the Son
>
> and believes in Him
> shall have eternal life.
>
> That one
> I shall raise up
> on the last day . . . (John 6:40)

✦ ✦ ✦

We take heart, pondering the story of the raising of Lazarus, and the astonishing exchange that precedes (and illuminates) the miracle (John 8).

Lazarus comes forth in the flesh, out of appointed time and place to be sure—time and place being on the heart's impulse, ruptured;

> Now Jesus greatly loved
> Martha
> and her sister
> and Lazarus (John 11:5)
>
> Fate is not late,
> Nor the speech rewritten,
> Nor one word forgotten,
> Said at the start

About heart,
By heart,
For heart.

(W. H. Auden, "To You Simply")

✦   ✦   ✦

In effect, Martha and Mary are assured that the raising of their brother is by no means a unique event. It is the drama of Everyman and Everywoman.

Jesus is at pains to underscore the vast implication. The grieving sisters stand at a closed tomb. And a stupendous work is immanent, of which they are to be witnesses. What He is about to do, what they are to witness, is a matter of human destiny as such.

Is it the sorry fate of us humans to be abused and dragged off by the principality named death? Does death, stopping all mouths, have the last word?

The summons of Lazarus is a clue to the contrary; it is the ultimate denial of death.

Resurrection, in the flesh? Yes. A gift to all who believe;

I am the resurrection
and the life;

whoever believes in Me,
though that one die,
will come to life;

and whoever is alive
and believes in Me
will never die (John 11:25–26)

✦ ✦ ✦

This Master of life is also, and by close consequence, the reinterpreter of death.

Let us, He implies, together take a closer look. Let us chasten that fearsome power and domination!

If all shall "come to life," it follows that death is tamed, its power reined in, broken. Death loses its grip, the power of awakening dread and paralyzing fear.

Look; here, now He will show it, the supervening power that flows from the God of life;

> He called loudly,
> "Lazarus, come forth!" (John 11:43)

✦ ✦ ✦

As for Job, he is in a twilight—or a dawn. He must wait and wait, for light, for life.

He is no Lazarus, no Savior looms over his plight, intervening, assuaging.

Except by invocation and hope; "my Defender," "my Vindicator," "my Redeemer."

✦ ✦ ✦

The translations of the honorific titles, thundrous, intuitive as they are—fall short.

The original, "Goel," is a technical term in Israeli law. It designates a relative, generally the nearest such, on whom certain obligations fall; this one "buys back," "repossesses" goods lost or improvidently sold (Leviticus 25:25).

Or more weightily, the "Defender," "Vindicator," "Redeemer," delivers from slavery (Leviticus 25:48).

Further nuances; the Goel succors the victimized and powerless (Jeremiah 50:34).

Best, highest of all offices, the Goel delivers from death (Psalm 103:4).

Finally, the term is applied by the rabbis to the Messiah.

With reason, one concludes, St. Jerome, the hero of our hope, adopts the latter usage; "my Deliverer."

✦ ✦ ✦

Job has been lost in a reverie of longing, of ecstasy amid worms. But his waiting is hardly to be thought sterile or passive.

No, he is infused with passionate longing for justification. The gift has been denied him. Three awful events block its bestowal; losses of family, of material benefits, and of bodily integrity.

And that chorus of derision, a tide all but riding him under—how is he to end it?

✦ ✦ ✦

He rouses himself, and the awful world sweeps in on an icy wind. His friends bulk there in the half light, sour and vigilant as mastiffs. Their stance speaks for them; when will he come to his senses, and confess?

They must be dealt with, again and again. Immobile in the darkness as steles of adamant, they are immune against wisdom and compassion.

Is one among them about to seize the cudgel again?

✦ ✦ ✦

Let them be warned. He has shocked them before; he would turn the tables and indict them;

You who say;
How shall we persecute him
seeing that the root of the matter
is found in him?

Be afraid
of the sword
for yourselves,

for these crimes
deserve the sword

that you may know
there is a judgment (Job 19:28–29)

✦ ✦ ✦

20:1–29 Zophar is a master of insult and scorn. The verbal lashing goes on.

He would finish Job off, would inundate the tender hope that found utterance in "I know that my Goel lives . . ."

Zophar, in effect counters; let us clinch the argument. Let us have done with this attempt to construct a crude shack of rhetoric, a hideout for the guilty. Seeking as they do (as he, Job, does) an exception to inexorable law.

Let us drown this vanity in images that bespeak, like a drumbeat of doom, judgment of the wicked.

Thereby, let us shore up the Original Inference; Job is numbered among the wicked. His woes are an evidence, written in supporating flesh; guilty. Irrefutable evidence.

✦ ✦ ✦

So, on to the images.

One after another he contrives them. It is as though he sharpened a quiver of arrows on the spot, tipped with poison. And launched them.

The sinner "perishes like the fuel of his fire," "like a dream," "like a vision of the night." His wickedness shall be "like a venom of asps inside him."

Invention sweeps Zophar up and aloft. A nameless evil is before him;

> Because
> he has oppressed the poor,
> and stolen a patrimony
> he had not built up
>
> therefore
> his prosperity
> shall not endure
>
> and his hand
> shall yield up his riches . . . (Job 20:19)

Are we bewildered? What has the indictment to do with afflicted Job?

The sum of the babel of images would seem to be this; Job, take warning, lest you be found in company with the wicked, lest you go under, in ruin beyond remedy.

✦ ✦ ✦

The pertinacity of these hectors!

A religion that kills hope—of what point? What motive drives their assault works?

What does it achieve, that a suffering human be stretched on a rack of dark argument, until his integrity fails him, and he confesses to—airy nothings, fantasies of sin?

These adroit torturers weave a mirage of criminality. They would force Job to inhabit it, as sober reality.

✦ ✦ ✦

Perhaps this would offer a sound rebuttal; to strip the trio of religious pretention.

This is their biblical usefulness; to play to the hilt the role of adversary. They speak for no god we know of. They speak for the world, for the fallen creation. For ha-Satan.

Thus, from them we learn much of the ways of this world.

Their argument is carefully wrought. Under a rubric of "religion," accusations multiply, metaphors of death abound. They speak on behalf of death, testing, probing this lover of life and of the God of life.

✦ ✦ ✦

The drama is terrifying. It is also truthful. Which is to say, in close accord with the Fall.

In such a world, faith must submit to a contest, a tragic one.

The faithful one is summoned to a legal proceeding. The trial is loaded from the start.

Job must withstand these acolytes of a fallen world who would criminalize and punish.

✦ ✦ ✦

In the struggle, much is clarified; implications, guises, pretentions, outright lies. The degradation of language, windy rhetoric concerning "justice," even the "justice of God."

✦ ✦ ✦

We breathe a brimstone atmosphere, as a palpable fear takes possession of the hectors.

A clue to their belligerence; their fear of Job. They fear tripping up, suffering his fate. They fear a faith that implies such loss, such anguish.

Shall they one day be burdened with such "friends" as themselves, mounting a similar assault?

They fear death, whose champions they are.

They fear the death they would deal Job—death of honor, of
integrity, of sanity, of the truth of God.

✦ ✦ ✦

Let us take note of another anomaly, one that invites attentiveness. A strange duality exists in the text concerning God; the
god revealed at the book's start, and the God of Job.

On the one hand, we saw a not altogether admirable bargainer with ha-Satan. One who concedes round after round
("spare his person"; then "do what you will; but spare his life"),
as he gives Job over to the untender mercies of his opposite
number.

✦ ✦ ✦

It is as though the author were inviting us to look in two
directions.

First, a god reminiscent of a murky, vindictive past, the god
of Samuel and the Kings, a deity useful to the designs of tyrants.
This god demeans and betrays, striking bargains with the wicked.

✦ ✦ ✦

Then the other God, the "my Redeemer," who "lives." The
God before Whom Job stands face to Face—though a veiled Face
to be sure.

The God "wise in heart and mighty in strength," to Whom
Job cries out; "Let me know why You oppose me!" The God "with
Whom I long to reason."

Who in despite of my fidelity "has given me over to the
impious" . . . "has dealt unfairly with me."

Such faith! Passionate, contentious, daring, giving the lie to closed systems of crime and punishment, rejecting out of hand the suffocating universe of the "friends."

✦ ✦ ✦

This God of Job is the faithful, compassionate One, the God of the great prophets, those healers and amplifiers of our humanity, stricken and triumphant, both.

This God of continuity, a Midrash drawn from the noblest Jewish Scripture and on to our own, whether we summon Paul's letters or the gospel of John.

God of Jews, God of Job, God of Jesus. Our God.

✦ ✦ ✦

21:1–6 How wearying for Job (for ourselves!) Woven about him is a close web of insinuation.

21:7–22 They would persuade him that the wicked are quickly tripped up, and fall. Judgment, judgment, a juggernaut!

✦ ✦ ✦

They state it all but obsessively; the wicked bear the seeds of their own destruction.

And the good, the virtuous? By implication these stand vindicated in time and this world.

Does one seek evidence? Behold the modest prospering of the instructing trio!

Therefore. Job, take warning.

It is never said, it goes without saying; be warned.

✦ ✦ ✦

Stronger than we our sins,
a weight as of worlds
rides us under.
Sterile that burden,
wintry
the heart's lucid flow.
Stockstill we stand,
hope gone to seed,
seed flung to winds.
O despite all, be
our winter's end,
solace and solstice.
Mere shadows we are
lengthening, death-miming.

Rumors appall us,
the seas are in flood,
earth cannot bear
our intolerance, folly.
Forbear.
Send a new season
our way, a new will
breaking the shell
of our ill-doing.
We rue, would repair.
Create us anew! (Psalm 63)

✦ ✦ ✦

But how shall Job be warned, and of what?

His eyes lead him in a contrary direction. He sees what the adversaries refuse to see, or are blind to.

Are the wicked brought low? They are not; borne on high, were closer the truth!

Nor do the just prosper.

Behold himself, his plight, his litany of loss—evidence of a far different outcome.

Therefore the mystery remains, the torment, the "why?"

> Why
> do the wicked survive,
> grow old, become mighty in power? . . .
>
> They live out their days
> in prosperity,
>
> tranquilly
> go down
> to the nether
> world (Job 21:7, 13–14)

He has borrowed the "why" from a kindred spirit, Jeremiah (12:1–2);

> Even so, I must discuss the case with You;
> Why does the way of the godless prosper,
> why do the treacherous dwell in contentment?

And one cannot but conclude; concerning the fate of the wicked, it makes better sense to attend to Job!

Job knows his own heart, light and darkness mingled; more, he knows the heart of evil.

✦ ✦ ✦

Ironically, Job conjures his friends addressing God; but with a kind of refined contempt, dismissively;

> Depart from us,
> we have no wish
> to learn your ways.
>
> What is the Almighty
> that we should serve Him,
>
> what gain if we pray to Him? (Job 21:14–15)

Has Job hit on the nub of the matter, the dark spirit that animates their rhetoric?

This would seem the most direct affront possible—implicitly to confess faith in God, only for the sake of practical disbelief. To address God in order to dismiss God.

✦   ✦   ✦

Perhaps Job too has mastered the art of innuendo.

A flick of the whip? Does this trio of practiced debaters prefer argument over encounter, self-aggrandizement over submission, judgment over mercy, talk, talk over listening and learning?

The go-around comes around. They have sedulously defined, categorized, tagged him. Then let him too hold up a mirror, showing his view of the viewers!

✦   ✦   ✦

21:23–26 Job issues an overt denial, a judgment against their harping theme of—judgment.

He puts the matter baldly; there is no justice to be found in this world.

From on high, there is no discriminating between an evil life and a holy.

His image is vivid, devastating;

One dies
in full vigor,
wholly at ease,
content . . .

another
in bitterness of soul,
never tasting happiness.
Alike
they lie down in the dust,
worms cover them both (Job 21:23–26)

Behold the mystery, which the friends would deny.

Job speaks of it openly. The mystery is intact, it is atrocious.

Job suffers under the mystery, whose existence the trio blithely, piously deny—meantime passing a harsh judgment on himself.

✦   ✦   ✦

Job is like the victim in the parable of Jesus. He lies in the ditch, robbed and wounded. And the trio are "the priest and the levite" who "pass him by" (Luke 10:25–35).

✦   ✦   ✦

21:27–34 Job knows their arguments, sadly, he has them by heart. According to these indefatigable moralists, the wicked are soon erased from the memory of the living, no trace of them abides. (And if such live on for awhile, it is only for sake of a heavier judgment to come).

Job; come now, how foolish. There is strongest evidence to the contrary!

Consult any who have traveled the earth; they view the crowds that follow the corpse of the mighty to its grave, the great monuments, the steles, statues, inscriptions so quickly raised;

Your "consolations" are vain, deceitful, perfidious.

✦　✦　✦

22:1–11 In no wise daunted, Eliphaz takes the offensive even more strongly. His quiver hardly depleted, he launches arrow after arrow.

He produces his indictment, a long list of defaults. And we are astonished; is this the Job who was introduced at the beginning as "a blameless and upright man, who feared God and avoided evil"?

✦　✦　✦

Is envy at work? If so, the "evil" of Job lurks in the eye of the beholder.

Child of a culture of abuse and heated debate, Eliphaz would unveil a radically different Job than the one commended by God.

Another Job, another than Job?

Someone merged in moral darkness stands there.

✦　✦　✦

In effect we have in hand an utterly new book of Job, this one "According to Eliphaz."

The original praise is twisted around, to its exact opposite, this; "a sinful, wicken man, who feared no one, not even God; one who courted evil."

✦　✦　✦

The catalogue is devastating; it is also disconcertingly near to prophetic. And so wrongheaded!

Eliphaz has no interest in cultic niceties, as sources of default. No interest in the "tent rubrics" set out in excruciating detail in Deuteronomy.

His indictment, his version of sin, is new upon the human scene; perhaps it was elaborated in his own era.

And it is awesome.

✦   ✦   ✦

Isaiah it was who spoke for God, the God of prophets—the newly born God, one dares say. The God no longer "useful" to tyrants, the God liberated from wiles and wars. The God who pleads on behalf of victims and outsiders, the "widows and orphans," the expendable ones of this world.

✦   ✦   ✦

Formidable Eliphaz! With a view to indicting Job, he has borrowed whole cloth the ethical insights of Isaiah.

The charges strike at the heart of sin, as elaborated in the same era.

The charge in sum; Job has violated charity and justice toward the neighbor—the helpless neighbor, underscored.

All excusing causes must be demolished.

Has Job pled innocence? He must be mocked, set back.

He is not innocent, not for a moment;

> Is it
> because of your piety
> that He reproves you,
>
> that He enters
> with you
> into judgment?

To raise the question is to imply an answer, a truthful one. This alone is medicinal; bitter as it is, the potion must be taken —the truth;

> Is it not rather
> your manifold wickedness,
> your endless iniquities? (Job 22:4–5)

Thus the cruel reversal of fortune. Job's good name and honor are dealt a disabling, if not a mortal, blow. His sins are laid out plain; his "virtue" was a bootless cover.

To come to cases, as adduced.

The indictment is relentless, exhaustive. Job is guilty of every sin in the prophetic account of conscience.

Item. He has unjustly kept kinsmen's goods in pawn, and left the deprived to go about naked.

Item. He has withheld food and drink from the needy.

Item. He has seized land from the poor to hand over to his cronies.

Item. He has sent away widows empty-handed, and left orphans without recourse.

✦   ✦   ✦

These are the classic sins denounced by Isaiah (58).

Ezekiel has taken up the theme, he too stands against Job (18:7).

✦   ✦   ✦

In face of such manifold transgression, is such as Job to be held approved of God?

Eliphaz brings to the court a formidable witness for the prosecution;

> This is the fasting that I wish;
>
> releasing those bound unjustly,
> untying the thongs of the yoke,

setting free the oppressed,
lightening every burden,

sharing bread with the hungry,
sheltering the oppressed and the homeless,

clothing the naked when you see them,
not turning your back on your own (Isaiah 58:6, 7)

✦ ✦ ✦

Does the prosecution of Job issue from malice, or from passion bespeaking the truth?

We are shaken by the hideous charges. Publicly they tar Job's honor.

Multitudes love and honor him and seek in his example, precious lessons in holy living.

But the allegations, if proven true, would destroy all claim, all repute of righteousness.

✦ ✦ ✦

Deep waters, and bitter. Eliphaz' are hardly to be thought general charges, or evidence of a friendship gone sour.

Are they to be taken seriously, are they not?

Seriously indeed. The text will meet the eyes of generations. Job must answer, refute the cruel assault.

And he shall.

✦ ✦ ✦

Indeed as matters unfold, the art and intent of the author are clarified. In all seriousness, he allows malice its dark hour. Let the adversary, like ha-Satan himself, quote Scripture to his own advantage.

Set down the indictment, and in detail. Heap the allegations on his head like live coals.

And the soul of Job is set afire. He cries out like a Pirandellan hero; Reality, reality!

We shall see the arousal, the quickened anger, the splendid rebuttal. And vindication will shine the more brightly.

✦   ✦   ✦

Such splendor rides his soul!

Centuries pass, the church will borrow Job, will embrace this image of suffering and vindication, will hold his light high—for Christ's sake and our own.

More light, give us more light! Job the light-bearer.

✦   ✦   ✦

But for the bitter present, the charges stand.

They fester there on the page, like sores on the flesh of Job.

But wait; he will have his hour.

✦   ✦   ✦

22:12–14 From bile to altitudinous god-talk; this Eliphaz, stony of face and heart, is a manipulator of moods, a skilled sophist.

He misconstrues Job, to stunning effect—for a time.

Until one scans the text closely, marveling at the skilled feints and ploys, the tendentious conclusion. Against Job;

> Yet you say;
> "What does God know?
>
> Can He see
> through thick darkness?

> Clouds hide Him,
> He cannot see,
>
> as He walks
> upon the vault of the heavens" (Job 22:13–14)

Job of course, has not once denied God's omniscience.

The offense that gnaws at Eliphaz is; Job dares question God. To a parched, abstract religious sense, questions are inadmissable, offensive.

Job's torment; how can it be—that God remains indifferent to the fate of the just?

Eliphaz draws his own conclusion, and attributes it to Job.

The one who dares question God is by implication, blasphemous; he implies that God is ignorant of, or indifferent to, the human predicament.

✦   ✦   ✦

Clearly, Job is an affront, a torment to his tormenters. That interrogation of God!

Is Job not sowing questions in minds obdurately closed, questions that lie close to the bone?

Or his queries are like a worm in a pleasant-seeming fruit, a worm well-hidden, omnivorous.

What is the worth of the religion of the three, this melange of philosophy, ideology, formulas tripping on the tongue, apodictic dicta, their Bible a kind of debater's handbook?

To justify, they must attack.

The allegations of Eliphaz stand on the page, an argument blind from birth.

✦   ✦   ✦

22:15–20 He will go further, this wordy, weighty man.

In effect, Job has aligned himself with the wicked ones of old, in their (purported) cynicism and pride of place. As though (implication, innuendo again) Job too, in his impetuous questioning of God, were daring say in effect;

> "Depart from us!"

and

> "What can the Almighty do to us?" (Job 22:17)

Let him take warning. Job and his religion are not simply placed in question; he is besmirched, aligned with the historically irreligious. (The religion of Eliphaz, we note, is strong on warnings, threats of punishment, as on bribes held out, dangling).

Job (another implication) risks a fate once meted out to wicked ancestors;

> They were snatched away
> before their time,
>
> their foundations
> a flood swept away (Job 22:16)

✦   ✦   ✦

Job, it would seem, must undergo the awful fate told of by Isaiah (53). Job, likewise a suffering servant;

Spurned and avoided by all,
accustomed to infirmity . . .
counted among the wicked . . .

✦　✦　✦

22:21–30 Can we credit it?

After a dose of woe and wormwood, Eliphaz offers a roseate ending!

Beyond surmise, a pure surprise; and typical one thinks, of his method.

First, weigh the page with more or less veiled threats.

Then change tack; offer largehearted (bribes?) rewards, visions of restoration, renewal, reconciliation, all good things impending!

✦　✦　✦

Promises, promises.

The rhetoric is persuasive, seductive, urgent, straight-faced. As presented, irrefutable.

And how could it not be so—does he not speak for the deity?

✦　✦　✦

There are of course conditions to be met; invariably there are. Job must repent of his errant ways;

> Come to terms with God,
> be at peace. . . .
>
> Receive instruction
> from His mouth
>
> and lay up His words
> in your heart . . . (Job 22:21–22)

Awesome. A saint, a just man before God, a servant mysteriously afflicted, a light unto generations, Job. One before whose
pain, only silence and companionable grieving would seem to
befit—Job must endure a catechesis designed, in accord with a
certain cast of mind, for the conversion of—sinners!

✦ ✦ ✦

Thus the mystery reaches us, the harsh drama, the humiliation of the great protagonist.

Truth told, his opponents (and ourselves as well) are unworthy to bind his sandals.

✦ ✦ ✦

And yet, and yet, strangely against the grain of logic, we are
grateful—even for the censorious graceless clamor that besets
the stricken one.

Turn by turn, we have seen it. The trio step forward, they
explore and exemplify the way of the world, refined and cruel,
united in oppression of the just.

And then, something unintended, unpredictable, majestic. It
is as though they seized the wheel of a wine vat, pressing out a
noble elixir—the soul, the poetry of Job.

Without the provocations and proddings, we would know Job
the less. For our sake also, for our biblical literacy, for insight
into stature and holiness contending with the Fallen world—he
suffers at their hands.

✦ ✦ ✦

Only concede their world, their god, their obsessions; and the
universe is stood on its head. The friends take possession; of Job,
the world, and the god. They own reality.

This purportedly just man? Just, not at all! Touched by the
finger of their god, his good works go dank and rotten.

✦ ✦ ✦

Relief, recourse? Let him confess; and lo! all will be changed—
for the better, to be sure.
For the better, if Job resembles them?
No. Night will fall.

✦ ✦ ✦

Astonishingly inventive, this Eliphaz. How close, perilously
close his arguments come to the real thing, the truth. We note,
and are shaken;

> . . . God brings down
> the pride of the haughty,
> but the humble
> He saves.
>
> God delivers the innocent (Job 22:29–30)

✦ ✦ ✦

One thinks of televangelists today; how closely they resemble
Eliphaz. Correct message, wrong context.
There lingers about such bully pulpits an unpleasant odor of
manipulation, magic, money. A single deed, a "coming forward
for Christ," yields miracles on behalf of the acolytes, brings in its
shining wake something known as "salvation."
A like gesture is urged, dangled before Job;

> Come to terms with Him
> and be at peace . . .
>
> If you return to the Almighty,
> you will be restored (Job 22:21, 23)

✦   ✦   ✦

Magic, or mystery? We are uneasy.

We ask, as we must—and what of others? Is Job to be saved, and the world condemned to its ruinous way?

What of the death of the innocent, and wars unending, and vast moneys accumulated in few hands? What of the principality of violence enthroned, the shadow of misery large across the land, across the world?

And what of our Job, this great refuser of magical gestures?

✦   ✦   ✦

Job offers only a cold consolation. This; in such a world as ours his vocation must continue.

"Such as ours"; which is to say, "fallen." "Must continue." The law of the Fall.

And does continue. Wherever alert consciences refuse to yield before the vainglorious empery of death.

Of the consequence of such resistance, the "four against Job" know much. So do we, seeing them again and again mustering their dire arguments, their dark-browed threats.

Know it or not, they stand with the powers of this world. They would punish the just, in accord with the law of the Fall.

Of which law, the god of Eliphaz stands as surrogate and upholder. His deity all said, is strangely akin to the deity of pharoahs and Sauls and Solomons, an Atlas upholding the massive pillars of "things as they are."

✦   ✦   ✦

For the trio, time dissolves. So does hope. We humans are condemned to a kind of nightmarish pseudo-eternity, in which "things as they are, shall be, *in saecula saeculorum.*"

We must not underestimate them and their like, their eonic

enticement. Were not Job courageous and firm of spirit, giving them the lie, the three, their logic, their god, their version of the world and time—these would be proven hideously correct.

These would prevail. But for that small and saving factor, that suffering servant and his "No."

✦ ✦ ✦

Neither should we overestimate them, these biblical antagonists of the holy and just. They join the kings and chiefs of armies and tricksters and fomenters of wars and murders—these malingerer on the page, indentured beings. They serve, by clash and contrast.

These serve Job and the God of Job.

Job, not they, stands at center stage.

Which is to say, holiness, not evil (not evil, as here, aping goodness, pilfering its language)—holiness is the point of all. The point of God, the point of the word of God.

The point of struggle. Today.

✦ ✦ ✦

We have suggested an image; Eliphaz, Bildad, and Zophar are indentured, their task is the turning of a wine press.

Another image occurs; they are slaves. With a creaking winch of argument they draw up from a well the waters of grace.

chapter seven

"Rebels against the Light?"
(23:1–28:28)

What is vulnerable as we
who cave in at a blow,
who fall like kicked sacks?

We die in an hour,
like insects, flowers,
drifting downwind,

we are shadows in armor,
death our portion,
our menu, our bleak house.
And the God of life?
like a master potter,
heart-shaped clay,
shaped it with Breath.

And we stood there
children, animals,
insects, flowers.

The diurnal planets
spinning on fingertips,
let all, all go—
a feather downwind

—Psalm 33

✦   ✦   ✦

23:1–7 We take in the scene, and are appalled. The look of the four falls on Job—such scant compassion, so meager a sense of justice.

Let us absorb the look, and be chilled to the heart.

In our time Job has become a social image of an interpenetrating "third world," those within and without the borders of power and affluence.

And a like gaze meets their suffering; the look, icy, forbidding, bystanding and bypassing, a look of guilt and bad faith—the gaze of the world today, falling upon its victims.

Job, baffled, stalemated, cries out in near despair; let us look beyond, let us look to God!

There to be sure one would gain a hearing, would learn the terms of argument.

Then at last, justice, vindication!

The sense of time past is fragmented. Job, as though swamped in fever and chills, loses his grasp on a truth he had long cherished.

To wit, vindication alas, is not to be, not in this world. The God of faith is hidden, God of the Cloud of Unknowing.

Job knew it, and he does not know it. Once the bitter fact was like a spar in a stormy sea, a bare hope; he gripped it close.

Now he loses hold, it floats away.

✦   ✦   ✦

In soliloquy, Job considers the terms of the game we call faith. God knows his every footfall, how he has walked in Godly ways, observed to the letter, holy commands;

> The words
> of God's mouth
> I have treasured
> in my heart . . . (Job 23:12)

✦ ✦ ✦

Thus ever so subtly, the author of our book reveals his Jewish roots, firmly set in the Law.

But what a crashing irony also!

Everything concerning Job's ancestry is cloudy. No geneology is offered. In the prelude he is presented as a non-Jew, an Edomite, born of the perennial tribal enemy of Israel.

The prophets repeatedly railed against the Edomites as cruel and murderous. According to Ezekiel (35), they were the despoilers of Jerusalem.

Worse was to follow; after the fall of the city, they proceeded to devastate the land, subduing the populace by main force. To crown their crimes, they settled among the conquered, a hated occupation force.

✦ ✦ ✦

And here the saving contrast; a Jewish poet presents as hero, saint, model of faith, an "enemy" of his people.

Even as, in the same passage, our poet hints at his own life of prayer, placing on the lips of Job words of utmost import to himself (Cf. Psalm 17:5; 139:1–6, 7–10; also Jeremiah 11:20).

Ever so gently, imperceptibly, Scripture grows before our eyes, life upon life. A truth is set down by one hand; later, impelled by a like faith, another underscores it or adds an inspired codicil.

✦ ✦ ✦

24:1–17 How praise this wondrously tender plaint, its theme the plight of the poor and victimized?

Praise it, linger over it.

We are to infer something of moment. There existed at the time of Job, an entire generation of Jobs, of "widows and orphans," of the "needy of the land," of "the young among them." And finally;

from the dust
the dying groan,

the souls
of the wounded
cry out (Job 24:12)

✦ ✦ ✦

Nothing of this misery, be it noted, is arbitrary, or occurs in the course of nature, or is to be laid to something (foolishly) referred to, then or now, as "God's will."

No, there exist "the wicked" and their systems of betrayal, greed, violence, and oppression.

These, as faith and right reason agree, must be indicted. Job does so; scorchingly.

✦ ✦ ✦

Such tenderness, such passion, so finely attuned he is to the sufferings of the innocent! He is of their kind, he dwells amid the shambles of a Fallen creation. Again and again, he sees the unfortunate brought low by systems of greed, envy, violence.

The ruin, the crime, the human perversity—the Fall—has entered Job's soul, it clings like a parasite to his skin and bones, to his existence.

✦ ✦ ✦

And why, one wonders, this continual reference in the prophets and in Job, to "widows and orphans"? It is as though these existed in such numbers as to form by themselves a class of misery and want.

We have noted how the era of Job marks a breakthrough, as the prophets appear, speak, suffer, and die.

It is also an era of wars and rumors of wars; each prophet

testifies at length to the horror. Jeremiah, Ezekiel, Isaiah, endured the siege of Jerusalem under the Babylonians. Jeremiah was punished as a faineant, even a possible wartime turncoat. Ezekiel and Daniel were exiled, together with their people.

Beyond every human folly, war was and is, the relentless widow- and orphan-maker.

✦ ✦ ✦

Job denounces the "wicked"; he indicts a political system under which he suffers, victimized along with others. The system condemns, impoverishes, defrauds, evicts, starves, exposes to death, declares of no value multitudes of Job's people.

In sum, the politics and practice are marked by utmost contempt, toward God, toward creation. Toward other humans—with a concentrated, distilled malice reserved for the poor.

✦ ✦ ✦

The Economy Is Bullish

From the woman on the street
who has nothing but the street.
I learn how Mammon prospers.

Each night she rolls up the pavement
like a goose-down blanket.
All weathers, she's cozy there.

Each day, hidden
in the brows of power brokers
she wheels and deals
humming along
with the whirring Stock Exchange.

She wears triage like a billboard,
tricked out in ticker tape,
laying bets like Mother Courage—
a hundred-to-one odds—
a square meal?

She moans—
C'mon baby, give!

Then
off she pushes in harness.

She's tomorrow
pushing today away.

Not far.
She's the next war.

DB

✦   ✦   ✦

Toward the end of World War II, the allied armies neared the bunkers of Berlin's rubble.

And in face of defeat and death, one of Hitler's henchmen announced that his Fuehrer had actually won the war. The proof; Nazi tactics had taken hold, were widely imitated by the enemy.

There is a kind of vicious insight here.

In the country of the author of Job, the tactics of the pharoah had taken hold and were sedulously cultivated.

Grown prosperous, the Israels flexed their muscle, waged wars abroad. These were wars similar to those of pharoahs; wars of expansion, of control of world markets.

✦ ✦ ✦

Domestically meantime, the would-be pharoahs, Saul, David, and Solomon and the like, created a new slavery, a class system, with forced labor, and a standing armed force.

In a sense, Egypt came home. The Israeli kings dreamed pharaonic dreams, raised a temple and palace to rival the pyramids, went "down to Egypt" seeking pacts of military protection.

It was a bitter pill, this capitulation. Isaiah refused to swallow it;

> Woe to the rebellious, says God,
> who carry out plans that are not Mine,
> who weave webs not inspired by Me,
> adding sin upon sin.
> They go down to Egypt
> but My counsel they do not seek.
>
> They find their strength in pharoah's protection
> and take refuge in Egypt's shadow.
>
> Pharoah's protection shall be your shame . . .
> (Isaiah 30:1–3)

✦ ✦ ✦

In consequence of such trafficking, Israel has come more and more to resemble Egypt. Isaiah sees it, and issues his warning;

> You have abandoned Your people,
> the house of Jacob. . . .
> Their land is full of silver and gold,
> there is no end to their treasures.
>
> Their land is full of horses,

there is no end of their chariots.

Their land is full of idols;
they worship the works of their hands,
that which their fingers have made (Isaiah 2:7, 8)

And the idols were not to be thought a third in a list of moral ills. The idols were precisely the "chariots" and the "silver." The violent and greedy worship at such shrines.

✦   ✦   ✦

And what of the great temple? It was eviscerated of meaning, of true worship. It became a "front," all decor. "The temple of the Lord, the temple of the Lord." Ezekiel raised his voice in mockery of the priestly establishment and its liturgy, as they fell prey to magic and incantation.

Shortly, after the golden heyday of Solomon, the political, military, and economic systems went to rot. The kingdom was ruled by predatory adventurers, would-be restorers of ancient glory.

Tawdry hubris; there was to be no restoration. The realm split in two like a rotten fruit.

No solution, worse. The "two kingdoms" were ruled by a series of murderers and malcontents; they disposed ruthlessly of the hapless, the recusant, those who objected or refused the game. When it was not expedient to kill, they crushed the deviant, prophet or no.

✦   ✦   ✦

Why is the justice of God delayed interminably in this world? Why do crimes of injustice go unrequited, to all intents unobserved by God?

The wicked proceed with their crimes, and prosper. And Job asks in effect, where is God?

He never once is led to ask; is there a God? Nor are his friends.
The root of their conflict is elsewhere, in this; the wildly diverse
understanding of a God each confesses faith in.

✦ ✦ ✦

Seizure of land from the poor is the first offense of the powerful. The crime is sternly forbidden in Deuteronomy 27:17. The
guilty are subject to one of the famous twelve curses;

> Cursed be he who moves his neighbor's landmarks. And
> all the people shall answer; Amen.

Those in possession afflict widows and orphans, seizing what
meager sustenance the poor lay claim to—an ass or ox.

This in plain violation of covenant, and disruption of communal memory as well (Deuteronomy 24:17, 18);

> You shall not violate the rights of the alien or the or-
> phan, nor take the clothing of a widow as a pledge. For
> remember, you were once slaves in Egypt, and your God
> ransomed you from there. That is why I command you
> to observe this rule.

Thus memory is invoked as a powerful spur to ethical behavior. Or the opposite may occur. Memory falls short, fades, affects
nothing of moral behavior.

There exist institutions, as Job understands, whose prospering requires the suppression of true memory.

In such circumstance, the Exodus and the saving acts of God
might never have occurred.

✦　✦　✦

Do the people recall those "acts of God" in the cycle of the liturgical year, most vividly in the recurring feast of Passover? Of course they do.

But time passes, prosperity rules. People forget. The central, saving events of history are reduced to mere pageantry, folklore, perhaps a harmless form of theater. One attends, one departs unchanged in heart or behavior.

All said, we owe God nothing. Nor the neighbor.

And yet it is commended in the law again and again, like the summons of a drumbeat—care for the well-being of the needy;

> If he (the debtor) is a poor man, you shall not sleep in the mantle he gives as a pledge, but shall return it to him at sunset, that he himself may sleep in it (Deuteronomy 24:12, 13).

To the contrary. The cloak is seized as surety; night falls, and it is not returned (Job 24:7–8);

> They pass the night naked, without clothing,
> for they have no covering against the cold;
> they are drenched with the rain of the mountains,
> and for want of shelter must cling to the rocks.

✦　✦　✦

So be it.

And we also, children of American culture, have learned a less exigent way in the world than that of the holy law.

This is the word of the culture; Americans have come, not out of Egypt and slavery; we come from—what shall we name it— nowhere? From a realm of fantasy and desire. From the moment just before the present moment, from one image just vanished to another, in full bloom.

The media, like a bottomless cornucopia, spawn a multitude of such images, momentary flashes of appetite, rebirth, ideal beauty, brio, youthfulness, advantageous possession.

The images come and go, their siren call strong and loud; Enter the dream, it is yours!

✦　✦　✦

From nowhere. Therefore we go—nowhere. We exist in a kind of moral haze, bereft of such memories, stories of liberation as would summon us to rejoice, to give thanks, to bend our lives to succoring others.

✦　✦　✦

They force the needy off the road,
the poor of the land are driven into hiding (Job 24:4)

Such people, the homeless, those who bare their misery in public, are inconvenient, embarrassing. They impede the passage of the great ones, the "chariots and horses" denounced by Isaiah, the panoply of power and greed, the accoutrements of war.

More; these impoverished ones offend eye and nostril. Sight of them is vaguely discomfiting. They stir the soul with dread, with a stark reminder; all is not well in the land, the commonweal has fallen short.

They are best out of sight, out of mind!

✦　✦　✦

Not easily done. The law of Moses stands in the way, a mighty impediment against the rage of power, a fortress protecting the despised and deprived (Deuteronomy 15:11);

> The needy will never be lacking in the land; this is why
> I command you to open your hand to the poor and
> needy kinsmen in your country.

And we note the concession to a "wicked" system.

Justice demands that there be no "needy in the land." But justice is a chief casualty of the Fall.

That being sadly true, we must reform and patch and improvise as best we may. We substitute charity for the exigent call to incarnate the justice of God in the world;

> Who has stirred up from the east the champion of
> justice, and summoned him to be His attendant?
> (Isaiah 41:2)

> Upon this one I have put my spirit,
> who shall bring forth justice to the nations.

> A bruised reed he shall not break,
> and a smouldering wick shall not quench

> until justice be established on the earth,
> and the furthest coasts await this teaching
> (Isaiah 42:1, 3, 4)

> I, God, have called you for the victory of justice
> (Isaiah 42:6)

✦   ✦   ✦

Jesus will make a like point, and with a sharp thrust of irony (John 12:7). He assembles with friends, a banquet is prepared. A woman, Mary, enters the room. Wordlessly she anoints Him with precious nard.

Judas, thief in secret (but the secret is out!) and traitor-to-be, protests;

Why was not this perfume sold? It would have brought
three hundred silver pieces, and the money have been
given to the poor.

To this Jesus replied; "The poor you have always with
you, but Me you will not always have."

Judas stands within a system of greed and betrayal, the Fall
and its generational, institutionalized "systems" of sin.

In effect, his behavior offers a kind of befouled guarantee of
the truth of the saying; "the poor you have always with you."
He would have it so.

Jesus makes a further, subtle point, no less telling. The effects
of the Fall, as they touch on this scene, are twofold;

1) The poor you have always with you,
   and
2) Me you will not always have.

The two are conjoined. Systems of injustice guarantee the
perdurance of the first and the connection between the two.

The point is not often made; the same systems will set in
motion the awful event that will remove Jesus from this world.

✦   ✦   ✦

The poor are driven from the land. Probably by night, a
wealthy neighbor has moved the boundary stones to his own
advantage. At dawn he points to the stones that conveniently
enlarge his holdings; behold, proof positive of ownership!

And for the evicted, what recourse?

None. Possession, nine points of the law.

✦   ✦   ✦

A personal note, as these reflections are set down.

The simpatico of Job for the homeless strikes close to the Jesuit community in which I live. In the summer of 1998 we were

served with an eviction notice. In effect, we must either vacate our modest apartments in a working-class neighborhood in New York, or consent to the doubling (or more) of rent.

Thus a wealthy landlord seeks, and may well win, legal sanction for "moving the boundary stones to his own advantage."

Up to the present our lease, renewed periodically for some thirty years, has been protected by law. No longer, if the landlord prevails.

From our eviction, vast moneys will accrue to this fanatical financeer.

Like Job, and unlike his carping friends, we are tasting in small measure the plight of the poor. How fittingly one thinks, for those who name themselves "companions of Jesus."

As to the outcome, we shall see. The landlord has assembled a powerful, expensive coven of lawyers; their record of prevailing in like cases is impressive.

✦   ✦   ✦

There are those
who rebel
against the light;

they know not its ways,
they abide not in its paths . . .

For them,
morning is darkness,
It is then
they discern its terrors (Job 24:13–17)

Murderers, adulterers, thieves; these are the enemies of the light, who would if they could, overturn the natural sequence of night and day.

Darkness favors them, light is their enemy. Dark deeds require the dark; there no eye falls on them, identifies them, charges and convicts them of crime.

Is not a linkage implied with what has gone before, the indictment of the warmaking state? War includes implicitly all these crimes, and on an unimaginably vast scale; murder, adultery, theft.

✦   ✦   ✦

The image of light-darkness is frequently dwelt on by Jesus. First in His nocturnal discourse with Nicodemus;

> The judgment, the condemnation is this;
> the light came into the world
> but they loved darkness rather than light
> because their deeds were wicked.
>
> Everyone who practices evil
> hates the light;
> he does not come near it
> for fear his deeds will be exposed.
>
> But the one who acts in truth
> comes into the light
> to make clear
> that his deeds are done in God (John 3:19–21)

✦   ✦   ✦

Jesus stood in the light.

And this was His crime; He cast light into dark places, He enlightened others, He banished the darkness in which the powerful throve.

This was criminal behavior, according to the "law of the land," a law, truth told, of iniquity, pure darkness.

In tormented human history, have there come forth darker minds than those who wrought His death—Judas, Herod, Pilate, the chief priest?

✦   ✦   ✦

The outcome is a matter of communal benefit; so the verdict is agreed on beforehand. Officials of church and state must end "the case of Jesus Christ," and close the dossier.

They must have done with the godly One.

The Fallen world that they dominate, their eminence in a system of domination, violence, and greed, together with the oath that seals their office as sanctioned, inviolate—and more, as willed of God—all these weighty realities, titles, credentials, demand the removal of the Light-bearer.

And the law of the land, blind at noon, supports the decision.

✦   ✦   ✦

See, brutes huff and puff—

the Lord of life
keeps them at edge of eye
They crumble like a
faulty tower.
At center eye—the apple of His eye
blossoms, swells, ripens—
the faithful who fall
straight as a plumb line
into
His right hand (Psalm 33)

✦　✦　✦

Another episode of John's gospel enlarges the metaphor of light-darkness, even as it tightens the irony.

Light and darkness, sight and blindness; the imagery offers a self-conscious prelude to events in the offing. Jesus knows what forces are gathering, and to what purpose.

Evidently the story is of prime import; John dwells on it at great length.

It is as though the evangelist were asking his soul; why this overmastering fear, this hatred of the light? Why the passionate embracing of the dark—a dark that admits nothing of the light of truth?

✦　✦　✦

Jesus will push the questions close; all but rudely, all but unbearably.

How comes it that darkness penetrates, possesses civil and religious authorities, in them flourishes, grows palpable, thick, an atmosphere of the soul, an affliction "from birth," native, as would seem, to high office, resistant against healing?

An awful eventuality, a warning.

We are told of a man, a near nobody, blind from birth. Jesus heals him. He goes about announcing freely, rapturously, the wonder worked by his Healer and Friend.

And for this, for naming the Benefactor, he is cast out of his religious community.

The eviction in no wise puts him down. Feisty, undaunted, face to face he condemns the authorities of the synagogue.

Jesus seeks him out. The healed man bows down in worship and gratitude.

And the response of the Healer is—surprising.

We might have expected some form of praise, an acknowledgment of wonderfully courageous behavior.

✦　✦　✦

Nothing of the kind; instead, Jesus turns in our direction.

It is as though his vision penetrated time, touched the uninstructed and unborn.

As though a distant age had arrived. As though we stood there.

The miracle becomes the medium, the medium becomes an utterly unexpected message.

Jesus utters a confession, vast in scope and shocking in form.

From the heart it is shaped, *"cur Deus-Homo"*; "why, this Incarnation of God";

> I came into this world to divide it,
> to make the sightless see
> and the seeing blind (John 9:39)

✦　✦　✦

Thus in the episode, Jesus takes a double part. He is first of all, the protagonist, healer—provoker. And he speaks as a chorus, commenting on the healing, driving the truth home.

Home? But in this world the truth has no home;

> Some of the pharisees around Him picked this up, saying, "You are not calling us blind, are you?"

> To which Jesus replied;

> "If you were blind
> there would be no sin in that.
> 'But we see,' you say,
> and your sin remains" (John 9:40–41)

Take it or leave, thus Jesus, Healer and Chorus.

End of episode.

✦   ✦   ✦

Paul for his part seizes the pastoral implications of the imagery, sight-blindness.

He even personifies both, light and darkness, as though each exerted a claim, each were seeking possession of his beloved Ephesians;

> There was a time when you were darkness, but now you are light in the Lord.

> Well then, live as children of light. Light produces every kind of goodness and justice and truth . . .

> Take no part in vain deeds, done in darkness; rather, condemn them . . . (Ephesians 5:8 ff.)

✦   ✦   ✦

25:1–6 Another question. Is God, as far as events go, revealed to us humans as the Powerless—or as the All Powerful?

The answer is dredged from the guts of Job, from tragedy.

God has led him by the *via negativa*. God would be known as the Non Intervener, Non Savior, Non Vindicator, Non Healer. The All who is—near Nothing.

Shocking! To Bildad such implications, let alone their expression, are errant nonsense, dangerous, near blasphemy.

✦   ✦   ✦

Let him, this impeccable critic, say it loud, clear, and for a change, mercifully brief; God is the All Powerful!

And this, with imagery heavy with terrestrial implication—the Deity as celestial Warrior.

And we humans?

In comparison with the All, we are near nothing; we crawl the earth like earthworms, blind, barely sentient, vulnerable to the beak and claw of mischance or malice.

Dour Bildad, and his theodicy of gloom & doom! He must exalt God at the expense of the human—of us, the declared image of God.

✦   ✦   ✦

26:1–4 Job has heard them out, the coterie of relentless interrogators.

Now comes his turn.

He would have the trio "test the spirits."

What impels them so to malign him as the "powerless" one, "feeble" and "ignorant"?

> With whose help have you uttered these words, whose
> is the breath that comes forth from you? (Job 26:4)

✦   ✦   ✦

27:1–6 We follow BJ here, attributing both chapters to Job's rejoinder—

> By the living God
> who denies me justice . . . (Job 27:2)

In the prelude, we heard the estimate of God; of "just," "noble" Job.

And here in a phrase stands his sublime oath; he is afflicted but unbowed.

And above all, and dwelling as he must in the dark night of providence—he is steadfast, true to God's estimate;

> By Shaddai,
> who renders my life
> bitter—
>
> So long
> as life remains
>
> and the breath of God
> shall pass my nostrils
>
> my lips
> shall not speak falsehood . . . (Job 27:2–4)

They have accused him precisely of this; consciously or not, he has uttered untruths.

What greater offense against the truth, than that a human would dare utter an accusation against God?

Still, in face of the (to them) incontrovertible evidence of affliction, he maintains his innocence. Admirable pertinacity! No untruth passes his lips, he passionately seeks the truth of life.

He insists, and insists again, mulishly; and they are forced to hear it, his stubborn holding of ground;

> Far be it
> from me
> to account you right;
> Till my last breath,
> I shall maintain
> my innocence (Job 27:5)

Incorrigible, or unconquerable?

We for our part, act as witnessess of a different kind. We are awed, led to deep pondering.

Are Job's afflictions deserved, as adduced? Or they are the evidence, negative, night ridden, terrifying—of the presence of God, the God whom Job acknowledges with all his riven heart;

evidence of the God Job would serve, if only he were summoned.

He has been summoned. We long to amend the text, to his comfort.

✦ ✦ ✦

But Who is this God of Job's?

Is this the God of the prelude, bargaining in secret, making of prosperity and health negotiable commodities?

Does this God not impede faith, scandalize, test and probe, strike blindly and without provocation the innocent and just?

As though, as though Job were in actuality unjust.

As though the carping chorus were correct in their indictment.

As though the four were empowered, delegated to announce the judgment of God. As though their allegation of Job's sin were endorsed from on high.

✦ ✦ ✦

27:7–12 The trio may take it or leave; Job will cling with a last breath to his honor. Will cling to his innocence; before God, if not before his friends.

He turns the tables, in a pivotal cry;

> Let my enemy be
> as the wicked
>
> and my adversary
> as the unjust! (Job 27:7)

✦ ✦ ✦

Job hardly urges innocence before God as a universal claim. He, perhaps he alone, is innocent.

To a point, Eliphaz is correct; of course evil is abroad in the world. Of course God will not attend to the prayer of the wicked. Of course God is no delight to the wicked. Of course, of course.

These are home truths; in them Job is in no need of instruction.

✦ ✦ ✦

One hears a sigh, riving Job's frame. If only they would attend to him, for a change would choose silence, become teachable—

> I am showing you
> what is in God's power,
>
> concealing from you
> nothing
> of the deep thought
> of Shaddai (Job 27:11)

Signs of ruin and reversal lie heavy on Job. And yet he retains, magnificent and close, his self-possession.

And more. We note how the light of his spirit burns ever more brightly. It is as though reversal and loss served to kindle and feed the flame of his soul.

✦ ✦ ✦

He offers a summary, in effect, of the profound truths he has drawn from adversity. No illusions, no longings transmogrifying the bare truth!

The hidden God, the God of Job's dark night, is announced— as such. God of Darkness. God whose native element is night.

And more; a God whose presence to the just is—a cloud of unknowing, is wounds, darkness, reversal, ambiguity, pain.

From on high, from near—only silence, only evidence of— absence.

One lingers over the astonishing couplet;

> I am showing you
> what is in God's power . . .

> the deep thought of Shaddai.

Indeed this holy portent, this epiphany of the human, Job, beset by verbal harpies, continues to show forth in his suffering, the glory of God.

Continues down the ages to instruct, to enlighten, to hearten multitudes.

That we too may groan and hope on, against the monstrous odds of the world.

✦   ✦   ✦

Does the adversarial chorus seem immune to wisdom?

They do. And yet, all unwitting they impel the action forward.

Absurd and ill-tempered, dark against light, they act as a foil, a setting. Through them, the incomparable jewel of Job's faith gleams the more brightly.

✦   ✦   ✦

Darkness is Job's (and God's) native element, while time lasts.

In contrast, the "light" of the adversaries, their confidence in their own powers, their sere logic and abusive rhetoric, their obsessive claiming of a god who sides with them against Job— such "light" is a mirage.

They stand in it confidently, they walk abroad in it.

But all the while they are led into vagaries, baseless claims, assaults on the truth and truthteller.

✦   ✦   ✦

How strangely familiar is their God of strict justice and small mercy! The trio has become a multitude; such acolytes are numerous today.

What a blessing, that certainty of one's merit and worth, one's exalted pharisaic status in a world of publicans and sinners!

✦   ✦   ✦

27:13–23 (We follow BJ here, attributing these verses to Cophar).

He elaborates, often in quite beautiful images, the fate of the wicked.

The wicked. By implication, Job himself? We have seen the tactic before. One or another of the adversaries launches heavy innuendos against Job.

So once more; let him take note and grow wise, even at this late hour.

Behold Job, close to view. Behold misfortune incarnate, his sores and losses open to the light of day, a rubric, a text.

Read it. He stands under heavy judgment; his contrary claims are vain illusions;

> He builds his house
> as of cobwebs,
>
> or a shack
> knocked together
> by a vine keeper (Job 27:18)

Bold talk indeed, and invasive, and derogatory. The images fall like a stoning;

This
is the evil man's
portion from God—

the lot
the ruthless
receive from Shaddai;
should he have
many sons—
they are marked
for the sword;

his descendants
will lack
their fill of bread.

Should he pile up silver
like dust,

and store away
mounds of clothing,

he may lay it up,
but the righteous will wear it,

the innocent
will share his silver . . .
He lies down,
a rich man,
his wealth intact;

when he opens his eyes,
it is gone . . . (Job 27:13–19)

Such mockery! A puny soul, thin in spirit, his mood sour and envious, derides a greatness beyond reach or measure.

✦ ✦ ✦

28:1–28 A renowned hymn follows; it celebrates the perennial "dwelling beyond" of wisdom, its inaccessibility to humans. Or so it is said.

✦ ✦ ✦

One dares suggest that the contrary is indicated. Everything in the prior and subsequent texts points to a splendid oxymoron.

Which is to venture; wisdom, declared inaccessible in the hymn, has been conferred on at least one human; on Job.

And the rub that rubs his soul raw is this; he remains ignorant, in darkness. He knows only the pain of life; he does not know that he bears it aloft, the jeweled crown of wisdom.

The gift relieves not a whit of the darkness he must dwell in.

✦ ✦ ✦

Still, out of that darkness, unrelieved, palpable—a dawn arrives.

And after dawn, a high noon. This light is kindled for others, for the unborn. For ourselves.

✦ ✦ ✦

A series of incomparable images celebrates the power, skill, genius of humans. They probe and possess, plumb the depths of earth and stream, draw forth incomparable riches. Silver, gold, iron, copper, jewels of all kinds, these the creation yields up before desirous tools and hands.

Human greatness, ingenuity, these are conceded, even celebrated.

But wisdom—another matter entirely, of a different order;

>   whence
>   does it come?
>
>   Where
>   is the source
>   of understanding? (Job 28:12)

Among humans the prospect of discovering the "source" is hardly encouraging. Have not Job's adversaries shown how slight is the chance that wisdom will alight on human lips, set minds ablaze?

>   We know nothing
>   of the way,
>
>   it lies
>   undisclosed
>   in the land of the living (Job 28:13)

Whence wisdom? Let all creation be surveyed.

Alas, neither air nor inhabited land nor the abyss nor hell itself can claim it—or so much as describe it. Nor can the mighty principality known as Death or Abaddon, the angel of hell personified. This mighty angel has heard no more than a rumor of the existence of Wisdom.

To resolve the riddle, to announce the meaning, is the work (and the word) of God;

>   Wisdom
>   is fear of God,
>   to shun evil
>   is true understanding (Job 28:28)

✦   ✦   ✦

Are we true to God's word concerning God?

One hopes so. In that spirit, we suggest that 1) wisdom is transcendant, perennially evades the grasp, the capacity, the genius of humans.

And despite all, 2) wisdom is not altogether withheld; it is conferred on a few, on the saints and martyrs and confessors of each generation.

Among whom must be included the suffering servant, Job.

Who despite all dark allegations, shines the more brightly in the firmament of holiness. Who "fears God," who "flees evil."

chapter eight

"I Was Eyes to the Blind and Feet to the Lame" (29:1–33:8)

Who knows whether death,
*   which in fear is named the greatest evil,*
may not be the greatest good?

*   May be, may not be.*

*   Expedient, to lose everything?*

The moon says it, waxing in silence, the fruit of heaven,
*   grape vine, melon vine.*
Autumn upon us, the exemplar, the time of falling.
* One who has lost all shall be born into all;*
*   buddha moon, moon of Job, moon of Jesus—*
light and planet and fruit of all;
"Unless the grain, falling to earth die, itself remains
*   alone."*

DB

✦   ✦   ✦

29:1–17 Memories, memories, how ambiguous they are; they haunt and torment, they bring unassailable joy, they strengthen the fiber of soul—or they attenuate it.

Job remembers.

Remembrance is a postulate of his being, a rule of existence in the world—and a deep cry of the heart.

Without memory and its ruling, enduring images, persisting despite obliterating time—deprived of images of a joyous past, of children and gracious weathers and nature's beauty and bounty, images of neighbors and friends, images of humans behaving humanly, ardently, compassionately—who is Job?

And who are we?

We are reduced to creatures of the moment, victims of appetite and greed and violence. We make of ego a mighty fortress, reduce the honored "neighbor" of the Bible to a rival, a potential threat to our possessions, a stranger—then an enemy.

We are ready for the next war.

✦ ✦ ✦

A command to "remember" is issued by Jesus Himself; and this at a solemn liturgical moment, the Last Supper.

"When you do these things, remember Me." It is one of few imperatives in the gospel.

We are commanded to "love God and the neighbor as yourself," and to "remember." And that is very nearly the entire burden laid on us. The rest, the works of love as these touch on situation and behavior, is left to us.

✦ ✦ ✦

As to Job, one would have thought that only misfortune was implanted in his mind and memory.

But are we to imagine that he was born on a dungheap, that he knew no better life?

Bereft of blessed contrary memory, Job might indeed be accounted a saint, but his holiness would be untouchable and remote, beyond our grasp. He would fall short of the tragic.

✦ ✦ ✦

Had he not known good times, sound friendships, a loving family? Repeatedly we heard his threnodies of loss. But did other, contrary images arise to stay and buoy him—faces, events, words, in warm detail?

Deprived of such memories, Job might well grow sour, his misery unrelieved.

✦ ✦ ✦

Blessed be Job, he could summon such memories, such images of joy. And presently they all but overwhelm him, images of the great and good days, when the sun of fortune stood at high noon, when he and those he loved sturdily flourished.

✦ ✦ ✦

He ruminates. Images tumble out, one on another.

What event brought his greatest blessing? Was it the favor of Shaddai, gracing his tent? Was it the presence of his sons, those signs, near and dear, of a steadfast future?

He summons yet another image; the honor that robed him about like a sheik's cloak, he a veritable king of his tribe. How the "assembly at the gate" awaited his coming, how his word was welcome as rainfall on parched soil. How he stood there in pride of place, a guerdon of wisdom and hope to his people.

A blessing indeed, that good name, the aura.

And be it noted; this was no empty or merely ceremonial response; he had earned an honorable name. He rightly wore it, an escutcheon.

✦ ✦ ✦

Thus he rejects in detail the imputation of Eliphaz.

Let his critic take note of the multitude Job has succored over the years; "the poor . . . the orphan . . . the dying . . . the widow . . . the blind . . . the halt . . . the nameless . . ." All have felt the power of his intervention.

✦ ✦ ✦

Of Job it is related that he made four doors to his house, so that the poor had not to be troubled to go around it to find an entrance. (Talmud)

✦ ✦ ✦

A particularly stark, energetic image occurs. Job in his heyday is a very Samson of strength. Imagine! It is as though he strikes a lion down, sunders the great bones;

I broke the jaws of the wrongdoer,
I wrested prey from his teeth (Job 29:17)

✦ ✦ ✦

29:18–25 All this being true, taking in account the works of compassion and justice that graced his youth—might Job not assume that age will bring him a continuum of honors, that he will live on and on, a blessing to his tribe?

Wrong, on every account.

He has come to this. From honors and prosperity, to loss of all;

dwellings and lands and herds and flocks, gold and silver.

His marriage turned sour, his spouse condemning him.

His children, every one, dead.

Among his peers, loss of an honored name.

✦ ✦ ✦

Useless

I wanted to be useless
as life itself, so
I told the president so
and told the pope so
and told the police so.
& one & all chorused,
like furies, like my friends;
AND WHO TOLD YOU SO?
The dead told me so,
the near dead; prisoners,
all who press faces against a pall of ice,
against a wall of glass,
a grave, a womb's thrall.
I read their lips, alas.
I told the poem. So.

DB

✦ ✦ ✦

A change of mood, a darkening. Out of Job's darkness and loss, second thoughts and reservations and doubts rise like a congress of demons.

We have witnessed their onslaught. The spirit of ha-Satan not only questions, it assaults and begrudges and implies sinfulness.

Bold and bolder grow the trio. They belabor him with verbal salves, lay on him massive assumptions of guilt. He is guilty before the fact, guilty before birth!

They mock his illness and humiliation.

They push the dark reality of the Fall. Fierce advocates of a Fall from which there is no rising.

And in this they go too far, even for the bargainer god, who in the beginning as we remember, declared a broad latitude of harm against just Job.

✦ ✦ ✦

Is not Job's plaint of innocence undeviating, firm?

No matter. The awful quartet harp on a presumptive guilt, declaring irrelevant his denials.

What dark-browed prosecutors, what would-be executioners!

✦ ✦ ✦

30:1–11 Among callow youths, Job has become a laughing-stock. Yet he dismisses them with a lashing stroke of fury; "their fathers I would have distained to rank with the dogs of my flock" (Job 30:1).

A strange passage follows.

Some among these mockers, it seems, have been reduced to misery and want, even as himself.

But while he bewails his own fall, he derides theirs. Have they not received just desserts, while he unjust?

Still, we wonder.

If the punishment that befell these mockers is just, what was their crime?

They mocked him, who (by implication) had been their bene-factor. Their fate is condign and brutal; let Job add to it a soupcon of vituperation;

> Want and hunger
> was their lot
>
> who fled
> to the parched wastelands . . .

> They were banished
> from among people
>
> with an outcry
> like that against a thief . . .
>
> From the underbrush
> they raised a rancorous cry,
> under the nettles
> they huddled together . . . (Job 30:3–7)

Is suffering inevitably a source of spiritual growth and benefit? We are well advised to doubt it, to examine every instance.

As here. In a strange reversal of roles, Job becomes the prosecutor of others;

> Such strength as they had, to me meant nought . . .
> (Job 30:2)

And again;

> Irresponsible, nameless men. . . . (Job 30:8)

They are brought as low or lower than Job, these mockers (LS1);

> They sing of me
> in mockery.
> I am become
> a byword among them . . .
>
> They abhor me,
> they stand aloof,
>
> They do not hesitate
> to spit in my face! (Job 30:9–10)

All mysterious. Flesh and blood hot with indignation, Job heaps living coals on his enemies.

Shall we speculate that we have, half-revealed here, the shadow, the less than heroic side of greatness?

Is this what he wills in his outrage, are these the grim depths he would cast them in, landless, outlawed, starving—"if only this could befall them . . ."?

A low mood. And Job all the more complex and puzzling. And thereby, the more precious to us.

✦ ✦ ✦

A dark mood earns him a place among the great ones.

The psalmist too, at times grows recriminatory and seeks revenge of his enemies from God.

And occasion warranting, the prophets too unleash their fires, cursing like very fiends those who brought them low.

✦ ✦ ✦

Christians have at hand another, far different response.

Christ met with an evil that must be termed consummate. It would claim His life.

And His response, as he stood dying on the nails?

> Father
> forgive them,
> they do not know
> what they are doing (Luke 23:34)

✦ ✦ ✦

Perhaps in the rage of Job a moral is implied. No other cause can match the justice of one's own, no wound so rankles as a wound in one's own flesh.

And further; no greatness of spirit but must endure dark nights.

✦ ✦ ✦

30:12–17 Military metaphors spring up, like warriors from dragons' teeth. It is all, one thinks, excessive.

But understandable as well is Job's mood, clinging, claiming him for its own.

He is a veritable city under assault;

> They attack,
> with none to stay them,
>
> as through a wide breach
> they advance . . .
>
> amid the uproar
> they come on in waves;
>
> over me
> rolls the terror (Job 30:13–15)

30:18–31 Surreal. In a flash, the "enemy" is changed, becomes Another.

Now the combat is One against one—and God is the assailant!

> One
> with great power
> lays hold on my clothing;
>
> by the collar of my tunic
> He seizes me.

He has cast me
into the mire;

I am level
with dust and ashes (Job 30:18–19)

And then, and then, the "He" is erased, a "You" is invoked.
Job raises a prayer, a cry of the heart.
Far from comfort, faith must wander an icy world, naked;

I cry to You,
but You do not answer;

You stand afar
and gaze at me.

Then merciless,
You turn upon me,

and with a strong hand
You buffet me. . . .

Yet should not a hand
be held out

to aid a wretched man
in his calamity? . . . (Job 30:20–24)

✦ ✦ ✦

The Jesuit Gerard Manley Hopkins seems to have suffered a
dark night akin to Job's;

Thou art indeed just, Lord, if I contend
With thee. But, sir, what I plead is just.

Why do sinners' ways prosper? and why must
Disappointment all I endeavor end? . . .

Mine, O thou lord of life, send my roots rain.

And again, wild, untamed as Job, this questioner;

But ah, but O thou terrible, why wouldst thou rude on
   me
They wring-world right foot rock? lay a lionlimb against
   me? scan
With darksome devouring eyes my bruised bones? and
   fan,
O in turns of tempest, me heaped there; me frantic to
   avoid thee and flee?

(*Poems of Gerard Manley Hopkins*)

Job for his part pleads for the compassion he has lavished on
the needy;

Have I not wept
for the hardships of others;

was not my soul grieved
for the destitute? (Job 30:25)

His argument is daring. His detractors would say, he is offensive, verges yet again on the blasphemous.
Thus Job reasons; virtuous behavior is urged by the holy Law.
But then comes the rub; how can the same Law exact no
equivalent of the deity, no *quid pro quo* of compassion?

. . . when I looked for good,
evil came;

> When I expected light,
> darkness descended (Job 30:26)

And more in the same dark vein. He will not be conforted, least of all by his "comforters."

He will not be comforted, even by God.

How can he be? Long before, he senses that God has joined with his tormenters.

✦   ✦   ✦

31:1–4 The question returns and returns. It recedes for awhile, then rolls in again, a bitter tide. Why is his life in ruins; what was his offense?

He is conscious of no sin, not the least sin of omission. He has taken to heart the moral instruction of the prophets; in his heart, in his behavior the love of God and of neighbor are one.

As he was instructed, so he has done, and so instructed others.

✦   ✦   ✦

The depth and range of Job's moral understanding!

His *apologia* is a sublime peak, a Himalaya of the Hebrew Bible.

Prophet among prophets, Job is also a lucid, ardent forerunner of Jesus and His ethic; "Love God and the neighbor as yourself; in this is summed up the law and the prophets." The summation is crucial, and quoted by all three synoptics (Matthew 19:16–19; Mark 12:28–34; Luke 10:25–28).

✦   ✦   ✦

Job's protestation of innocence has been compared with the Egyptian "Book of the Dead." In some respects the likeness is striking. But the Egyptian work is a liturgical text of set formulas; through its instruction one confessed to faults, reciting the magical formulas. Thus after death, one would win entrance to beatitude.

Job's confession is far different; it owes nothing to rote or prior text. No hint of ritual transgression, but a spontaneous account of conscience.

Job struggles against the dark will of God that beats him down. His protest rings through the book like the intoning of a bell of passing; why me, the innocent?

✦   ✦   ✦

> Midwife You were, You drew me
> out of the guts of my mother.
>
> Red as a budded rose I lay
> at Your breast and hers.
> You held me at knee, Your first born.
>
> Now my life is pure nightmare,
> my days a dance of death,
> nights a welter of beasts.
>
> They circle me, hem me in.
>
> Do I live? I lunge toward death
> Die? I am cast in the pit of Sheol
> My veins run in full flood,
> my bones are a random fall,
> my heart melts like a snow,
> my tongue a rattling gourd,
> hands, feet, a criminal prey—
> O save me, my Savior!
>
> As once You drew me
> from the womb of oblivion,
> bring to a second birth
> out of hell's guts, this hapless one! (Psalm 22)

✦ ✦ ✦

The literary form is a hypothetical "litany of curses" against himself; "If I have done such and such . . ." The sense invites a negative response; "I have not . . ."

The charges are launched, but they strike against a firm wall and ricochet off. Job's sense of innocence cannot be impugned, not for a moment, by no barrage of insult or imputation.

✦ ✦ ✦

So his sublime account of conscience begins with a kind of "pact." He enjoins care of his eyes, will yield before no carnal desire, even the most secret. In this he goes further than the Law, which forbade adultery (Exodus 20:14) and any attempt on a neighbor's spouse (Numbers 5:20–22).

✦ ✦ ✦

Jesus, we note, seizes on the delicacy of Job's conscience, and elevates it to a law;

> You have heard the commandment, "You shall not commit adultery."
>
> What I say to you is; Anyone who looks lustfully at a woman, has already committed adultery with her in his thoughts.
>
> If your right eye is your trouble, gouge it out and throw it away! (Matthew 5:27–29)

✦ ✦ ✦

31:5–12 Now to public sins. Let the following be known of him; he nas never cheated through use of false weights and measures.

(If he has, let his life be placed on a scale of justice, and weighed to the most exact, and exacting, measure!)

Never has he seized goods of another.

(If he is guilty of such, let others benefit from his labors, let them seize his increase!)

And as well, no adultery.

(If such, let a terrible curse fall—and on another than the delinquent. Let it fall on his wife. Let her be reduced to slavery— let her become a concubine!)

But what will be exacted of the adulterer? In a fiery image Job describes the outcome for the hypothetical guilty one, himself. Adultery is;

> a criminal offense, a fire burning
>
> down and down
> to Abaddon,
>
> consuming
> the roots
> of all my prospering (Job 31:11–12)

The image echoes Deuteronomy;

> By My wrath a fire is enkindled,
> that shall rage to the depths of the nether world,
>
> consuming the earth with its yield,
> licking with flames the roots of the mountains (32:22)

✦   ✦   ✦

31:13–15 And what of Job's rapport with servants, including handmaids? Has he regarded these in accord with the law, which keeps a solicitous eye on these vulnerable "neighbors"?

Job avers that he has so behaved; justly.

The motive goes deep. If he loves and cherishes servants, it is because he and they are drawn from the common clay of creation.

Is he master, are they servants? The distinctions are arbitrary; toss them aside. Human rankings and hierarchies, judgments as to worth—if these are made the basis of domination, they become sinful.

✦   ✦   ✦

Job's Midrash is beautifully elaborated, a borrowing from the imagery of Genesis.

Out of indistinguishable fine-grained earth, God has fashioned some to be servants, Job to be—Job.

The communality is everything; a lifeline, a mutuality. Of each it signifies, on each bestows dignity.

It is also the basis for responsibility on the part of the one appointed as master.

Let the need govern the response, the wound the healing. If some are vulnerable and at least relatively powerless, let Job be all the more conscious of justice and compassion.

With all his heart, he embraces the strict norms of justice repeatedly set down in the Law (Exodus 22:2 ff; Leviticus 25:39 ff; Deuteronomy 5:14 ff).

✦   ✦   ✦

Paul points to a similar communality of the faith, though his vision, like Job's, remains limited in scope (Ephesians 6:8, 9). According to him, too masters remain masters, slaves slaves;

> You know that each one, whether slave or free, will be repaid by God for whatever good is done.

> Masters, act similarly toward your slaves. . . . Remember that you and they have a Master in heaven who plays no favorites.

✦ ✦ ✦

More than the Law, above and beyond the Law, God is surety for the well-being of those at the bottom of the societal pyramid; slaves and servants.

✦ ✦ ✦

We take note in the regard, of God's dire word to Jeremiah; the word trembles with outrage.

An oath was uttered on behalf of the powerless, pledging to free the slaves in the Jubilee year.

Then the sworn promise was reneged on (Jeremiah 34:8–32); the masters renounced their sworn word.

Let them hear this;

> You changed your mind and profaned My name by taking back your male and female slaves, to whom you had given their freedom; you forced them once more into slavery.
>
> Therefore thus says God; you did not obey Me by proclaiming your neighbors and kinsmen free.
>
> I now proclaim you free; says God, free for the sword, famine and pestilence! . . . (Jeremiah 34:16–17)

✦ ✦ ✦

31:16–23 If I, Job, have violated justice in this or that way . . .

Principles are applied to the living; "the widow . . . the orphan . . . the poor." Examples illumine precepts, faces loom before Job, eyes scrutinize his behavior.

And what a strong heart beats on, bestowing clarity and right purpose!

✦ ✦ ✦

Job offers another analogy, immensely moving; Could I Job, in a time of prosperity eat my bread in satisfaction, while the hungry stood at the door? Could I so do, when from my childhood, God was father to me, from the hour of my birth guiding me aright?

As to the naked, let them speak; did not their loins bless me, as they warmed themselves with the fleece of my sheep?

A practical morality, an ethic firm grounded in this world, in this time, in these needy ones.

Did I raise my arm in anger against the innocent, knowing I could even summon a supporter, to supply an excuse for the vile deed?

I am in terror of God's glance upon such perfidy! If I did so, let that arm fall from its shoulder.

✦ ✦ ✦

31:24–28 Social injustice and idolatry; in prophetic teaching the two are intertwined, like convolvuluses of a poisoned vine (Jeremiah 7:1–11; Ezekiel 18:5–9). Entirely fitting then, that idolatry and socialized sin be placed side by side in Job's moral categories.

There is a subtle juncture here; in greed, did I worship gold? In secret, did I worship the golden sun, the splendid moon and stars?

> Had I put my trust
> in gold,
>
> named fine gold
> my security . . .
>
> Had I looked on the sun
> as it shone,

the moon on its course
in full glory

and I in secret
succumbed

and hand touched mouth
in a kiss . . .

that too would be criminal,
offensive—

I would have denied
God above (Job 31:24–28)

✦   ✦   ✦

In a poem of G. M. Hopkins a strikingly similar image occurs, but with a difference. The image is void of any tinge of nature—worship.

In "The Wreck of the Deutchsland";

I kiss my hand
To the stars, lovely—asunder Starlight, . . .

But the gesture is raised, not to nature-as-god, but to Christ;

. . . wafting him out of it; . . .

And the ecstasy mounts, the sky is literally the limit. Everything on high bespeaks Christ;

. . . and
Glow, glory in thunder;
Kiss my hand to the dappled-with-damson west;
Since, tho' he is under the world's splendour and wonder,
His mystery must be instressed, stressed; . . .

Beauty and majesty in nature leads beyond itself; it is "his mystery." In creation, the poet encounters that Word in accord with Whom all things come to be;

> For I greet him the days I meet him, and bless when I
> understand.

✦   ✦   ✦

Elsewhere too, Hopkins offers the same insight, effortless seeming (but what painstaking skill!), a modest tribute to a truth self-evident.

Nothing exists "on its own"; everything is openhanded-with, fecund-with, beautiful-with. Everything in creation offers analogies to the seeing eye, leads thought and heart's desire beyond;

Pied Beauty

All things counter, original, spare, strange;
Whatever is fickle, freckled (who knows how?)
With swift, slow; sweet, sour; adazzle, dim;
He fathers forth whose beauty is past change;
Praise him.

Hurrahing in Harvest

I walk, I lift up, I lift up heart, eyes,
Down all that glory in the heavens to glean our Saviour;
And eyes, heart, what looks, what lips yet gave you a
Rapturous love's greeting of realer, of rounder replies?

And the azurous hung hills are his world-wielding shoulder
Majestic—as a stallion stalwart, very-violet-sweet!—. . . .

✦ ✦ ✦

Job, one thinks, would understand. He knows, as does Hopkins, that is a "superior" form of greed. To worship sun and moon is to slaver over a heap of gold.

Idolatry blocks the soul, blinds.

To lose hold of analogy is to lose meaning itself.

Meaning is a hand placed in our hand, leading beyond.

✦ ✦ ✦

31:29–30 A further matter, hard and practical, arises.

Facing enmity and hatred, Job renounces the tactics of the adversaries who stand before him—or whatever others.

He will go further. He will take no pleasure in the misfortune of an opponent.

Let others curse an enemy; not he.

An admirably sound beginning, and a stark reversal of the world's ways.

In a fallen world, Job summons a fragile flowering—the human itself.

✦ ✦ ✦

We grieve. Centuries have passed since the era of great Job.

Another millennium has passed. And the flowering summoned by each of these supreme seers, Job, Isaiah, or Christ, has yet to occur. The world, by turns sere and frozen of spirit, is held in the grasp of a chief principality named death.

✦ ✦ ✦

Behold our cultural—better, our religious—plight in the U.S.; a superstate armed to the teeth with guns and cruise missiles and nuclear weapons. And worse horrors to come.

Hatred and the works of hatred are the norm, and love a lost art.

And yet, and yet. In the bristling face of "things as they are," "the world, the way it goes," Christ lays down a gauntlet, gently, firmly;

> You have heard the commandment, you shall love your countryman but hate your enemy.
>
> My command to you is; love your enemies, pray for your persecutors.
>
> This will prove you are sons and daughters of your heavenly Father, for His sun rises on the bad and the good, He rains on the just and the unjust (Matthew 5:43–45).

✦   ✦   ✦

The Promise is of both light and darkness, reward and dishonor, unmasking and shame.

Some, the martyrs, will appear at the feast of the Realm of God, their clothing drenched in blood.

And others will be cast into "external darkness," blood on their hands.

Meantime, we live through the awful crepuscular "meantime," the closing years of an unspeakably ensanguined era.

Everything we cherish, every institution we were once taught to believe would cherish and sustain us—education, medicine, workplace, most of all the "protective cover" of the military—these are transformed, some in degree, some utterly, unrecognizably.

Severally they turn neutral, no longer serving human need; they grow self-contained, self-centered.

Or they turn hostile—or murderous.

And a desperate need arises; that the teaching of Job and Isaiah and Jesus be rescued, hearkened to, taken seriously.

As in the example of the Plowshares activists, whose "crime" was this; they took the teaching seriously.

✦ ✦ ✦

31:31–32 The absurd allegations of Eliphaz against Job—

> To the thirsty
> you have given
> no water to drink,
>
> and from the hungry
> you have withheld bread . . . (Job 22:7)

—and so on, and so on; the litany of untruths rankles in the breast of Job. It is as though the father of lies, ha-Satan, had taken possession of the tongue of this "friend."

Job must repossess the truth; his honor is due no less.

Therefore say it plain; his household will testify that tent and table were open to all;

> Indeed the men
> of my clan said;
>
> "Who has not been fed
> with his meats?"
>
> No stranger
> must pass the night
> out of doors;
>
> I opened my tent
> to wayfarers (Job 31:31–32)

✦ ✦ ✦

31:33–34 We near the end of Job's appeal and (what relief!) of his harrassment as well.

Despite all, his spirit remains unbroken. His self-knowledge is like an undistorted mirror. He holds it up, looks in his soul and discovers no defect, no cause for shame or concealment.

See then, his travails are endured in public, before all.

Let rumors fly, those birds of ill omen. Let friends and enemies judge his cause as they will; his conscience is untrammeled.

✦ ✦ ✦

31:35–37 Proudly he will turn the shame around. He will wear his enemies' indictment like a diadem, walk firmly toward God, a prince approaching a king.

✦ ✦ ✦

And what of God? The Deity plays a double, ironic role.

God who is "my adversary," who from on high (let us not forget) plays hobs with Job's well-being, with his very survival—this God is also a God of love.

Live with the irony, Job! God decrees the testing, and God preserves your spirit, firm and unbroken.

✦ ✦ ✦

Why then (we too raise the question)—why? why these insults, this scorn, why is Job beaten down, why are health and possessions and loved ones snatched from him, and he reduced to a near nothing?

✦   ✦   ✦

The question beats on, as though it were the tormented cry of time itself.

And the response? Only a vast silence, no heed paid, for Job's sake or our own.

✦   ✦   ✦

And we reflect (and the thought brings no relief, quite the opposite)—there cannot but be—silence. This Providence is dark as a cave's mouth, opaque against all questioning.

The testing—is.

As God—is.

And the testing of Job is an image, socialized, perennial, of God's behavior toward us as well—toward all.

Dare we yield before that Will, confessing that dire events are aimed like a cloud of arrows, to this purpose, the awakening of the godly in us?

Or shall the testing create the ungodly in us?

Misfortune can do either. Ha-Satan himself, it is said, was tested, failed, became the ungoldly one.

Job will be reminded of these matters. In due time.

✦   ✦   ✦

32:1–36 And at long last, the chorus of friends withdraw.

Their reason for the exit is obscure—and perhaps fruitfully so.

Do they end their dudgeonous vigil because Job appeared as just "in his own eyes," because no argument of theirs could shake his will?

Or has Job won them over, they seeing him at last, as just "in their own eyes"?

Either way, after the interventions, wearying, abstract, ill-tempered, interminable, silence is indeed golden.

✦　✦　✦

The silence, alas, is a brief respite.

And we are astonished once more.

It appears that a fourth member of the vigilers has entered the scene.

Or perhaps all the while he has stood there?

In any case, one cannot but note his enormous self-restraint. This Elihu has kept silent, on the sidelines of event and speech.

The arguments went pro and con; he stood by patiently.

Now at length, he must burst out;

> I am full
> of matters to utter,
>
> the spirit within
> compels me.
>
> Like a new wineskin,
> its wine under pressure,
>
> my bosom
> is filled to bursting! (Job 32:18–19)

✦　✦　✦

Let us grant it; Elihu has the tribute youth owes to age and experience.

But presently—do his ears deceive him—does he hear aright, the trio of jurors has decided to wind matters up, to allow the "case of Job" to rest?

It is beyond bearing!

Is Job then to prevail, even by implication, as though there remained no argument to counter and crush him?

As though indeed Job, not God, were in the right?

By main force, Elihu thrusts himself into the text, another purported advocate of the Deity.

Impetuous, a bit foolish, his tied tongue all but exploding, he demands a hearing.

✦   ✦   ✦

Elihu, redoubtable.

Grant it; wisdom has failed the elders.

Let youth thrust itself into the fray!

Six chapters of the book are handed over to this rhetorical genius.

✦   ✦   ✦

And we yield; give him place.

The wisdom cultivated in Israel, we are told, was a formidable achievement, a composite of reflection, experience, and the distilled sagacity of the Orient.

This, together with the acknowledgment that Divine Wisdom is preeminent over human, and that the Gift of God may be granted or withheld, no reason adduced.

✦   ✦   ✦

For a start, Elihu grants much to his compatriots.

Then he proceeds to demolish them.

His discourse, truth told, is—windy, sesquipedalian.

Let us foreshorten his theme, which comes to this; let wisdom be heard from, that charism depending not at all on shaky pillars of age or experience.

This wisdom resides in—himself.

✦   ✦   ✦

33:1–8 What ho! He is about to speak!

> Behold now, I open my mouth,
>
> my tongue and my lips
> form words (Job 33:1–3)

He is both arrogant and inept of speech. *En garde*, Job!

> If you are able,
> refute me;
>
> draw up your arguments,
> stand forth! (Job 33:5)

And some 29 verses follow, an airy interminable exordium to be sure—wordy, pretentious, offering little or nothing of substance.

What a contrast!

The vanished trio were a formidable congress, the baiting and hectoring of Job marked by enormous skill, tropes, and images apt, telling, now and again sublime.

But here—pedantry and bravado. Adversary Elihu is flat of foot and tedious of mind.

chapter nine

"God Is Great, and Who Job, Are You?"
(33:9–37:24)

Remember

Because we remember,
let us dismember
the demon-haunted will.
Because we remember,
let us bind up
wounds we never dealt.

Unbungled, courageous,
birth and second birth—

a thighbone
wreathed in its laurel flesh
walks on and on.
Toward.

Alive, remembering,
incandescent, soul.

Toward.

DB

✦ ✦ ✦

33:9–11 At last Elihu shows his hand.

He has the gravest objections against Job's plaint. He, Elihu, will quote, only to refute.

And what we are hearing, one thinks, does not greatly differ from prior objectors and arguments.

This is it that rubs wrong; the insufferable claim of Job, his clinging to an illusion of innocence and integrity.

The rub festers, and the wrong as well.

Who can claim innocence before God, we humans being an essentially flawed lot?

✦ ✦ ✦

33:12–30 Bolster the argument, shore it up strongly.

No "explanation" of the ways of God can be rightfully sought. Life in this world is a proving, a testing on the part of the utterly Other. No one of Whose decisions can be called in question.

Far from us be such presumption!

God allows for two ways of warning and turning us around. The first is through dreams and nocturnal visions.

The second, the way of suffering and loss, is of far greater important—and longer dwelt on by our speechifying savant.

Suffering and loss; opaque means to be sure.

But wait; the one who suffers is not alone;

> He finds
> at his side
> an angel,
>
> one
> out of a thousand,
> a mediator
> to show his duty,

to take pity,
to declare;

"Deliver him
from the pit of hell,

I have found
a ransom
for his life" (Job 33:22–24)

✦   ✦   ✦

And, for a change, we are on serious ground, and inclined to take our monologist seriously.

This original angel of his! We had not thought Elihu capable of imagining so grand and majestic a creature—let alone of announcing the angelic designs.

Designs the angel surely has, and on such as Job, to be sure—duties, helps, as well as required hindrances.

✦   ✦   ✦

Elihu proceeds to enumerate these.

The angel will cast light on travails that otherwise appear absurd, senseless.

He will open the eyes (of such as Job) to delicts long hidden, and intercede for him before God.

✦   ✦   ✦

The present angel is in good company, and ample. Forerunners and kin appear in both the Hebrew and Christian Bible.

Ezekiel and Zachariah celebrate the angelic intercessions.

The psalmist sings of their protection (91:11–13).

In both testaments, angels bring the prayer of humans before God (Tobit 5:4; 12:12; Revelation 8:3 ff.).

And more; our Scripture testifies to angelic guardians (Matthew 18:10; Acts 12:15).

✦   ✦   ✦

Quite an angel, and quite a success story follows!

The reasoning would seem to go like this. The word of the good angel reveals the truth of sin and repentance. If one (Job, to be sure) hearkens to that word, all will be well!

Nothing new, we think; the old semi-magical sequence. Repent, and (repeat) all will be well!

✦   ✦   ✦

Young Elihu, it appears, is at one with the former trio of necromancers. Each is a great speller-out of the "good life" sure to follow chastisement of the delinquent (sic)—if only he confess;

> Then his flesh
> shall become soft as a boy's;
>
> he shall again be
> as in the days of his youth (Job 33:25)

Has Elihu taken note of the sores that lie like a stigma on Job? In any case, the youth promises physical healing, surely no small matter to the afflicted one.

But more than this. Like the others, Elihu is a would-be doctor of the soul. Only let Job submit, and God's favor will shine on him once more;

> He shall pray
> and God will favor him;

> with rejoicing
> he shall see God's face (Job 33:26)

It never fails to astonish, this assurance.

We have seen it repeatedly in the pronunciamentos of the famed trio.

Their version of reality; God and creation form together a precise team, Engineer and engine, premise and consequence. Thus is the moral universe constructed, thus does it function.

Job disagrees, vehemently, feverishly.

Show him; what logic rules his predicament?

Better still, let him be! Imitate the trio of friends, withdraw from the fray!

But Elihu will not give up. Job is intellectually muzzy, he complicates and fabricates; prisoner of feeling and mood, he tinkers with an essentially faultless universe.

✦   ✦   ✦

The trio have vanished, but the memory lingers on. And more than memory. Expanded to a quaternity, Elihu and friends strike one as strangely modern in spirit, a clutch of born-again believers.

We too have heard the incontravertable message; only repent, confess to the Savior, and all will be well with you.

And what, one asks, of the human community?

We note the omission, deliberate, enormously significant.

✦   ✦   ✦

What of the world of humans? This is the question of Job, not of his interlocutors.

What of the God who "so loved the world as to give His only Son . . ."(John 3:16). And who presumably, abides in that love—even as wickedness perdures through the centuries, and the code of Job and Isaiah, so compassionate, insistant on justice and charity, is spurned, violated.

That world, perennially echoing the tormented cries of Job. And seemingly empty. The silence of God.

✦　✦　✦

The human community, created in the image of God?

Dare we modify the image? Dare we say; created in the image of Job? And thereby Godly?

✦　✦　✦

33:31–33 Elihu is nothing if not—cocky, a long-winded sage, vast stores of wisdom at his disposal.

Let him then freely instruct!

And let Job for his part be silent. Chastened, let him receive instruction gratefully.

Or perhaps Job wishes to speak? Elihu seems wary, unsure of himself;

> Be attentive,
> O Job,
> listen to me.
>
> Keep silence.
> I have much to speak.
>
> Or
> if you have aught to say,
> answer me.
>
> Speak out.
> I would have you justified.

If not,
then listen to me.

Be silent,
while I teach you wisdom (Job 33:31–33)

One imagines Job in face of this barrage. Shall he dignify the
occasion, deigning to answer? Shall he keep silence, as urged?
Either course is humiliating.

The effrontery of the youth takes one's breath away.

He goes the trio one better; he would push a shallow "wisdom" at Job. At one whose dire suffering has made him
supremely wise.

✦ ✦ ✦

What constrasts! The foray of Elihu, his ploy of infalliblity,
his stupifying speeches, serve only to heighten the moral greatness of Job.

Job must suffer a fool—if not gladly, then gently, and at wearying length.

✦ ✦ ✦

34:1–6 No one escapes the punishing whip, the rodomontade.
Elihu turns his basilisk eye on the trio, who by inference are still
present, listening in silence.

In effect, they have failed, have yielded the contest to Job.

Shame! they fail to vindicate the justice of God, so wantonly
assailed.

Elihu then, must take up the cudgels.

In this wise. It violates sanity and faith, that God be casti-
gated as unjust. For is our God not the Fabricator of creation
and the Sustainer of all beings, the God of Providence, all-
powerful and all-knowing?

✦   ✦   ✦

So far so good. Yes.

But, but (and Elihu sputters with dismay)—then the pernicious reasoning of Job intervenes. According to him, other considerations loom large. He would diminish the sovereign One, introducing analogies. God's activity must be compared with merely human behavior.

He would even dare hail God into an earthly court!

Is the Holy then, to be indicted by the likes of him?

Let Job take serious note. Such tactics are a subterfuge, an attempt on the part of a delinquent (unnamed, but as previously, close-resembling yourself)—an attempt to avoid the truth of the situation; sin, and the call to repentance.

✦   ✦   ✦

34:7–12 Elihu overreaches himself. He likens Job to a mocker, one who lives as though God did not exist, in scorn of religious truth.

The indictment is broadened. In wickedness like seeks like; the Jobian complainers are legion;

> Job
> drinks in blasphemies
> like water,
>
> keeps company
> with evildoers
>
> goes along
> with wicked men (Job 34:7–8)

Such as these, we note, are often condemned in wisdom literature;

Arrogant is the name
for the man of overbearing pride
who acts with scornful effrontery (Proverbs 21:24)

✦   ✦   ✦

The rhetoric of abuse is in full play. Elihu speaks as though a
jury of peers were present, as though a judge granted or sub-
tracted points to this or that attorney. In sum, a mere contest of
wits is in progress, independent of, indifferent to the truth of
whatever assertion.

The punishing rigorist strikes hard and quick, this Elihu; and
all, be it noted, for the greater glory of (his) God.

But whether his God corresponds to the God of the prophets,
or more nearly, to the God of Job, this must remain moot.

✦   ✦   ✦

Whose God, Job's? Elihu's?

If Elihu's, our world is monochromatic, post-lapsarian, with
no relief in prospect. No color, no verve, small hope. We stand,
we fall, under the judgment of a merciless deity, whose heart is
hard as diamond, who loves not the work of His hands.

For Christians, faith eviscerated of its central event. In effect,
no Incarnation, no consequence; hope, wild, viable, visible, tac-
tile. The palpable God, and we, coming alive;

What we have heard,
what we have seen with your eyes,

what we have looked upon
and our hands have touched—

we speak of the word of Life.

This life became visible;
we have seen
and bear witness to this . . . (1 John 1:1–2)

✦ ✦ ✦

The debate might be likened to the brushfire of history itself, fanned by winds of special interest, bigotry, domination, contempt.

Fanned as well by winds of holiness and heroism.

Whose God? The god of Elihu, or the God of saints and martyrs?

The conflagration is never extinguished. It burns and burns; we humans are its pyrotechnists—and its tinder.

✦ ✦ ✦

In the eyes of his adversaries, Job's contesting with God is unacceptable, scandalous, combustable.

The fire rages, a destroyer. Like a stallion from heaven or hell, the flames leap boundaries, destroy all in their path. A fiery leveling, smoke and ash.

Then mysteriously, under smoke and ash the world springs to life once more.

✦ ✦ ✦

As for Elihu, throughout the centuries since his epiphany here, the intemperate objector has attracted a legion of disciples—and when required, rigorous defenders.

Today too, they turn a stern face to Jobian sufferers. They poke about in lives, utter innuendos and covert accusations.

Where there's fire, there must be inflammatory material. Look to yourself, you afflicted with AIDS, you homeless poor . . .

✦ ✦ ✦

In sum, to the Elihus in our midst, the Fall, not the Incarnation, stands pivotal to our history.

Human evil stops God short, God's forgiveness and reconciliation. The Jobs? they languish there amid the detritus of their lives, unforgiven and unreconciled.

Worse; the Jobs are unable to forgive and reconcile; with God, with others. With those who would save them from their worst enemies; themselves.

✦ ✦ ✦

Given the ironbound suppositions, given the god of ferule and strict logic, a god who concedes to ha-Satan so large, even so prevailing a place in the human heart, in the heart of the world—given all this, our tribe is indeed a rich soil for the archeologists of evil. The dig yields a hundredfold.

✦ ✦ ✦

34:13–32 Confronting, rebuking the passionate outcry of Job, who must undergo the rigors of the God he addresses—we have the bloodless dispassionate theodicy of Elihu.

The youth lives solely in the mind. It is a walled place, without light or air or access to the world.

He has discarded his heart somewhere; he grants it, a traitor, no place. No place as well to the feelings, those meandering enticing tempters!

Elihu is like a plowboy in a field, following a team of horses in harness. Arms and eyes steady as a quadrant, in a square field in the round world, he plods on confident. Back, forward, right angles, row upon straight row. Life is like this!

✦ ✦ ✦

His reasoning is tight, airless, parched, his logic irrefutable.
And he is wrong.

✦ ✦ ✦

Would Job deny for instance, the assertion of Elihu that God
gives to no other the governance of creation?

Or that an all-knowing, all-powerful God is of necessity a
just God?

And what of this, closer to the present contention; does Job
dare tax Providence with an accusation of injustice?

Does Job imply that the moral universe is incoherent, enig-
matic, unguessable?

To Elihu's understanding, he does.

✦ ✦ ✦

Let us grant the youth his due; he is in good company, his
reasoning is consonant with that of the Sages;

> Indeed before You, the universe is as a grain of sand,
>
> scarce able to tip a pair of scales,
> or a drop of dew on the morning ground.
>
> But You have mercy on all
> because You are all-powerful,
>
> You overlook the sin of humans,
> that they might repent.
>
> For You love all things that exist,
> and loath nothing of what You have made;

for what You hated,
You would not have fashioned.

And how could something remain in existence,
unless You willed it,

or be preserved,
were it not called forth by You? (Wisdom 11:22–25)

✦ ✦ ✦

Elihu is correct; an all-knowing, all-powerful God implies a just God as well.

Only thus is the universe governed by—sanity, and ourselves by moral responsibility.

Then, but then; Elihu raises the stakes. He magnifies like a thunderhead instances, images—God, in despite of the evasive wicked, judging equably all comers; the high and mighty, the nobodies.

But the thunder dies on the air, the examples fall short.

His instances are heartless as a thunder.

They grant nothing to Job's afflictions.

If Job is taken seriously in his claim of innocence (and by Elihu he is not taken seriously), then the counter-argument— that only the wicked suffer—falls to pieces.

✦ ✦ ✦

For *in casu*, there must be thought to coexist in the world two radical incompatibles; a God of justice, and the suffering innocents.

✦ ✦ ✦

Making Something

The blind man
longed passionately to see,
but wish was vain
while dawn delayed—
a false savior, no sight
from that miraculous store.

The cripple dreamed
dancers and tumblers all night long; at dawn
lay there, dumb
as the world's wood or winter,
no volcanic man.

Tears are an only poem.
I spread out
like a blind fakir, on the mat of the mind
sorry magic;
two scored stones for eyes,
broken sticks for limbs;

for man—
sans eyes, sans hands, a century's
empty locust shell.

For oracle, only
"be content, be like."

DB

✦   ✦   ✦

Is the suffering of the just willed by God? Or is the affliction merely allowed by God?

In the breach, in Job's predicament, the distinction seems meaningless.

His question remains, we are never rid of it. The arguments multiplied by Elihu and his cohorts help not a whit.

✦   ✦   ✦

It haunts, it scalds the heart, then and now. To presume that the question is laid to rest by adroit arguers, that they have "clarified" the moral universe, have mitigated the plight of the innocent (or are we to conclude with these rigorists that there exist no innocents, then or now?)—this, one thinks, is in plain denial of the evidence of one's own eyes.

✦   ✦   ✦

To this day and hour, the race of Job abounds in multitudes across the world. To them, life is pure horror. Disasters multiply, in nature, in war, in the ruinous greed of empires, in war and seizures, in loss of possessions, health, loved ones, life itself.

The plight is hardly lightened or wounds healed, by the sweet or bitter talk of theological theorists.

✦   ✦   ✦

Happy the one You raise up
to esteem Your law;
evil days, will they touch him?
The wicked—
their thoughts are a mockery; this God
sees nothing, hears nothing, says nothing!

They carry their heads on high,
they weave cunning words. To hear them talk
oppression, warmongering
greed, duplicity—these were noble endeavors!
In their kangaroo courts, the just
stand condemned out of hand.
"Law and Order!" they cry—
lawless they are, disorder their skill.
God of strict requital, judge them,
lest they prevail forever—torturers, liars,
mockers, mimics of justice
piling their booty
on the bowed backs of the poor . . .
There is One who speaks for me,
One who judges in justice;

Does an evil snare all but trip me?—
He is there, rescuer, consoler, friend (Psalm 94)

✦   ✦   ✦

34:33–37 Nothing daunted, Elihu charges on. Does Job presume to judge God; and thereby to play god?

Should God requite
as you see fit?

But
you have despised Him (Job 34:33)

And worse; Job adds insult to injury;

To his sin
he adds rebellion,

> brushing off
> our arguments,
>
> multiplying statements
> against God (Job 34:37)

Thus the just one stands accused of hardness of heart; his conscience is impermeable, adamant against conversion.

Add to physical and psychic losses this final accusation; Job chooses to stand outside the domain of the saved.

Indeed God has provided him with occasions of grace—(presumably the four friends?) These are the "men of understanding," the "wise ones" summoned by Elihu.

All in vain. Job rejects them. He stands in the realm of darkness.

✦   ✦   ✦

35:1–16 Onward, relentlessly onward, Elihu presses his lengthy monologue. He will refute Job—and the three interlocutors as well.

Words, words—in face of the silence of Job.

Elihu hardly pauses for breath, never wondering in a kind of awe; what might that silence mean?

Scorn, default, concession?

No matter, to this human battering ram.

✦   ✦   ✦

You. Job. Your justice or sinfulness holds little or no interest to God. Such matters affect only your fellow travelers.

And forebear saying—

> God sees
> nothing of my case,

which lies
open before Him.

With trembling
should you wait upon Him

✦   ✦   ✦

We are bewildered; is "waiting" not the chief occupation of
the stricken one, indeed the only one?
Is any other possible to him?

✦   ✦   ✦

Since Job drastically falls short of Elihu's estimate of a just
one, a question occurs; What form would his "ideal Job" take?
Elihu and his cohorts suggest the form rather consistently;
the paragon would resemble—themselves.

✦   ✦   ✦

The case closes like a dossier, the claim is proven.
They are the ideal humans, these logicians. For them, God,
omniscient, omnipotent, just, presents no problems, no ambiguity, no darkness.
For them the creation, as constructed and conducted, makes
perfect sense. For them (how often we have heard it!) an impermeable logic governs human life; virtue is blessed of God, crime
brings punishment in its wake.
And the logic is applied, like a branding iron upon flesh. Job
suffers loss and torment, therefore Job must be guilty. Let him
look to it.
Does he refuse to look to it? Then he is twice cursed; in this
life and in prospect of another.

✦ ✦ ✦

36:1–4 Elihu continues to bewilder us.

A blunderbuss for tongue, mightily confident and self-commended, he abruptly takes aim at Job's contention and suffering.

Then—Fire!

In his own eyes, his presence is strictly providential.

Even as he angers us, he intrigues.

✦ ✦ ✦

36:5–15 Now for a windy resume of familiar arguments; God seeks the conversion of sinners. Once a change of heart is evident and sincere, punishment is withdrawn, the quondam sinner is restored in possessions and preferments.

✦ ✦ ✦

36:16–20 A mutilated text allows minimal light.

Has Elihu borrowed a leaf from his predecessors? The text wobbles, its theme can only be conjectured.

But it would seem to imply a rehashing of old charges made by Zophar (Job 20) and in more detail by Eliphaz (Job 22).

The attack is outrageously vindictive, empty of all evidence.

The charges; Job is guilty of sins of omission, committed in a thoughtless heyday;

> Once
> your prosperity
> was boundless,
> your table groaned.
>
> But you ignored
> matters of injustice,
> paid no heed
> to the rights of orphans . . .

✦ ✦ ✦

36:21 No doubts surround this verse, or its meaning. The theme of the famous trio, driven home at great length, is restated briefly. Once more, a throttling logic governs Job's plight.

Stated flat out or venomously implied; no mystery exists under the sun. None surrounds the sorrows of Job. Only apply the power of the mind; correct reasoning "explains" God's action.

As for Job, let him repent at last;

> For the future,
> avoid conduct
> that breeds injustice—
>
> the root and reason
> of your travail (Job 36:21)

✦ ✦ ✦

36:22–37:24 The extended hymn to wisdom follows. Its majestic tone, the wisdom implied in the hymning of wisdom, such sagacity laid to so lofty a theme!

Both subject and style would seem on the face of it, beyond our youth Elihu.

Does so ardent, even recondite a song lie seemly on brash lips?

Prior to this utterance, he had seemed oversure of himself, contemptuous of the greatness before him.

Now suddenly, he is transformed. The narrow accusational mode vanishes, a diaphenous spirit of celebration, even of ecstasy, seizes on him, tongue and soul.

✦ ✦ ✦

It is as though the callow logician were possessed by a sibyl of the wisdom he invokes.

Praise the wondrous deeds of God! Those "deeds," not of liberation (Job has scarcely been "delivered"), but of creation itself.

Still, we note; the finger continues to wag, a metronome of guilt before Job' face.

The hymn bears an instruction for (the likes of) him;

> Who
> is to prescribe
> God's conduct,
>
> who to dare say;
> You have done wrong!
>
> Rather,
> you should extol His work,
> which everywhere
> is praised in song (Job 36:23–24)

Which of course Job has "extolled," "praised," with surpassisng skill and at great length.

✦ ✦ ✦

What holds the eye here is a spiral of mystery, whirling up and up.

The word of God on the lips of Elihu. He declares that the word of God lies beyond human scope. Therefore beyond the scope of such as Job, not to speak of lesser mortals.

Still, the "beyond" does not forbid a certain access; one approaches the "burning bush that is not consumed"—though surely in fear and trembling.

Thus Job's questioning is put in context; he searches for access, ever so slowly, timorously, approaches the Mystery.

◆　◆　◆

To the afflicted one, the matter is simple. He must so live, must attempt access to God. Or he dies before death.

The access, the light that extinguishes darkness—this is his birthright, the dignity of this Suffering Servant;

> I God have called you for the victory of justice . . .

> I have grasped you by the hand;

> I formed you and set you
> as a covenant for the people,
> a light for the nations,

> to open the eyes of the blind,
> to bring out prisoners from confinement,
> and from the dungeon, those who live in darkness
> (Isaiah 42:6, 7)

◆　◆　◆

An atrocious fate has brought Job down.

Then something else, something beyond imagining, pure gift.

A vocation is bestowed on him. The hand of God that brought him low has other designs, other skills—for Job (for ourselves, we dare hope).

He is anointed, an Abraham of the spirit. Chosen, the father of a vast tribe.

The hand that withheld mercy to Job (but only for a time)— that hand will draw the least and lowliest, the offscouring of earth, the victims and martyrs, into stature, grandeur and glory.

This is the apotheosis, the summons, the vocation; first

offered in the very withholding, to Job.

And on and on; to the Jobs of our tribe, on whom salvation rests, though with a hand of iron. On those who bear the gift through time.

The gift of the cross.

✦ ✦ ✦

And what of the arguments, the charges and stipulations and innuendos? They fall away like tissues in a storm of rain.

They were useful, those harriers and their verbiage, to this degree; they tested, weighed, probed, shamed, denigrated, usurped, lacerated.

And finally, contrary to design and dark skill, they verified the greatness of Job.

✦ ✦ ✦

What a gift!

At whatever cost, under whatever frown of disapproval, Job plods on. He must learn why he, a just man, undergoes grevious loss.

Undeniably he is stubborn and self-willed.

Granted. But God has not forbidden the questioning, even as He permitted the torment. Let Job proceed. His queries neither violate nor cheapen the Mystery.

Cheapening, violating—these are the vain works of his friends, as they attempt in vanity of spirit, to "explain" the One Who admits of no explanation, no onset of mere, sere, "right reason."

✦ ✦ ✦

Thus the dilemma, the delicate, all-but-impossible balance demanded of Job.

On the one hand, no human intervention assuages. He is

bidden simply to submit before the Mystery; It lies beyond the scope of humans, beyond his probing faith, his sublime poetry.

And yet does God not invite Moses to approach the "Bush"? Isaiah (30:13) echoes the wonderment;

> Who has directed the spirit of God?
> Who has played counselor of God?

✦ ✦ ✦

Paul takes up the theme; God is the One who dwells "beyond"—but not so distant as to deny all access.

Indeed, such denial would offer a blank page to believing, seeking eyes. Our Scripture would be a blank scroll.

The hymn is an invitation. Come, you who believe, approach the burning Bush—but warily, in fear and trembling;

> How deep are the riches and the wisdom
> and the knowledge of God!
>
> how inscrutable those judgments,
> how unsearchable those ways!
>
> For who has known the mind of God,
> or who has been God's counselor?
> Who has given God something,
> so as to deserve return? (Romans 11:33–35)

✦ ✦ ✦

It is as though these great ones, from Isaiah to Paul, were admonishing Job (and ourselves)—you are on holy ground, dangerous terrain. Be mindful, go slowly, prayerfully, in fear. Walk in a spirit that acknowledges scope and limit.

You are not to play god before God.

The friends of Job, for their part offer no right way.

But neither are you to play dumb. As though in despite of
Job, you accepted the inference of the "friends"; that you must
willy nilly venerate their mechanistic god, their inductions, the
guilt they would tar you with.

As though by reason of fear or loathing or self-abasement—
or large doses of each—you must abandon the quest for light.

"No" to them.

✦　✦　✦

For sake of a greater "Yes."

The "Wisdom" celebrated by Elihu is yours, Job. It is justified
by the quest itself. Even as It is conferred by the quest.

Come then, warm yourself at the Bush. In the flare of that
Mystery, compose a better text than the adversaries'. Better, more
truthful, more in accord with the heart's deep stirrings.

✦　✦　✦

A double mind be far from me,
I love Your commands,
my hope is Your promise.

A lying tongue be far from me,
I love Your promise,
my hope is Your law.

Far from me a double will,
Your will is my hope,
I love Your commands.

To witness Your law,
to love Your commands
be my first love (Psalm 119)

✦ ✦ ✦

This holy Wisdom, how praise It?

It pervades nature, it is the soul of visible creation. It is the measure of wind and rain and snow, ample and unexcessive, of tempest and frost as well, of the passsing seasons, day and night.

These offer rich analogies, metaphors, images of the One who is secretly at work in and through creation.

"Secretly" is the operative word. Wisdom is inscrutable, impartial. It is also shot through and through with goodness.

✦ ✦ ✦

How rankling is the alleged offense of Job! Elihu again hints at it, and more than hints.

Job attempts fruitlessly to penetrate the divine Will; worse, he would call God to an accounting.

Elihu is mortally offended;

> Shaddai!
> We cannot discover Him,
>
> preeminent
> in power and judgment;
>
> great Justice owes no one
> an accounting (Job 37:23)

And he ends with a doxology, an implied rebuke;

> Therefore fear God;
>
> to God,
> the veneration
> of the wise (Job 37:24)

✦ ✦ ✦

And we breathe deep. The lengthy attempt to refute, indeed
to convert Job, comes at last to a close.

Nothing has been resolved. The four have spoken, then they
step back, frozen in place.

Familiar tactics have abounded; abuse, denial, overbearing
rhetoric.

Still at times, they have summoned images of a vast grandeur—such images of God remain seductive through the ages.

✦ ✦ ✦

Their God, irrefutably set in time and place, summons an
image; an iron deity upon an iron throne.

He is judge, an inscrutable overseer of creation, surpassing
beyond measure the law to which humans are bound.

✦ ✦ ✦

But Job is adamant. No such god.

He will question God, or die; it is that simple. And his God
will submit to being questioned, though He denies all response.

Job's heroic purpose is torn from his throat, it lives and
breathes on the winds of time. Echoed and amplified to a great
cry, the voice of multitudes of victims and martyrs. Why must
the innocent go under, the guilty prosper?

Why must Job's torment become a social, generational, com-
manding image of the fate of humans?

We are never done with this questing of Job, with his unflag-
ging, faithful heart. He haunts our days and nights, tormenting,
strengthening, whispering; let ill circumstance rage, do not fall
prey to dumb acceptance.

Cry aloud to that Enemy and Friend, cry against Him!

And so be renewed. Dare one say; reborn?

✦ ✦ ✦

I will cry to Thee and cry to Thee and cry to Thee,
until the milk of Thy kindness boils up.

(Rumi, Sufi poet)

✦ ✦ ✦

That cry of Job.

It rants aloud in the pages of Revelation, all but tearing the page to rags. The Lamb has broken the fifth seal;

> I saw under the altar the souls of those who had been martyred because of the witness they bore to the word of God.
>
> They cried out in a loud voice; How long O Master holy and true, before you judge our cause and avenge our blood . . .
>
> Each of the martyrs was given a long white robe; and they were told to be patient a little while longer until the number was filled of their sisters and brothers, to be killed as they had been (Revelation 6:9–11).

It is all there, from Job to the third millennium, the like pattern; the outcry of faith, the silence of God.

✦ ✦ ✦

38–41 How far we have come, we and our God, from the opening scene, craven and secretive as it was, public before all save Job.

The game! It made of just Job a hostage to ego-on-high, giving free rein to the malice of ha-Satan.

We have come so far, we and Job! Toward the end of the narrative, a far different Jawe takes center stage.

His rejoinder to Job and the trio is majestic, replete with thundering intuitions, a poetry beyond praise.

Deliberation and forethought are supposed; a central issue, previously obscured, is summoned, revealed. How does God regard the version of God offered by Job, how the contrary image of the friends? Whose God speaks from the whirlwind?

✦   ✦   ✦

From one point of view, God's monologue is a nonresponse, beside the point of Job's plaint.

As though God meant to imply; your questions remain. You and your descendants are free to raise them again and again, as long as time endures. As I, Jawe, am free; free in My refusal to respond, to unveil the Mystery.

To your "Why?" there is no answer. There is only the burning bush.

✦   ✦   ✦

Thus the dilemma and its anguish abide.

Thus the book of Job approaches its end. Job suffers, he speaks at length, is restored in health and goods, and dies.

So by all accounts do the friends die. As for their world, which is our own, Fallen—that world continues its bloodshot, bloodletting way. For century upon century, Mars lays claim to humans. Under his chariot the innocent perish, war following on war, a monstrous folly unending.

And yes, in distempered nature, plague and flood and quake tear the fabric of earth and air to a shambles.

✦   ✦   ✦

All this. What you Job, endured in the flesh, in loss and death, in suspicion and contempt—these mount and multiply, a plague, a fearsome social reality.

The world of Job is our world. It expands to a vast abattoir; multitudes have no other fate than suffering, no credential but their wounds. Have no name but—Job.

✦   ✦   ✦

And what thoughtful human would not be appalled, not be led to question such a world, and its God—if God there indeed be?

But the "if" must immediately be modified. It is a gloss on the text; it cannot be laid to Job.

Let the condition be applied elsewhere; to the god of the indomitable quaternity; "if" their god exists.

How can we not, in face of the God of the whirlwind, the God of Job, not doubt the existence of their god, the meticulous, overbearing judge of the living, the deuteronomic metronomic god, this magister of sere logic?

Doubt on, one thinks—and all to the good!

chapter ten

Out of the Whirlwind; "Where Job, Were You?" (38:1–41:34)

I lift my eyes to You
my help, my hope

the heavens
(who could imagine?)
the earth
(only our God!)

the infinite starry spaces,
the world's teeming breadth—

all this. I lift my eyes
—upstart, delighted—
and I praise.

—Psalm 121

✦　✦　✦

38:1–21 In the here and now, in time and this world self-revealed at last, is the Deity.

The Hasid
hears the voice of becoming

> roaring in the gorges
> and feels the seed of eternity
> in the ground of time,
> as though it were in his blood.
>
> And so
> he can never think otherwise
> than this moment and now.
> This
> will be the chosen moment.

(Martin Buber, *Hasidism and Modern Man*)

✦ ✦ ✦

How far removed we are, in the God of the whirlwind, from the "preliminary" deity; from Him of the supreme court and the inexplicable handing over of Job to the wiles of ha-Satan.

And how far removed from the god of the quartet who have so tried the soul of Job—and ours as well!

✦ ✦ ✦

The dazzling monologue that follows is a sign; the rehabilitation of Job is underway. Though in a manner sure to be thought puzzling, and painful as well. In the processs, turn about is fair.

We have heard Job's lengthy, tormented questioning of God. Now Job himself will be subject to close inquiry;

> Gird your loins like a man [sic]. I will question you,
> and you tell me the answers! (Job 38:3)

✦ ✦ ✦

So it begins, this uninterrupted eruption, a monologue of utmost irony, even of abuse, one dark device heaped on another.

"Were you there when I . . . —when I was performing one after another, the *magnalia Dei*, the grand works of creating and sustaining all things? Where were you, Job?

The "where" is a trope. Implied; do you then think yourself co-eternal, co-omnipotent, co-omniscient? In the moral sphere, does it please you to play God?

✦ ✦ ✦

Relentlessly Job is cast back and back.

This is as far—not very far!—as the inquiries concerning God's will for the world (and for Job himself) will be granted place, honored, answered.

Not answered at all, granted least place.

And yet, most strangely honored.

✦ ✦ ✦

Throughout the preceding episodes Job has repeatedly, sometimes intemperately sought light on the mystery of his gratuitous suffering. And by implication, has sought light on catastrophes that roll through time and space, witless as tumbleweed, lethal as an avalanche, afflicting the larger world and the unborn. Afflicting ourselves.

The living are buried alive, so will the unborn be buried—in darkness. Lives half-realized, anonymous, their stories untold. Hopes dashed against rock.

So are the ancestors buried.

An image. No light will be granted. Or so little as hardly to matter.

✦ ✦ ✦

Nonetheless, let a mystery be underscored. In holding to the Great Refusal, God greatly honors Job.

Greatly honors ourselves. By refusing to unveil the Mystery. By setting limits.

We sense the enormous tension. In the dialogues, Job has challenged those limits. And for such daring he has paid dearly, in the tongue lashings of tormenters, in reproof and insult and moral fabrications.

✦ ✦ ✦

And yet the questing faith of Job is admitted to Scripture, as the warranted word of God. Is admitted there, confronted there.

Admitted (we ask), only to be reproved, or worse—stigmatized as unruly, unbefitting? Admitted to the text, only to be denied validity?

In a negative sense only (i.e., *caveat lector*, "let the reader beware") are the words of Job set down "for our instruction"?

Is this implied—that believers are forbidden to follow his example or embrace his image of God—along with the example of ha-Satan, or of the coven of "friends"?

If such were true, the entire text, including the minatory Voice from the whirlwind, would be a kind of "Handbook of Forbidding," a "Book Concerning the Way Not to Proceed."

✦ ✦ ✦

Surely this is not the intent.

This, rather; God speaks from the whirlwind. The violence in nature is a symbol. God seeks to break a pattern asunder, to shift and shake the status of the question.

Job, cease asking; Why?

Approach the burning bush. In it, all questions are consumed, a straw.

Instead of questions, far more exalted than answers, I give you My voice, My self-revelation. And to you—ecstasy.

✦   ✦   ✦

A setting of limits will also be implied in what follows. The method of God will greatly differ from that of the friends. No covert attacks will be launched against the integrity of the just one. No justifying on shaky, logical grounds, his atrocious sufferings. No more of this.

✦   ✦   ✦

Limits, one thinks, on all sides. The friends will stand condemned. They have wilfully missed the mark—in regard to God as well as Job.

And alas, rebuke will meet Job's anguished search for light. But "rebuke" hardly says everything.

A momentous breakthrough occurs, a loving, immediate Presence. And a lengthy discourse is granted the suffering one.

And finally, a summing up; unqualified approval and praise are bestowed on Job.

✦   ✦   ✦

The vast-ranging, majestic monologue, unprecedented in Scripture, is underway.

It is as though a father wildly confronted a son who has launched a threat against absolute paternal dominion.

Would the upstart dare unseat his parent? His grievances form a long litany of woe. He has been robbed of his possessions, his loved ones were snatched from the earth. And for what reason?

Silence reigns at the throne. Others prosper, he must suffer, he is told nothing.

And now, is accounting at hand? Will a revelation unlock the grim secret of the world?

It will not. To the contrary, Job's plaints are accounted inappropriate, presumptuous, even impudent. Let him be reproved, and strongly.

Still, one thinks, God speaks to Job; as though Job, his wounds and losses, stood surrogate for all humans. He must be taken with utmost seriousness. (So must we?)

The root of love holds firm.

Admitted on high; Job has endured much.

Shall he have no requital? He shall.

✦ ✦ ✦

Elihu, the fourth objector, has disappeared from the text, whether through a lacuna or a deliberate snub.

In any case, as he came he went, intemperate, an intruder, echoing to the end the abuse of his elders.

Then he simply ceased to matter.

As for the notorious trio, they will shortly be reproved, and in draconian terms. God it would seem, wants no part with these harrassing "true" believers. Credibility is stripped from them; their sterile deuteronomic morality is declared awry or redundant or both.

✦ ✦ ✦

In sum, God finds faith elsewhere than in them, and authentic trust as well.

For these qualities, grand, consistent and true—God turns to Job, that bare survivor of the blows of unaccountable providence.

How the title "just" has stood under fire, infernal or celestial—and how it has been vindicated!

✦ ✦ ✦

And what of that barely admissable (or inadmissable) "why" of Job? To the end of the story named for him, to the end of his life as well, Job will not be granted to know.

Of that, nothing.

And yet—something. Something unprecedented, awesome, an epiphany.

Something? An overwhelming Event, God self-revealed, Presence and Voice.

For Job's sake, no other; honor, privilege, access, grace unparalleled, divine serendipity come to earth. A lustrum, a rapture.

✦ ✦ ✦

As for the multiple queries, they will not die with Job. They are not meant to, quite the opposite.

For this reason they lie in the text; that they may rise, amplify to a tide, elusive and tormenting.

Articulated, translated in every tongue, the questions of Job will become a common patrimony, the choral ode of humans, confronting God—or evading, denying God, raising humans to moral stature, falling in despair. Condemning us to ape a fallen world, transfiguring us through the world.

To the end of time, we will not be granted to know.

But we will be granted this, the text, the torment of Job. And the Event; God and Job.

✦ ✦ ✦

From the opening, frosty and fiery both, of this final, majestic pronunciamento, the decision is plain. God rejects every attempt on the part of humans, even the most favored, to win a clue as to the divine Intent.

Job, for all his dogged virtue and forebearance and fidelity, is granted no exception. Nor are we.

✦ ✦ ✦

One side of the coin; one side only; darkness unrelieved.

Turn the coin over; it blazes, pure gold.

✦ ✦ ✦

Is God uneasy in his dominion? Is this why secrets must be kept?

Such has long been speculated.

The Deity here emerging is the God of creation, the God of the prophets. He seems assured, transcendant, dynamic in every corner of creation.

His imagery sweeps through the cosmos in a storm of self-vindication.

This God knows humans, knows Job. The argument is irrefutable—at least to Himself.

✦ ✦ ✦

Limits, limits. The finite vis-à-vis the Infinite, the mortal one seeking out the Immortal. I am not you; so goes the argument, leveling all claims before. I know you, heart, soul, frame, family, possessions. And loss of all. I know, I allowed. In the decree of loss my glance pierces heart and loins.

And you? I behold Job, needy, a near nonentity.

Forbear. You can never for a moment's folly or daring, presume to know Me.

✦ ✦ ✦

Moses learned it. Face to My face, humans die. Your sole access, Job, is My voice "from the whirlwind."

The "access" must be thought a terrifying epiphany of power, designed to strike you prone, to inspire awe and trembling.

The words touch on little or nothing of Job's cause. Or of ours.

We have heard only the firm shutting of a door. Our plight remains, entire, awful, set in place, deep founded.

And for relief? Only the whirlwind, the Voice.

✦　✦　✦

The author of the epistle of John reports on a far different epiphany of the Holy. The whirlwind is stilled, we are in the realm of the dear and familiar, of God our Brother.

How, after the thunder and lightning that played about Job, the majestic, scornful distancing—how credit our eyes?

> This is what we proclaim to you,
> what was from the beginning.
>
> What we have heard,
> what we have seen with our eyes,
>
> what we have looked upon
> and our hands have touched—
>
> we speak of the Word of Life . . . .
>
> What we have seen and heard
> we proclaim in turn to you,
> so that you may share life with us (1 John 1:1–3)

✦　✦　✦

A further note. No excuse is offered, no linkage attempted, between the God of the early exchange with ha-Satan, and the drastically different God whose lightning bolts play about Job.

Ha-Satan had craftily suggested that under duress, Job would show his true face, peccable, despairing.

Then all agreements are off. The "prosecutor" flees the stage, possibly sensing defeat in the offing. Demon, begone!

And Job for his part, emerges strangely victorious—over the accuser, as well as the coven of friends, those champions of deuteronomic morality.

✦   ✦   ✦

The book of Job might be summed up as a contest—between
God and the god.

And on the human plane, a contest between the Law as preeminent (how God would have us behave ethically) and the
prophets (how despite all God would hold us, an asp in His bosom, close, in love).

✦   ✦   ✦

The God of Job, and a sublime epiphany.

Not yet, one thinks, not the God of the prophets. Not a God
whose "mighty works" are recounted in Exodus and elsewhere.

Rather, the God of Genesis. The God who glories in the works
of the first week. Glories in the bliss of the absolute, in the contrast; the pale contingent human, a mote amid the infinite, an
atom amid the firmament.

✦   ✦   ✦

A comparable "showing," we note, marked the lives of the
great prophets, Isaiah, Exekiel, Jeremiah, Daniel; marked them
as God's own, bound over for His work in the world.

And yet, with what a difference! Here, the monologue remains
majestically self-centered; God dwelling on the works of God.

And could one claim that Job is marked for God's work in the
world? In his moral stature he greatly resembles the prophets;
they and he undergo and survive torment and scorn.

And he is unlike them in this. He is bidden to suffer, withstand, persevere—and nothing more. His life halts here, on a
dungheap. He is anointed for no vast public vocation, he is without effect on the world's course. In the seats of power he is
unheard, unknown. His story is simply told; he is harshly set
apart, in near anonymous torment.

✦ ✦ ✦

Job is an anomoly in the world, as convention would view the human norm. He is like one terminally ill, subject to a long dying, no relief in sight.

He is assigned only to suffer.

And what sort of vocation is that? It awakens only revulsion, a sense of scandal.

Worse; in the judgment of his friends, who echo the larger world, he suffers badly, unreconciled, wild and in chains.

✦ ✦ ✦

Strange also, how the order of time is reversed here.

Job's "showing" comes at the end rather than the beginning. First he is tested sorely; then finally, a vision is granted, gratuitous as dawn after an endless night of the spirit.

Contrarily, the prophets' vision came at the start, presumably to strengthen them for a great and awful vocation; truthtelling, witness, rejection.

✦ ✦ ✦

> Cut my cloth
> to a human measure—
> big schemes, big follies,
> the dark ground of connivance
> be far from me!
>
> come my soul,
> like a bird to the hand
> like a child to breast
>
> I will nurture you, mother you.

As my soul hastens
to breast, to hand,
May I to my God hasten, abide (Psalm 131)

✦   ✦   ✦

The Deity marshalls a showing of wondrous power and might. And Job cowers under a firestorm of poetry.

A mighty pageant passes before his eyes, recalling the wisdom and power that brought creation into being.

First to the foundation of things.

The cornerstone of creation is laid. And the momentous First Week is underway; all things are in good hands;

The morning stars
sang in chorus,

the sons of God
shouted for joy! (Job 38:7)

In a strange bending of time, it would seem as though evil spirits already lurked in remote corners of the earth, preceding the creation of humans.

Are these shadowy ones to be thought the acolytes of ha-Satan?

Have you
in your lifetime
commanded the morning

and shown the dawn
its place,

for taking hold
of the ends of the earth,

till the wicked
are shaken from its surface? (Job 38:12–13)

A homely image; as though the fingers of dawn were those of a housewife, standing out of doors, shaking a dust of crumbs from a cloth.

✦   ✦   ✦

Strange. How comes it that the theme of evil so permeates the recital of creation?

The question arose before; does Jawe sit his throne with a measure of unease?

In this grand ode, a "stain of original sin" lies there on the palette of creation, the dark "color of things to be," preceding the firm origins.

The theme continues; dawn arises, a metaphor. Earth takes on a subtle variation of hues, lent by the rising sun.

But darkness lurks; no light rises upon the wicked, sunk in night unending.

More, and worse; for such, dawn is a shattering reversal of everything the night held close and protected.

✦   ✦   ✦

That reign of Jawe; is it to be thought tranquil, unopposed?

One has an opposite impression; from the start a harsh contention is underway. Evil is all but "in the nature of things";

The earth is changed
as is clay
by the seal,

and dyed
as though it were
a garment;

> But from the wicked
> light is withheld,
>
> and the arm of pride
> is shattered (Job 38:14–15)

✦ ✦ ✦

The poetry pours on and on, declamatory, exalted—and strangely ill at ease.

That relentless, questioning Job!

A skilled riposte; let God turn the tables, question the questioner.

Job, shall one presume, perhaps was present when "the abyss" and "the gates of hell" were set in place? He knows the domain of "light" and "darkness," so as to lead them about in proper order? Surely he knows such matters, since, ironically;

> you were born
> before them
>
> and the number of your years
> is great (Job 38:21)

It is as though God were withholding and granting, all together. What are the boundaries that surround the human, that are not to be crossed? Has Job dared cross them, or has he not?

And if in fact he has violated a taboo, has not his daring won an epiphany and vindicated his freedom—even freedom to transgress?

Has he compelled this unparalleled self-revelation of the deity, urging God to come forth, to justify His ways?

✦ ✦ ✦

And God spoke.

God would not justify His ways; but He would come forth.

He would emerge for sake of Job (for our sake?)—if only to proclaim that His ways are beyond our comprehension—and shall remain so.

Job has prevailed; and Job has lost. So have we.

✦ ✦ ✦

God has spoken, but it is as though He has not spoken. Job's afflicted flesh presents no argument against God, against divine Goodness.

Or it does offer an argument.

Let Job if he so choose, continue to urge the argument. It will go nowhere. The Mystery must remain intact, sealed.

Behold the word from the whirlwind of time and this world, and beyond. Take this comfort, cold and scalding at once; Job, be certain—you will never be granted to know.

Indeed your best word, your most enduring, was uttered early on. It questioned nothing, told of an abandonment pure and self-blinded;

> God gave,
> God has taken away.
>
> Blessed
> be God's Name! (Job 1:21)

✦ ✦ ✦

With this difference—which Christians, for all our defaulting, reverence as momentous. And rightly so.

And the difference, be it confessed, is due to no merit in ourselves.

The difference; the Mystery has been illustrated, as though in blazing color and full round, in the passion and death of Christ.

No thunders, no voice from the whirlwind; rather, a Human assailed, accused, found guilty, capitally punished. No "explanation" of the "why" of suffering innocence. Only an illustration, a testing of the Divine in the fires of the inhuman.

✦ ✦ ✦

We note that the three friends are granted no such thundrous visitation as is given Job.

Could they have welcomed it, learned from it?

At least this is implied; they and their hidebound logic are simply off track. So their version of God is ignored, and yields mightily before Job's.

✦ ✦ ✦

And Job prevails, though with no fanfare or reward. God comes into his presence angrily, all but aggressively.

In Person. To suggest; from the start, your God, Job; the God of anguish and no response, the God who left you to fend for yourself, who granted the tormenters equal time with yourself.

Yours was true God. I heard.

✦ ✦ ✦

But also, a strong reproof; you violated boundaries; stubborn and willful and vertiginous, you walked a dangerous ground.

You neglected to put off your sandals, the habiliments of ordinary life. You would not strip yourself of your "Why?"

✦ ✦ ✦

Unlike some other rebbis,
the Kotzker did not teach
that one should under all circumstances
be meek, because one was a nothing,
quieter than calm water
and flatter than mown grass.

On the contrary,
one should hold one's head high;
for a feeling of meekness and inferiority
is the worst trait
in the fight for truth.

(Abraham Heschel, *A Passion For Truth*)

✦ ✦ ✦

It comes to this; God must set limits to the questioning of God. For if I allowed access to the Mystery that plays darkly in time and this world—what then of the matter called faith?

What then of the sublime faith of a Job, a very model of faith?

The faith of Job would be redundant, would evaporate, in the—"answer."

✦ ✦ ✦

38:22–38 Memories, the memories of the Deity are summoned (or at least it is so adduced, by an author whose own memories, it would seem, remain unexorcised).

God remembers the role of snow and ice in the outcome of ancient battles.

Thunder on the left; memory brings regression. The "old god," the notorious god of Exodus and Samuel and Kings, the god who prior to the era of prophets accredited the sordid affairs of the mighty—that god emerges from the mist like a ghost in armor.

Now the god is dangerously heard from.

Job, take warning. The God of nature is untamed—untamable, even by such as yourself. Hear him speak;

> Have you entered
> the storehouse of snows,
>
> and seen
> the treasury of hail,
>
> which I reserve
> for times of stress,
>
> for the days
> of war and of battle? (Job 38:22–23)

✦ ✦ ✦

The tone of the questioning shifts, generalizes. For a few verses, it is as though Job were a surrogate. Now his limitations extend to all humans;

> Who has laid out
> a channel for the downpour . . .
>
> to bring rain
> to no man's land? . . .
>
> to enrich waste
> and desolate ground
>
> till the desert blooms
> with verdure? (Job 38:25–27)

Plainly, no human can lay claim to such mammoth earthworks.

Jesus will echo the theme, with a difference; His is the God "who makes the rain fall on the just and the unjust alike."

✦ ✦ ✦

Do we humans account ourselves the crown of creation? We read so in the story of Origins, and rejoice.

In God's own image He created them (Genesis 1:27).

But here and throughout the great monologue, the human tribe is given short shrift—indeed hardly any at all.

Job alone is addressed, with no reference to human ancestry. It is as though he were a monad, a sport; as though of all humans, he alone mattered or merited.

And he "matters" finally, because he can be held up, a shamed specimen of the decline and fall of humans.

A Midrash here, and a mocking one, on Genesis. That divine image is no more. Closely, ironically, even mockingly, Job is questioned as to his status in the ranks of living beings, his role in the vast scope of the works of creation.

✦   ✦   ✦

He submits to the searching, often humiliating inquiry. His moral measure is being taken.

Is he to be accounted no more than a schoolboy under a hard master? He is silent.

The monologue is a clue. He must be found teachable under the ferule of God. If so, all will be well; from lesser to greater wisdom he will come.

✦   ✦   ✦

38:39–39:18 The tactic is plain. The relentless questions imply, one after another, their own answer. Any response on Job's part would be redundant, even impertinent.

Not a word therefore; none is required. One has a strong sense; none would be tolerated.

✦   ✦   ✦

Job and his kind are accounted by the Deity a lesser, ignorant tribe, much in need of instruction as to the human condition.

The instruction; we humans stand near the bottom, or at best, toward the middle of the hierarchy of being.

Imagine then, be teachable—consent to be humiliated!

Thus is your true status, your condition laid out; impossible that you estimate or celebrate, let alone attain—the clairvoyance, beauty, grandeur of the fauna and flora of creation.

✦   ✦   ✦

Inanimate creation likewise; it surpasses you unutterably.

Look up, gaze in wonder at the heavens. The stars evade human reach, evade all but an entranced gaze. They range the heavens far and wide, in an all but infinite arc.

Is it humans who set them on their illimitable path? Can we cause them to veer from it?

Idle to question; to claim part in the great works would be the chatter of fools.

✦   ✦   ✦

The creation proceeds in full majesty. Life calls to life, like to like; in a moment, living beings are summoned from the void.

Then another task of the Creator; an unending susurration, a breath of life, mouth-to-mouth with the living, sustains and upholds all;

> Like a cooper of barrels
> You bind the mountains with ribbing.
> Your hand rests on rambunctious seas—
>
> they grow peaceful,
> the brow of a sleeping child.
>
> Autumn, a king's progress,
> largesse lies ripe on the land.
>
> Up, down the furrow Your midas touch
> rains gold;
> rainbows arc from Your glance.
>
> Fall of rain, evenfall, all, all is blessing! (Psalm 64)

✦ ✦ ✦

And what is our knowledge of the wild beasts of earth? Little or nothing. Mountain goats and hinds conceal their place of birth. Wild asses and oxen slip the hand that seeks to tame and subdue them.

The divine Wisdom, manifest in all things "spare, original, counter, strange"—is disconcerting to humans, proclaiming against all evidence, domination of the "lesser" fauna.

Humans dominating? A foolish, wanton claim.

✦ ✦ ✦

The "argument of dimunition" continues.

Shall we humans supply a provender suitable to lion cubs or newly hatched ravens? We cannot; those helpless ones must look to God.

✦ ✦ ✦

Another case in point; the ostrich. Behold this ungainly earth-bound creature, caparisoned with hapless flapping wings.

She comes to term; then she drops her eggs carelessly about, abandoning her offspring to chancy fortune, for

> God
> from her
> has withheld wisdom
>
> and given her
> no share in understanding (Job 39:17)

Still, her weapons of defense are formidable. This curious avian, flightless as a serpent of the fields—her vast ugly feet gather strength, spur on occasion a breathless speed, whether in onslaught or flight. Horse and horseman take note!

✦　✦　✦

God, it seems, is winsomely delighted with the creatures of His hand. He parades them before Job like a proud Noah at the door of the ark, stroking his favorite curiosities as they pass by.

✦　✦　✦

Need one add—it is by no means clear that an equivalent pleasure arises in the Creator at sight of humankind?

Job, and by strong implication, ourselves, are shown variously as ignorant, inept, bystanders at a splendid parade, poor specimens, falling short of the grandeur of the beasts.

Is human creation, as the book of Origins presents it, here stopped short? Are other champions displacing us humans?

✦　✦　✦

And a nagging whisper lurks in the mind, questioning; could the admiration of God stem from this; that the ark of earth, swimming in space, is silent, resounds with no questions?

Is there no Job aboard? If not, can this be accounted a blessing, whether on God's part or our own?

Is God wrapt in admiration for a world populated by the mute and subdued, whether humans or beasts?

Does God seek a human tribe without troublemakers?

Is God content with the works of His hands because, as night falls and the planet swims on, the great bestiary sleeps in peace, sweetly ignorant, content?

Is this to be the human ideal; we ignorant, content with whatever lot befalls?

✦　✦　✦

39:19–30 The procession continues; summoning horse, hawk, eagle, the paean of God rising to ecstasy.

It sounds in our ears strange, and strangely familiar—this ode of the divinity in praise of wild and wondrous creatures. Horse and mount, one; eagle and rider, one.

(Thus do Native Americans sing and dance and pay tribute to the unity of the tribes of earth, clothed, concealed under masks and robes drawn from noble creatures of earth and air and sea.)

✦　✦　✦

The scene is the ancient Mid East.

The horse, we note, is a beast of the era; a warhorse.

The image summons to mind a Greek centaur, a beast-human. The splendid charger all but takes to itself the qualities of a noble warrior-mount.

Has the horse become human, is the warrior transformed to a beast?

Of the mounted warrior we are told not a word. It is as if he grew irrelevant or superfluous, in view of this preternatural presence.

The horse "leaps like a locust," "its snorting is terrible," "it laughs at fear, is not dismayed." "It does not turn back from the sword." "When the trumpet sounds, it says 'Aha!'"

Is God Himself become a mounted warrior, borne aloft on ecstatic imagery?

Does a battle rage in His mind, another phase of the wars that once delighted the deity of Saul and David and Solomon?

Does a war god mount his charger? Is the god impregnated with the blood lust of the passionate steed?

✦ ✦ ✦

40:1–5 An interruption—or perhaps God seeks a reaction from his interlocutor. How has Job received the opening salvo, this grand Beethovian "first movement"? Job holds his peace.

His silence is equivocal, one thinks. Is he overwhelmed, is he defiant? Or is he inured by now to the status of underdog, resigned to cease and desist shaking the cosmic scheme of things?

✦ ✦ ✦

It bears reminding; the atmosphere is that of the realm of Necessity, of the Fall. According to its supreme Arbiter, the consequence of human misdeeds are inevitable; a fallen realm is held together by ironbound staves of law.

And the law, its motivation, its exactions against innocent and guilty alike, in principle must be kept secret.

✦ ✦ ✦

Nonetheless Job is not easily put to silence.

We have noted it before, the perennial ancient question. How it abides, whether in him or others. How it is woven in the fabric of soul, and will not be done with, as long as time.

Hold it at heart then, cherish it, keep it close; why must the innocent suffer, why do the wicked walk free?

The question ranges the earth and time, a torment on the air.

And the question, one suspects, strikes too close; like a sword blade thrust through the veil of the Tabernacle, the Mystery.

✦ ✦ ✦

Thus a dilemma lies unresolved in the hands of Job, and the hands of the One who sits the throne.

In our hands as well, ourselves, the others, the yet-to-be-born "third party" to the scene of conflict. Limits are set from the foundation of the world.

And in the world we stand or fall to face, baffled, beset.

This, as implied, is quite simply the human condition. On God's part, no disclosure. On our part, no surpassing the question, no evading it.

To Job comes an implied word of God; Live with the questions.

✦   ✦   ✦

Still, another rhythm is in play.

Do we hear it, this counterpoint? Job's tormenters are shortly to be reproved, and in the strongest terms. In accusing Job, they have stoked the fury of God.

✦   ✦   ✦

The divine Decree is implicit throughout; in the sublime imaginative forays of God into creation, in the loving lingering attention paid all beings—with the notable exception of humans.

Does it come to this, the message to Job and friends; a plague on both your houses? I, the Creator, turn away from you?

✦   ✦   ✦

God; I take delight in the oddment and grandeur and quickened pulse of life in beast and bird and fish, in "all things counter, original, spare, strange" (G. M. Hopkins, "Pied Beauty").

I vastly prefer these, over your sour recalcitrant tribe, you and your theorizing, squabbling, joyless missing of the point of life and love.

Equally awful are you, Job, deep in acedia, baffled and obstinate, refusing to let dark matters be.

✦   ✦   ✦

And one ponders; is this a post-lapsarian God, with redemption and hope in short supply?

Beyond doubt a grim gaze rests on us humans. The "friends" are found excessive, fatuous, peevish; they miss the mark. And Job is a rueful fricative presence; he darkens God's brow, playing hobs with boundaries and taboos.

God turns away.

Humans are—deprived animals. We merit nothing of the praise heaped on us by the book of Origins, its organ note of approval and blessing;

> God created humans in His image; in the divine Image
> He created, male and female He created them . . . God
> looked on everything He had made, and found it very
> good . . . (Genesis 1:26, 31).

✦   ✦   ✦

40:6–8 Fully aroused, God mounts a further, closer question.

Job has dared doubt the integrity of the moral order, as well as the physical.

Who will rise to defend him, as his innocence is derided and held in scorn? Is his not a capital point, even as evil speeds, footloose and prospering in the world?

✦   ✦   ✦

The implication touches a raw nerve. If the Deity is not master of the moral order, is not transcendance a dead letter?

Job has kept silent for a long time; and this, one thinks, under heavy provocation. Why then the vehemence of the divine salvo?

An offensive innuendo darkens the air;

Would you refuse to acknowledge My right?

Would you condemn Me
that you may be justified? (Job 40:8)

A purported attack on divine sovereignty—it demands sharp, quick rebuttal.

By implication God likens Job to a fallen Adam. He has eaten of the tree of knowledge. Thereafter he is intoxicated with a new sense of power; he presumes access to matters altogether beyond his scope.

He would "see into heaven." His plaints are a kind of verbal Tower of Babel; he constructs it and mounts.

✦   ✦   ✦

The story is an unprecedented jousting match.

We stand at the climax. God enters the world of Job, utters a monologue unheard elsewhere by human ears.

We humans are both honored and set back, at times in the same impetuous breath.

The honor? God appears, God speaks, to one human. For hours on end the Deity issues a sublime manifesto.

Venturing on this, He ignores, even goes counter to commands issued elsewhere. He appears, is heard from, face to face.

✦   ✦   ✦

An image suggests itself. It is as though in the Pentateuch and historical books, a shingle were hung on the portal of heaven. Its message was dire, final; "Deity unavailable." Or worse; "Trespassers beware; death penalty enforced. See God and die."

For the nonce, for Job's sake (for our sakes), all is changed. Job, afflicted and vilified, at least (at most!) may hold aloft a sovereign moment, then gather it to his heart.

So by implication may we.

The moment, the kairos, the intersection of divine and human freedom. The freedom on both sides; on God's—"I choose to speak." On Job's, "I choose to hearken."

God speaks with him. The moment of epiphany is extended; at great length God speaks.

At whose summons, this unprecedented bending low? One thinks in awe; at the longing, beckoning gesture of a mere mortal.

✦ ✦ ✦

No wonder then, that God is led to improve the occasion, to counter sharply His immense concession, His all-but-stated confession of love.

Love for Job—a weakness in God? No wonder then that we humans are put down and the fauna and flora of creation are exalted.

These latter are safe, after all; they put no questions.

And Job—he is an embodied risk. Shall he be allowed to require of God justification of a murky moral universe? Shall he require God to justify Himself, to defend the suffering and loss inflicted, on Job, on nameless multitudes of Jobs?

The encounter must be thought transhistorical; shall God be summoned again and again to justify the incalculable anguish of unborn generations, in *saecula saeculorum*?

Deal carefully with this Job; he is larger than life. He stands there, or cowers there, an apt forerunner, a dire image of the many to come, cursed or blessed to dwell in a world discomposed by sin.

✦ ✦ ✦

Shall God be required to justify the world of the twentieth century, this brimstone mix of monstrous, wrongheaded, lethal power, a world organized against the God of life—and life itself?

Shall the monologue of the Deity be composed anew, required as God is by the likes of Job to justify catastrophes and losses? Shall God be held responsible for this Dantesque inferno, our century, an unextinguished firestorm of war, deluge, earthquake?

✦ ✦ ✦

Let us not push matters too far.

Let us grant this; a gracious God (though fiery) deigns to encounter Job—and ourselves. And this despite His knowing what we know; the sorry, blood-ridden human passage in time and this world.

God also knows that we know; know that in the encounter with Job, (better, the nonencounter) we hear all we will be granted to hear of "the ways of God."

✦ ✦ ✦

Until Jesus.

Until "God so loved the world as to give His only Son. . . ." Until God joins Himself to the sorry sum and story, and suffers in the flesh losses more terrible than those of Job.

And until, all unaccountably, and by a power surpassing the human—until He is restored to life.

✦ ✦ ✦

Nothing of the foregoing insight and implication, it goes without saying, is granted to Eliphaz, Bildad, Zophar, or Elihu, that woeful quartet.

As the epiphany opened, they grew silent—or absent? For reasons that may not be thought obscure.

As for us humans, it is as though we were a vanished tribe, or a tribe that never was. As though Job were the single, unique human, a new Adam.

As though Job alone counted. (And yet we count.)

✦ ✦ ✦

We have seen the divine Imagination in full spate, celebrating the vast range and rainbow of creation. And Job stands there; he alone is addressed, reproved, vilified, jibed, justified, embraced.

We are not to miss it, the honor paid one among us; in the emotional vortex and chaos, one human is paid attention, is clothed and crowned, as with gold and jewels, with the divine Attentiveness.

✦ ✦ ✦

The conclusion is crucial.

In humiliation as in ecstasy, Job stands surrogate for all; for us who dwell there in the shadows—the ancestors, the unborn, the uncelebrated, all-but-discredited, all-but-redundant humans.

What an implication! So puny in understanding and ethic, so hugely inferior to those we thought our inferiors, to Behemoth or Leviathan—as to be justly, even mercifully ignored.

✦ ✦ ✦

We do well to take Job seriously, amid his pitfalls and detours and false starts. Job, as adduced.

For this reason take him seriously. With many a reservation and second thought and third on the part of the Deity, with verbal thumps for presumption and importunity, for trespass and transgression—God takes Job seriously.

For this reason he merits reward; for abiding faithful in pain, for showing forth the full and awful range of human undergoing, for enduring reproof and insult, for being confessedly flawed and importunate, for wondering and wanting, for going too far, for stopping short—behold Job the human. God takes him seriously.

✦   ✦   ✦

May it not be inferred then; in taking Job seriously, God waits upon our taking God seriously?

And were we to inquire the meaning of that rather occluded phrase, "taking God seriously," would the Deity respond shortly, not a word wasted—something like; "For that, look to Job; as I look to him."

✦   ✦   ✦

Who enters Your dwelling, an honored guest?
Who wins Your handclasp, sister and brother?

The just one, who walks steadfast in truth,
whose tongue is a wildfire contained,

who sows no dissension abroad,
who honors the upright, despises the double deal

who turns the blood of the poor to no base gain,
whose word is bond, whose oath is adamant.

Behold God's faithful one, sister and brother!
(Psalm 19)

✦ ✦ ✦

40:9–10 This illimitable—yes, this unconscionable God!

We think of the sour monologues that preceded. In wearisome detail the trio of friends sought to define (and confine) the deity, to place and placate, once for all.

And Job in his own way overstepped. Did he not seek to probe the mystery, perhaps to master it, to force a revelation. To vindicate himself?

✦ ✦ ✦

Therefore God; let matters be clarified, once for all.

Neither the intrepid theologians and their closed, cramped "schools of thought," nor Job the torrid interrogator—none of you owns Me, God, none persuades Me to side with you.

I evade the nets you cast for Me, no matter how cunningly and closely woven.

None of you declares Who I Am.

Let this be known; I am unentailed, unowned, useless to your designs, indifferent to your moralisms, surpassing your religion. I wince at your incantations, your provoking, your sorry attempt to beckon Me forth.

How you have insulted and degraded My sweet creation!

How you would if you could, unmake Me! Would banish Me, declare Me irrelevant, unnecessary, an obstacle, an overweening tyrant—or simply nonexistent, done with, a noxious zero.

I am in effect a resident alien, an "undocumented" Deity, an exile in your world. "A tattered figure, moving from tree to tree in the back of the mind" (Flannery O'Connor).

✦ ✦ ✦

40:11–14 Let us indulge, Job and I, in a kind of fantasy. Let us stretch reality to the breaking point.

Imagine yourself (yourselves) in My place.

God being author of this unlikely game, you are henceforth allowed to "play God."

Glory be to Job!

You, Job, are sovereign also, of Sheol.

Who goes there? It is for you to judge, to weigh, to condemn;

> Bring down the haughty
> with a glance,
>
> bury them in Sheol
> all together;
>
> hide their faces
> in perpetual twilight (Job 40:12–13)

✦   ✦   ✦

And not a word is uttered, we note, of another, contrary power; that of crowning the just with beatitude. Nothing of this handed over to Job.

On, then, to the conclusion.

This dealing of death being granted you, this condemning the wicked to "death after death"—such would bring you praise and commendation; and from Me!

> Then I too
> will acknowledge
>
> that your right hand
> has triumphed (Job 40:14)

Which is to say, short of the unlikeliest turnabout in the universe, short of a simply unimaginable event—namely that Job were granted the power and wisdom (and the status) of God— short of this metaphysically impossible premise, which I God, choose for a moment to entertain—you Job, are well advised to know your place, your creaturehood, the boundaries of desire, the limits.

Read it again, ponder it well, the decree.

Honor the taboos. Watch where you trespass.

✦ ✦ ✦

40:15–41:34 We enter on the famous passages concerning the great land and sea beasts, Behemoth and Leviathan.

And the old, ironic question sounds once more. Who could have contrived this unlikely duet? Could Job?

God steps back, and invites Job to do likewise. Let them together take delight in these two untamable portents.

Let them delight also, God and Job, in the coruscating Magician who created them.

✦ ✦ ✦

As to Behemoth, only imagine! (and with a soupcon of irony);

> He is the first fruit
> of the works of God (Job 40:19)

Can we credit our eyes? In the order of excellence, this monstrosity is a "first," a "foremost"?

We had been given to believe otherwise; that it was ourselves who stood at the peak of creation.

Are we to be replaced by this infinitely ugly, pugnacious, iron-plated recalcitrant?

✦ ✦ ✦

We note the irony.

Unheard of. Face to face, God and Job compose together, and

record, sublime images, elegant tropes of admiration, words of upset and conflict, page after page blessing and shocking our eyes with the glory and terror of creation.

Images of who we are and are not, images of Who God is, and is not.

✦　✦　✦

A nagging thought intrudes; to what end the honor, the vast-ranging, incomparable poetry of the monologue?

To this purpose? That a vast caricature, a stalking nightmare of a beast be favored, praised, stroked, over and above Job and our kind?

We are in the realm of the archiac, the stuff of myth.

Let God conjure the unlikeliest of brutes, a mock-up of a beast, a beast all but beyond belief, one in whom ugliness and force collide and concentrate, whose brutal armor and will massively push all before, out of his path.

Whose visage is a terror in creation, a geologic tremor in the breast of humans.

Summon this one, the hippo. He ambles massively on stage; the earth trembles. Those vast legs propel the great body like four ambulatory pillars. He stands there, in pride of place.

✦　✦　✦

The praise is immediately qualified.

Must not unpredictable God convey an ambiguous intent, perhaps even (God forbid)—an error of judgment, in granting this portent so altitudinous a presentment?

It is as though a motionless Edenic scene were violently shaken. The creature, like a monster of Ionesco, crashes through the papery decor of beatitude.

✦   ✦   ✦

A mortal threat lies in the helmeted head of Leviathan, in
those inflamed pig-like eyes.

Danger! Suddenly the admiring Parent issues a warning.
Sword, bronze, arrows, clubs, spears avail not a whit.

The beast retires, submerges in a jungle torrent. He lies content there for the moment; he watches the watchers. Only his
eyes and great snout remain visible.

Let humans take warning; the vast carapace is pure danger;

> Can he be taken
> by his eyes,
>
> can his nose be
> pierced by hooks? (Job 40:24)

✦   ✦   ✦

Leviathan. Again and again Scripture pays tribute to the
monster, through Isaiah, Amos, the psalmist.

But it remains to Ezekiel (29:3 ff.; 32:2 ff.) to name, if not to
tame the beast.

The Hebrew tongue has no word for it; for want of a better,
Ezekiel names the beast tannin, the "sea monster."

✦   ✦   ✦

In a lurid extended parable, the prophet reveals the symbol,
the new Leviathan. The hideous primordial enigma is none other
than the pharoah.

That eminence too bestrides the Nile and the vast surrounding estuary. Making common cause with the enemies of Israel,
the imperial nemesis stalks abroad, claiming a vast area of waters and land, inspiring on all sides fear and loathing.

What is to be done?

We have an answer, through Ezekiel. The prophet is told of his task. He is to capture the armored horror, drag the beast ashore, hack it limb from limb. Then, part by part, let him dispatch the meat of the mail-jacketed ruffian to the great ones of earth.

In gore and livid flesh, let them read the "signs of the times"; their own downfall.

✦   ✦   ✦

Predictably, views differ greatly regarding the import of fearsome Leviathan and Behemoth.

Some would have it that the two fantastics embody wickedness, the evils Job suffers in the world and longs to have unmasked by God.

Perhaps, one thinks—and then perhaps not.

Such a dark interpretation ignores the tone of the passage, the divine admiration that bathes the beasts in an aura of delight and terror.

✦   ✦   ✦

Another view would see the two images as half-humorous caricatures of Job himself. Thus the tone; the passage is charged with broad humor, the smile of God.

Job is like that! He too struts about and wildly rejects limits and checkreins. He frets and fears the onslaught of chaos in and around him.

To describe the terror of his woeful, much regretted birth, he summons Leviathan;

> Let them curse
> that night [of birth]

>   who curse the Sea,
>   the appointed disturbers
>   of Leviathan! (Job 3:8)

And again, as though God judged him to be one with the forces of chaos;

>   Am I the sea,
>   or a monster of the deep
>
>   that You place
>   a watch over me? (Job 7:12)

Nothing of the kind! In this view God takes delight in Job, an unlikely marvel of creation.

✦   ✦   ✦

Another view; the portents, Leviathan and Behemoth, are vast sources of divine analogy and metaphor. They shed light on the mystery of God.

(As, it goes without saying, the trio of "friends" was radically unable to do. And as, by implication, Job was likewise unable.)

God turns elsewhere; let Job know of God from two altogether unlikely sources.

✦   ✦   ✦

In the Bible, Leviathan, figure of chaos, is never finally overcome.

Our book takes a totally different tack, and on reflection aptly; Leviathan has become a favorite of the Creator. In face of furious contrary evidence, this bizarre "favorite" of God is hauled bodily on stage.

For admiration. The Creator glories in its intrepid, ferocious cruelty.

And why not? Through the images of Leviathan and Behemoth, God manifests the divine Sovereignty, His own, over sea and land.

(No need of high-soaring winged symbols; of eagle or peridactyl or such; God is everywhere acknowledged Ruler of the "upper air," the "heavenly Jerusalem.")

✦ ✦ ✦

Thus the suggestion; the beasts Behemoth and Leviathan are presented as images of the Divine. The Creator regards the two with close affection, a sense of intimacy—and of likeness.

Reveling in the wondrous beasts, it is as though God stands before a mirror, glorying in the resemblance. Only behold, Myself and these fond others!

It is all left to our surmise.

Only this to guide us; Job (and we) had best prepare to be astonished. At the Creator, at creatures and their close place in the Creator's heart.

✦ ✦ ✦

And with regard to ourselves, something seems implied; we humans, the "original image" of God—willy nilly we require a counter, a corrective image.

We have gone too far, we have fallen from favor. Our delict was double; the sterile abstractions of the friends' quartet, and the presumptuous thrusts and parries of Job.

Enough of these humans, their intemperate tongues. The moment is at hand to call a halt.

To introduce others than humans, to place others at center stage; wild lives, beloved and bizarre—and this to the chagrin of would-be triumphant animal trainers.

✦   ✦   ✦

Humans, beware.

The images come crashing through the text, all horns and jaws, might, and brawn—carnivores, born killers.

Closer to God than ourselves, and corrective.

Images of God!

✦   ✦   ✦

It seems fitting too, that Leviathan has achieved an immortality of sorts. In the seven seas of time he cavorts and thrashes about, destructive, flourishing.

In the book of Beginnings he first appears. He multiplies, haunts the communal imagination, stalks the world, in person and in nature; a many-layered, many-splendored, many-horrored being.

Wonderful! Of the bewildering bestiary streaming from the quixotic mind of the Creator, this one owns the page, is given ample space, for play, for feeding. For battle.

Like his land-roving companion at arms, Leviathan is untamable. No human has laid a hand on him, and survived.

✦   ✦   ✦

A clue; it touches the heart, touches nature, and closely.

God much resembles His fantastic favorite, Leviathan.

God. Not to be tamed, boxed, defined, interred or disinterred, made plausable or incomprehensible, explained or explained away, reduced to polemic, located within or beyond creation, liberated or captivated, house- or temple-broken.

Beyond. Beyond language, enticement, placation, invocation, use or misuse. Beyond our wild desire or inertia, our hope or hopelessness, our rectitude or wickedness. Beyond category.

No telling.

✦ ✦ ✦

None of these; God.

Upon the earth there is not his like (Job 41:33)

An implication holds firm, a connection between wild Leviathan and wilder Deity.

The realism is astonishing, on the face of it. No hook, we are told, avails to lead the one or the Other about, no bit in the tongue, no ring in the nostril, no gaff through the cheek.

Neither can be captured or captivated; impossible. Neither to be cornered by sweet talk, by gentle persuasion, by a bribe.

Neither, must one add, is to be reduced to a plaything—a caged songbird forsooth, for the amusement of children.

✦ ✦ ✦

Shall you perhaps lead Leviathan about on a leash?

Or will he consent to play slave to your beck and call?

Or perhaps you would carve the great armored creature in pieces, selling chunks of crocodile in a market, like pounds of fish?

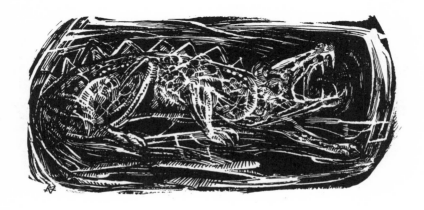

Careful; you sport with death;

> Once
> you lay hand upon him,
>
> you will never
> undertake battle again! (Job 41:8)

✦ ✦ ✦

In sum, the images are taken here as a commentary, by turns lighthearted and dark of mood, offered by God, concerning God.

As a wonderfully ironic commentary on the sea creature—and on the God of the creature.

A bestiary and a theological tract, both.

✦ ✦ ✦

And we wonder. What of the reaction of the friends; are they not confounded in mind, scandalized?

The tone is; they may take it or leave. And so, for that matter, may Job.

Here are proffered, for those with eyes to see, certain aspects of the behavior of God, a sublime and supernal Beast of all creation.

Let the trio take pleasure, interminably categorizing and analyzing; they are dismissed as vain and vainglorious.

And let Job fret and weep and malinger about, in rueful, perennial mourning for his unmerited misery.

God is on the spoor of larger game. He escapes the close-ribbed net of human tears, smiles, surmises, bribes.

✦ ✦ ✦

It bears repeating;

> . . . lay a hand upon him;
> you will never think of battle again! . . .
> Who has assailed him
> and come off safe?
>
> Who under all the heavens? (Job 41:8, 11)

And here the text grows deliciously uncertain.

It is as though a filter were lowered, deliberately blurring, even here and there merging with the primary image.

An analogy, one ventures, that only God would dare.

Does the reference point to the crocodile, fierce-jawed and armor-plated—or to God? Or to both?

Some would read;

> There is none
> so fierce as to rouse him;
>
> who then
> shall stand up to Me?
>
> Whoever confronts Me
> I will requite,
>
> for everything
> under the heavens
> is Mine (Job 41:10–11)

✦ ✦ ✦

Admiration prevails, rides all else under. Details of valor and intrepidity are heaped high and higher, an Etna of images topping an Olympus. Let all creation take note. And let Job be halted in his tracks.

The God of beasts crowns the king of the beasts.

So doing, not a facet of His own crown is dimmed or given over. Quite the contrary; praising the crocodile, bringing a hideous smile to those jaws, God is praising—God.

As in the first week of creation, He is once more "seeing that what was made, was very good" (Genesis 1:31).

Even horrid-stalking Leviathan, hierarch of depths and estuaries, of water and land, midway between nightmare and godling—even he is "very good."

Stand speechless, heaven and earth! Was it not the pleasure of God to summon the unimaginable, the unspeakable—into being? And into praise of being?

✦   ✦   ✦

No profit, it would seem, lies in allegorizing—as though details of crocodilian anatomy were meant to apply, by wit or will, to the Creator.

No, Job (together presumably with ourselves) is offered an example of imaginative theology, drawn from the bottomless wellspring of the Creative imagination.

No arguments here, no sterile logic, no bending to intellectual ego.

Nothing here of the preceding, wearying rodomontade.

✦   ✦   ✦

This splendid crocodilian ode! Pure, inspired (!) description, tropes, daring. The poetry pours out and out, an overflow of delight and lightness of spirit.

Lighten up, Job! By land, through water, your God is stalking you, an onslaught of terror and beauty and the heart's craving!

✦   ✦   ✦

The key image, verified anatomically in the eldritch beast, is one of power, invincibility.

In comparison with the majestic creature, human pretention to dominance or control are simply—laughable.

✦   ✦   ✦

Again and again, what surprises is the two-edged irony, the doubled force, the honor paid, the honor withheld.

Job is made privy (along with ourselves) to the divine Mind; analogies are drawn from creation, proffering a glimpse of the uncreated holy.

Then Job (and presumably ourselves) simply vanish as sources of analogy. Job and his friends are placed to one side, literally done with, poor specimens of a depleted tribe.

We are sterile pedants, beggars in the "realms of gold" where being is freely given—and gives itself away.

✦   ✦   ✦

There we stand in the text, naked, diminished, held in small esteem.

And yet, and yet, something else!

Upon whom but ourselves is loosed this torrent of truth and beauty, this tale of the two phantasmagoric beasts and their unforeseeable Lover?

God chooses to ignore us, to put us humans down—and this though He stand face to face with a rare and luminous spirit, a holy one of our line, just Job.

And yet, through Job, God attends to us. We have His word for it.

✦   ✦   ✦

Analogies leap to the eye.

Fierce, recondite, serendipitous, the King of the beasts celebrates the works of His hands—and by strong implication,
celebrates Himself.

Thus God pays subtle honor to His sole literate acolytes, lec-
tors—to you and me.

To our tribe, our by-no-means-altogether-Godforsaken human
clotting.

✦   ✦   ✦

The Beast is impregnable; which suggests a transcendant God,
a Mystery impervious to humans.

The mind is stilled, conscious of immortal power—and the
limit of power;

> Who can pry open
> the doors of his face?
>
> His bared teeth
> strike terror.
>
> Protective scales
> are his pride,
>
> locked
> with a binding seal.
>
> One scale
> touches the other,
>
> not even a breath
> can enter between them (Job 41:14–16)

✦   ✦   ✦

Subsequent images are all of fire; "light flashes forth" . . . "eyes . . . like those of dawn" . . . "firebrands . . ." "sparks of fire" . . . "steam, as from a seething pot . . ." "coals of fire" . . . "flames from his mouth" . . .

Does the fire of truth illumine at long last the crepuscular sojourn of Job (of ourselves)? Is a road all but lost, suddenly alight, a dawn, perennially delayed, here and now bestowed?

We seize on the image, it offers a rare hope.

✦   ✦   ✦

Leviathan is deathless.

Immortality! The beast, in jagged contrast to Job and humankind, is impervious to every onslaught of the principalities.

Leviathan perish? As well attempt to put God to death. What weapons laid in what hands could penetrate that hide, that flesh, "hard as a lower millstone," could reach that heart, "hard as stone"? What do "sword . . . spear . . . dart . . . javelin . . . iron . . . bronze . . . arrow . . . slingstone . . . clubs"—what do these avail? They are "straw . . . rotten wood . . . splinters . . ."

✦   ✦   ✦

Lounging luxuriously in his favorite ooze and mire,

> upon the mud
> he spreads
> like a threshing sledge.

> Sunken in the Nile or its estuary,
> he makes the depths
> boil like a pot,

the sea he churns
like perfume in a kettle.

Behind him
he leaves a shining path;

you would think
the deep
were white of hair (Job 41:30–32)

Admiration and its poetry. And a summing up;

Upon the earth
there is not his like,

intrepid
he was created.

All,
however lofty,
fear him;

he is king
over all proud beasts (Job 41:33–34)

An obvious implication of the poet; honor paid the king of
the beasts redounds to the king Maker.

chapter eleven

Submission; "No Purpose of Yours Can Be Hindered" (42-1-17)

42:1–6 At long length; Job has had enough; of contesting God and of grand designs. Enough to last a lifetime, and beyond.

He has been granted a survey of the round of creation, in company with a Guide of power and might.

Questions remain unanswered—and quite deliberately so.

All are agreed on this, the refusal.

(The consensus is unusual, among scholars and mystics alike. Could it be that in them too, the quest of Job lives, that his questions regarding the fate of the just and unjust, have become their own? That in them poor Job is transfigured?)

Thus the book must be accounted a mixed blessing. Mixed, underscored as mixed. But still, beyond doubt—a blessing.

We have in the first instance, what might be termed a "poetry of irresolution."

The central questions of Job are ignored by God, as we have seen. Shall the Creator yield before a creature?

Other matters issue from the whirlwind.

✦ ✦ ✦

The book veers about wildly, the original intent flies away on the wings of a storm.

Or a calmer image. It is as though a newly written literary masterpiece joined the immortals on a bookshelf. The older works are displaced, moved over. They must be evaluated anew, in light of the new arrival. What were the sources, influences upon the recent work? What new images emerge, what nuances of the human condition are underscored?

✦ ✦ ✦

Thus the theophany to Job; displacement, replacement! His questions, which by and large are those of the prophets—these are impetuously, stormily put aside—in favor of the concerns of God.

It appears that the Deity is intent on self-justification. So suave a skill, so prodigious a deflection!

The method is, as usual, implied, specific to Job; but it is also unmistakably universal.

The instruction; Humans must learn by unlearning.

Perhaps (as repeatedly noted) Job's questioning (and ours) of the Grand Master was wide the mark, impertinent, bound to go nowhere?

✦ ✦ ✦

It is as though Beethoven's Fifth Symphony had burst from the page. For the duration of the grand monologue, we are lulled, charmed out of our Jobian low mood, out of a dark sense of the world and our fate therein.

A sublime distraction! In poetry unmatched, creation is celebrated, savored on the tongue of the Creator.

✦ ✦ ✦

Job for his part appears chastened, put to silence. To all evidence, he submits;

> I know
> You can do all things,
>
> no purpose of Yours
> can be hindered (Job 42:2)

Is this to his credit, to our instruction as well?
Perhaps. Still, doubt lingers.
Can the heart be forbidden its pain, its slowed beat, its tears?
Forbidden or no, pain and the questioning of pain seem endemic to our soul, its substance and fabric.
The voice of Job is stilled and it is not stilled. An echo lives on, lives in mystics, scholars, believers of every age. Lives in ourselves. The "why"?

✦ ✦ ✦

We Christians are hardly bereft of resource. Indeed we are granted a far greater resource than was given Job.
A suffering Savior has walked our world, a God, protagonist of a tragic drama, an Innocent in torment.
Ours is a God who responds to human torment; and not primarily in words. In enactment, embrace.

✦ ✦ ✦

In words—and how much more!
In His flesh He embraces the fate of Job, and worse. *Passus, mortuus et sepultus est*; "He suffered, died and was buried."
The Latin phrase is laconic. But the agony of God lies there

in "tears and a strong cry" (Hebrews 5:7); God, tried on criminal charges, convicted, capitally punished.

✦   ✦   ✦

As for Job, he is altogether chastened, or seems so.

Henceforth he must take God and the world on God's terms, not his own.

So it seems. So the text would have us believe. At length, Job speaks;

> I have dealt
> with great matters
> that I do not understand;
>
> with things too wonderful,
> which I cannot know (Job 42:3)

✦   ✦   ✦

Has the great questioner been brought to heel?

And what of ourselves? Are we to take the instruction like a child's pablum, to cease all fretting?

To accept without question the bloody course of the world, Hiroshima, and Vietnam and the "contra" war and the School of Assassins and the Iraq slaughter? And on and on the ululation, the litany of our loss?

Has the faith of Job been discredited, a dying fall, he reproved and put to naught?

> I had heard of You
> by word of mouth,
>
> but now
> my eyes have seen You.

Therefore
I disown
what I have said,

and repent
in dust and ashes (Job 42:5–6)

Taking the conclusion as definitive, the "disowning," the "repenting," we close the book of Job.
But we remain confounded, steeped in perplexity.
An unhelpful ending, to say the least.

✦　✦　✦

Yet the last pages, battering us as they do with emulation and compliance, are hardly to be thought the entire book.
We take seriously the conclusion and its apparent capitulation. Still, we think; more must be taken in account.
In the early chapters, Job lay prone under the torrent of God's silence and surmise. Heady praise was bestowed, lengthy exchanges followed, by turns abusive, contradictory, stubborn on both sides. All this, one thinks, cannot be gainsaid or canceled by a dour outcome.
Along with his submission, other, contrary or at least modifying events are on record; the Passion of Job, his unswerving fidelity under fire, his integrity—these too are honored as the word of God.

✦　✦　✦

We dare construct a moral, to place at the conclusion of our inspired tale.
Dare say it. In the "nature of things," the nature of the fallen world and its omniscient, opaque Deity, in the nature of the mind itself—faith must include the questioning of God.

Why goes it so ill with the world's innocents, why the pain, the vanquishing of the helpless? "Why do the wicked live on, reach old age, and grow mighty in power?" Why the institutionalizing of murder? Why the obsession with war and killing?

Why the Pentagon, why the malignant justice system, why the vast apparatus of "death on demand"—from abortion mills to assisted suicide?

✦   ✦   ✦

And why is no light proffered in our book, no answer—though a query much resembling our own is raised by Job, again and again?

No answer. Instead, a poetic monologue, beckoning the questioner into an untouchable realm of power. Where enlightenment is denied, let Job grow giddy.

✦   ✦   ✦

The response (non response?) issues "from the whirlwind." This wild Deity, we learn, rides the storm like a rider of stallions, will not be tamed or brought to heel. This God is a very Behemoth for valiance, a Leviathan for mastery.

✦   ✦   ✦

So be it. But what of ourselves, what of faith? Shall faith be obliterated in the whirlwind?

Shall this be the outcome; enlightenment is forbidden, let humans grow subdued and safe?

But, but. Difficulties ignored or unanswered only serve to fester in the mind, to evoke more (and harder) questions.

Is God unable, unwilling, incapable of offering a clue, a hint, a nuance, a semblance of relief?

Does God suffer, when humans must suffer?

Is the trio that hems Job in, tormenting him with austere logic, correct after all? Is the world's central event the Fall, and no redeeming mercy?

✦   ✦   ✦

Job may submit; we cannot.

To decree that a show of power must do, is regression and vanity. The decree goes further, it touches on us. It would have humans regress to an acquiescent childhood.

✦   ✦   ✦

Indeed, could faith in God be thought to survive, with no Job in the world?

A community of faith survive, with no icon of unease?

Supposing such a community, mature and aware of its world—then the alternative, a mute acceptance of "things as they are"—this latter appalls. It closely resembles Job's fatalistic concession; a shrug, a "so be it."

Shall we name his conversion bizarre?

Is Job twice born, or does he seek a return to the womb?

His phrases haunt the mind;

" . . . no purpose of Yours can be hindered . . . I spoke without understanding . . . things beyond me . . . I recant and relent . . . dust and ashes . . ."

✦   ✦   ✦

Nothing prepared us for this.

It is as though Job's sublime clarity, his sense of justice out-raged, all had vanished on the winds of heaven—or hell.

Who among us would undergo so funerary a transforma-tion, and count it gain?

Does the God of Job count it gain, that He has subdued a valiant, protean opposite number? Count it gain, that an obeisant, laced with futility, prostrates before Him?

The hero has lost heart. Submission is exacted, and rendered.

It is like the wall-eyed fatalism of a beast with a blade at its throat.

✦ ✦ ✦

42:7–17 Yet the mystery beats on. And approval for the beat.

We glean what we can, meager though it be—the gain, the echo of that voice out of a storm.

The hectoring foursome, for their part, are set back, explicitly. They have not "spoken rightly of Me, as has My servant Job" (Job 42:7).

So after the palaver and poetry, the heights and stygian depths of mood, the clash of interests and ideologies, the issues not joined—after all this, is Job vindicated?

He has "spoken rightly of Me."

A mighty vindication, and a final? Is the sense intended general or particular?

As recounted, Job yielded and held his tongue. He confessed missing the mark, he repents his vivacious daring.

✦ ✦ ✦

But wait. A different judgment is issued.

That feisty behavior of his; was it not praiseworthy, was Job not after all rightly stationed?

Did he not walk in the light, even as he all but drowned in darkness, as he tested, tested the limits of the allowable?

✦ ✦ ✦

Back, forth, a weather vane in a storm, the mind races. Not only Job—we too are tossed about in that whirlwind.

Outcome? It is utterly unpredictable.

✦   ✦   ✦

Job behaved laudably, and is therefore crowned by the hands of the Deity.

In Person; crowned as human, sublimely so.

As a type; the human, best and noblest.

The human—dangerous as well.

Dangerous to the Deity?

Job, a living interrogation mark before God.

✦   ✦   ✦

He is also reproved, stingingly so. He must take in account the boundaries, the ground God will not yield.

Job is judged excessive, is humiliated.

He falls flat; "I disown what I have said, and repent in dust and ashes."

Dignum et justum—"worthy and right." But then, a turnabout.

Praise is pronounced, not once, twice; "My servant Job" has spoken rightly of God.

✦   ✦   ✦

Astonishing. The book is all but ended, and Job is incalculably disgraced, put down. Or so we thought.

By no means. Repentance is exacted of the adversarial malingerers.

And for Job, divine praise.

As guarantee of favor from above, all is restored to him, and more; a hundredfold of prospering, sons and daughters, flocks and herds, descendants to the third generation, his own life extended to twice the alotted years.

✦ ✦ ✦

Jawe is named at last, self-named.

Throughout the debates, neither Job nor his friends named the Divine. The trio was sunk in ideology, Job wandered in a daze of bewildered loss. Neither he nor they could pronounce the holy Name aright.

Now God names God. And something of divine behavior is manifest; God stands guard at the gate of the holy.

And what of time and this world?

Here, now, unlikely, everywhere, the holy takes the form of— Job. Just; and under the lash of circumstance. This it means to be human.

And this it means to be God; to be the Great Negation, un- owned, unentailed—even before "my servant Job."

✦ ✦ ✦

God refuses to give Himself away, to unseal the decrees of innocence and guilt, of who is to prosper and who go under, to answer the haunting "why" of humans—though the ones who cry out be heroes, martyrs, the noblest of our race.

Thus the unease, the drama, the tragedy implicit in this face- to-face commerce.

Job and God; each playing a part, each unsatisfied, unsure of the opposite number, standing warily at distance, each tak- ing the measure of a mysterious other, the adversary, the lover.

✦ ✦ ✦

Words die, suns set, grass blows, a dust.
What then?
We must learn
time and again

like infants, on hands and knees,
spasmodic wisdom.

Six months, sixty years—
all one—
at the empyrean.
one blind tug.
Teach us
to count our days—
multiple, scanty,
no matter.

But a voice of praise (Psalm 90)

(October 22, 1998; commemoration of
Maura O'Halloran, Christian Zen Monk)